MARIE ANTOINETTE'S WORLD

ALSO BY WILL BASHOR

Marie Antoinette's Darkest Days: Prisoner No. 280 in the Conciergerie

Marie Antoinette's Head: The Royal Hairdresser, the Queen, and the Revolution

Jean-Baptiste Cléry: Eyewitness to Louis XVI and Marie-Antoinette's Nightmare

MARIE ANTOINETTE'S WORLD

Intrigue, Infidelity, and Adultery in Versailles

WILL BASHOR

ROWMAN & LITTLEFIELD
Lanham • Boulder • New York • London

Published by Rowman & Littlefield
An imprint of The Rowman & Littlefield Publishing Group, Inc.
4501 Forbes Boulevard, Suite 200, Lanham, Maryland 20706
www.rowman.com

86-90 Paul Street, London EC2A 4NE

Distributed by NATIONAL BOOK NETWORK

British Library Cataloguing in Publication Information Available

Library of Congress Cataloging-in-Publication Data

Names: Bashor, Will, author.
Title: Marie Antoinette's World : Intrigue, Infidelity, and Adultery in Versailles / Will Bashor.
Description: Lanham : Rowman & Littlefield, [2020] | Includes bibliographical references and index.
Identifiers: LCCN 2020002703 (print) | LCCN 2020002704 (ebook) | ISBN 9781538138243 (cloth) | ISBN 9781538138250 (epub) | ISBN 9781538189443 (paperback)
Subjects: LCSH: Marie Antoinette, Queen, consort of Louis XVI, King of France, 1755-1793. | Marie Antoinette, Queen, consort of Louis XVI, King of France, 1755-1793—Family. | Marie Antoinette, Queen, consort of Louis XVI, King of France, 1755-1793—Friends and associates. | France—Court and courtiers—Social life and customs—18th century. | Queens—France— Biography. | France—History—Louis XVI, 1774-1793. | France—History— Revolution, 1789-1799.
Classification: LCC DC137.1 .B33 2020 (print) | LCC DC137.1 (ebook) | DDC 944/.035092 [B]—dc23
LC record available at https://lccn.loc.gov/2020002703
LC ebook record available at https://lccn.loc.gov/2020002704

*To my brother Randall Scott and the beloved memory
of Bertina Faye and Norma Blanche*

CONTENTS

AUTHOR'S NOTE

If it can happen that we feel thirsty and yet do not wish to drink, there must be something in our psyche that bids us drink, and something else that forbids it. The latter is reasoning or the calculating part of the soul; the former is the passionate.

—Plato, *The Republic*

For more than two centuries, historians have contemplated the psyche of Marie Antoinette, the iconic queen of novels, biographies, and the silver screen, who graced the halls of Versailles until her life was ended by the guillotine's blade.

In my previous works, I charted Marie Antoinette's life as seen through the eyes of her servants and jailers to present an unbiased account of the life of the last queen of France; however, in doing so, I neglected to delve into what historian Pierre de Nolhac called "the so little-known intimate life of the royal family." In this work, therefore, I attempt to present a more exhaustive picture of the queen's world, ranging from an analysis of her handwriting to an emotional genealogy of more than four generations.

Readers who are familiar with my previous objective stance regarding the queen will find it absent from this book. In contrast to many of Marie Antoinette's biographers, I cannot blindly assume her innocent of sexual promiscuity based solely on the lack of any hard evidence against her, especially in light of the numerous *alleged* affairs and licentious acts that scandalized her realm at the Château of Versailles. Put bluntly, Marie Antoinette's world cannot be styled as anything but conducive to intrigue, infidelity, adultery, and possibly, sexually transmitted disease.

Marie Antoinette's often thoughtless, fantasy-driven, and notorious antics have shown that there was indeed something in her psyche that bade her, in Plato's words, to drink, especially amid the self-indulgent entourage of her court.

In response to those who may accuse me of dishonoring the sacred memory of Marie Antoinette, I contend that I honor her more by depicting a real woman rather than a martyred queen of the French Revolution. And more important, am I not honoring her even more by placing blame where it belongs—on the influence of those in her circle, the vile environment of the court of Versailles, and on the sins of her fathers?

Protecting the queen's privacy should not be an excuse for sweeping unpleasant details of her life under the royal carpet. Readers will thus have the task of weighing all the evidence presented here, and because some evidence is stronger than others, it will also be their task to decide whether this new characterization of the last queen of France can be justified—beyond any reasonable doubt—as we peek behind the decorative screens, learn the secret language of the queen's fan, and explore the secret passageways and staircases of endless intrigue at Versailles.

INTRODUCTION

The throne is debased by indecency. . . . Versailles has become the palace of perfidy, hatred, and vengeance; wrought by intrigues and personal views, it seems that all sense of honesty has been abandoned there.

—Florimond Claude, Comte de Mercy-Argenteau,
Austrian ambassador to Versailles

Austrian-born Marie Antoinette and her husband, Louis XVI, being third cousins twice removed, were both descended from Louis XIII of the House of Bourbon. In fact, Marie Antoinette, the great-great-granddaughter of Louis XIII, was two generations closer in relation to Louis XIII than her husband. For this reason, the first chapter explores the intimate life of Louis XIII, who built a small hunting lodge in 1623 on what is the marble courtyard of today's Château of Versailles.

By focusing on the enigmatic Versailles from the reign of Louis XIII to Louis XVI, distinctive traits of social mores and behavioral patterns can be identified that had been handed down from generation to generation and institutionalized at the court of the last queen of France. Such an expanded angle of vision provides a guide for navigating the labyrinth of Marie Antoinette's psyche.

As we will see, her psyche will become intertwined with the Château of Versailles's raison d'être, where the closed society and court life only amplified traits inherited from generation to generation, making them more apparent and more easily discernable; this is called emotional genealogy when family behavior patterns are transmitted.

Although the palace was initially constructed as a hunting lodge, it soon served as a retreat for scandalous intrigues and rendezvous—all hidden from the public's eye. In later reigns, the royals would need to find other nearby retreats or hideaways for liaisons, of which the Grand Trianon, the Petit Trianon, and the Parc-aux-Cerfs would become most notorious.

THE STORY OF VERSAILLES

The plot of this narrative has always been simple: a foreign princess is betrothed to an heir of the throne of France. The characters, however, are all far from simple when playing their roles in this pervasive, inherited environment, which included royal possessions of land, immense wealth, palaces, titles, and even the *Cents-suisses*, the mercenary Swiss Guard who served the French court as royal bodyguards for almost four hundred years.

Very strict social norms also evolved at court to regulate the personnel of royal households for the education of the monarchs' heirs. Ages of majority were set at the age of thirteen, but princes were taken from governesses and put in the society of males with their own apartments by the age of seven.

Until the age of seven, however, a governess kept watch over a future monarch's health and welfare, swearing an oath to shape his predilections and provide him with guiding principles. She was called "mama" by tradition and held the post for life. As we shall see, Louis XIV's governess would take her rank to the next level when it came to the instruction of the young prince's education in the royal bed.

With respect to sex, the elaborate system of favorites and mistresses, which developed at court, allowed royals to have their cake and eat it too. Louis XIV would father more than a dozen illegitimate children, each given his or her own household, education, finances, and coveted positions at court. At Versailles, the policy of the monarchy became dependent upon palace intrigues and the taste of the boudoir, leaving the strength of the realm wantonly squandered. Folly and incompetence reigned in high places while an indignant nation remained sullenly aloof.

In part 1, we will thus discover that the intrigue and debauchery of the Bourbon kings from Louis XIII to Louis XV are closely intertwined with the physical development and expansion of the palace of Versailles as well as its intricate system of court life. Although Marie Antoinette was, in a sense, more Bourbon than her husband, Louis XVI, we must also remember that she was descended from the House of Habsburg-Lorraine.

Therefore, in parts 2 and 3, we will examine the scandals and intrigues that plagued the ancestors of the Habsburg princess at the Viennese court, where court etiquette was much less rigid than that at the court of Versailles.

Attention to Marie Antoinette's arrival and first years in France will then allow us to examine her conduct during this transition and her reaction to new trends and customs. The evolution of her personality will also be compared to that of her siblings, especially Maria Carolina, the queen of Naples and Sicily.

After Queen Marie Antoinette finally gave birth to a princess in 1778, we will see that motherhood did not discourage the queen from continuing her frivolous and flamboyant lifestyle, prompting scathing pamphlets to be distributed at the court of Versailles and throughout Europe. Part 4 will meticulously examine these pamphlets in relation to Marie Antoinette's psyche to discern what was false, what was possible, and what, although shocking, could have most probably been true.

Moreover, in part 5, newly discovered evidence suggests that the most shocking revelations concern infections that might have been transmitted through contact with the last queen of France's sexual partners.

In the first three reigns at Versailles, the kings were sinners and the queens were saints—not so, however, in the reign of Louis XVI and Marie Antoinette. It is only fitting that part 6 concludes with a discussion of shame, guilt, and confession.

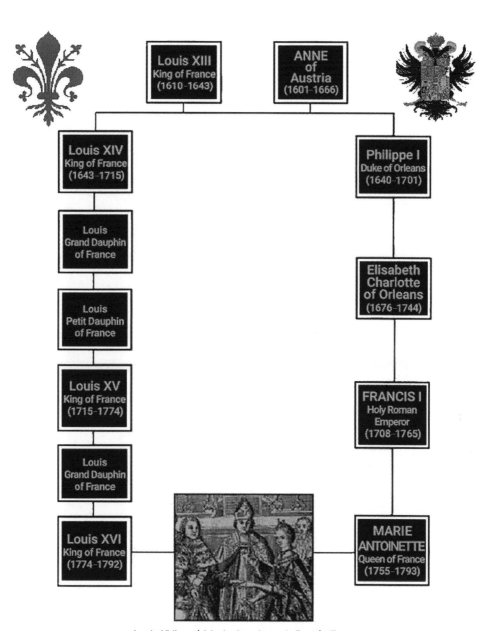

Louis XVI and Marie Antoinette's Family Trees

CHRONOLOGY

1755
November 2   Archduchess Maria Antonia Josepha Johanna von Habsburg-Lothringen is born at Hofburg Palace in Vienna, Austria

1763
February 15   Seven Years' War ends; to maintain an alliance between Austria and France, the marriage of Marie Antoinette and Louis XV's grandson is discussed

1764
April 15   Jeanne Antoinette Poisson, Marquise de Pompadour, dies

1769
April 22   Jeanne Bécu, Comtesse du Barry, becomes Louis XV's official mistress

1770
April 19   Marie Antoinette's marriage by proxy to Louis XV's grandson, Louis-Auguste
May 16   Marie Antoinette's wedding at the Château of Versailles

1774
January 1   Marie Antoinette meets "le beau" Count Axel von Fersen
May 10   Louis XV dies; Louis-Auguste and Marie Antoinette ascend to the throne
May 24   Louis XVI gives the Petit Trianon to Marie Antoinette

1777
April 18   Emperor Joseph, Marie Antoinette's brother, arrives from Vienna
August 18   The royal couple's marriage is consummated

1778

August 26   Fersen returns to Versailles; Marie Antoinette: "Ah, an old
                 acquaintance!"

November 19   Fersen enters Marie Antoinette's private apartments in
                 uniform

December 19   Princess Marie-Thérèse Charlotte of France is born

1779

July 14   Marie Antoinette's first miscarriage is reported

1780

May 4   Fersen sails for America and Swedish Ambassador Creutz
                 writes, "I own that I cannot help thinking that she had
                 a liking for him. The queen's eyes could not leave him,
                 during the last days, and they often filled with tears."

November 29   Marie Antoinette's mother, Empress Maria Theresa of
                 Austria, dies

1781

October 22   Dauphin Louis Joseph Xavier François is born

1783

November 2   Marie Antoinette's second miscarriage

1784

June 7   Fersen returns from America

June 27   Fersen enters Marie Antoinette's private circle

1785

March 27   Prince Louis Charles, Duke of Normandy, is born

1786

July 9   Princess Sophie Hélène Béatrix of France is born, several
                 weeks premature

1787

June 19   Princess Sophie Béatrix dies

1789

June 4   Dauphin Louis Joseph dies; his brother Louis Charles
                 becomes dauphin

July 14   Storming of the Bastille

October 5   March on Versailles

October 6   Royal family escorted to the Tuileries Palace in Paris

1791

June 21   Royal family arrested during flight to Varennes

1792

August 13	Royal family imprisoned in the tower of the Temple Prison
September 3	Princesse de Lamballe killed and decapitated
September 21	Fall of the monarchy official
December 11	Trial of Citizen Louis Capet

1793

January 17	Louis XVI convicted of treason and condemned to death
January 21	Louis XVI guillotined at the Place de la Révolution; Louis Charles is Louis XVII
August 2	Marie Antoinette taken to the Conciergerie Prison
October 16	Marie Antoinette found guilty and executed
October 16	Fersen writes about Marie Antoinette, "I thought about her constantly, about all the horrible circumstances of her sufferings, of the doubt she might have had about me, my attachment, my interest. That thought tortured me."
December 8	Jeanne Bécu, Comtesse du Barry, is guillotined
December 9	Yolande Martine Gabrielle de Polastron, Duchess of Polignac, dies in Vienna

1794

May 10	Madame Élisabeth of France, Louis XVI's sister, is guillotined
June 8	Ten-year-old heir, Louis XVII, dies

MARIE ANTOINETTE'S WORLD

Part I

ENIGMATIC VERSAILLES

A "resident" of Parc-aux-Cerfs, Marie-Louise O'Murphy

1

LOUIS XIII'S CHÂTEAU
OF DEBAUCHERY

*I am going to Versailles tomorrow for two or three days . . . anywhere
as long as I am far from these women.*

—Louis XIII, August 19, 1638

Twelve miles from Paris, the country village of Versailles prospered
in the Middle Ages, known then for its small castle, windmill, and
church of Saint Julien. After the Hundred Years' War, however, the castle
fell into ruin in a sparsely populated area of marshy land, an area known
locally for its "stinking ponds." The ponds, some of which fed into each
other, emptied into the Ru de Gally, a small river of sewer water widely
said to be "black as ink."

Henri IV regularly hunted in this area, bringing his six-year-old son
Louis here for the first time on August 24, 1607. After Henri's death in
1610 and by the time the child was crowned Louis XIII, the melancholic
Louis found joy in returning here for riding and the hunt.

One day in February 1621, when hunting for stag ran later than usual,
Louis found himself at nightfall on a small hill where an ancient windmill
stood. He slept here on a bed of straw while his men took shelter in a
nearby cabaret, and when he woke, the fresh air soothed his soul. Finding
the mill uncomfortable, two years later, at the age of twenty-one, Louis decided to build his own pavilion with a small park attached, and the mason
Nicolas Huaut began work on the site where the mill stood.

Dense woods and pestilent wastelands surrounded the original site
where Louis XIII began construction to create his haven—a graceful, but
small, castle that the Duke of Saint-Simon called a "little pasteboard box."
But Louis was content with the spot, which was neither too near nor too

far from his court at Saint-Germain-en-Laye. Saint-Simon also called the king's country retreat a "château of cards," and the Venetian ambassador called it "una piccola casa per ricreazione"—a mere folly. A courtier named Bassompierre said one could not boast of it, but it was better than sleeping on a mattress of straw infected with fleas, ticks, and vermin.

When the king stayed at the pavilion, he had his bed brought from Paris. He stayed for only a night or a week at a time until 1630, when he would take up permanent residence after his overbearing mother, Marie de Médicis, failed to displace Cardinal Richelieu as chief minister and succumbed to self-exile.

Louis XIII's physician, Jean Héroard, wrote, "Whenever the king arrived at Versailles, he hunted, dined, and afterwards went riding to take a deer or a fox. After supper, he would often exercise with his musketeers or create and perform ballets before retiring for the night." Before long, Versailles served as the king's treasured escape from his ministerial duties, his queen, and women in general.

A recurring theme in the development of Versailles began to evolve. The new residence was only intended for short stays with a small, all-male entourage to escape the women of the Parisian court of Saint-Germain-en-Laye.

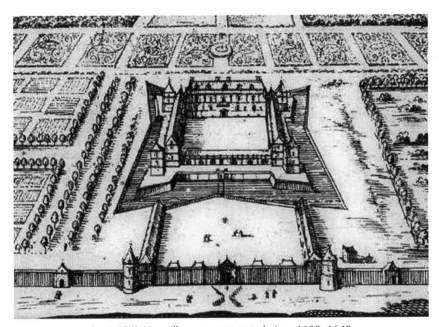

Louis XIII's Versailles, as constructed circa 1630–1640

To isolate himself from prying eyes, Louis XIII built square pavilions rising at the castle's four corners with a moat crossed by a stone bridge on the side of the gardens to the west and a drawbridge to the east. The structure was all brick and stone, most fitting for Louis XIII and his musketeers; it would become a site well secluded for the king to carry on numerous affairs with men in secrecy.

It must be noted that, although legal oppression against homosexuality was severe in France, the privileged status of the French nobility did ensure a degree of immunity. The proverb "in Spagna gli preti, in Francia i Grandi, in Italia tutti quanti" (in Spain the priests, in France the nobles, in Italy everyone) not only rang true in the reign of Louis XIII but would apply to the reigns of Louis XIV, Louis XV, and Louis XVI as well.

The hunting retreat at Versailles was truly a man's retreat, in more ways than one. Louis XIII's mother, Marie de Médicis, had enfeebled her stuttering Louis by rendering him effeminate, allowing her to keep hold of the reins of the monarchy. As a result, if it could be said that Henri IV loved women, then Louis XIII loved men.

The king's first affairs included his coach driver, Saint-Amour, and his kennel master, Haran. After these *passions d'adolescence*, Louis's first serious affair "that only death could extinguish" was with Charles d'Albert, Duke de Luynes.

After Henri IV's death, his widow, Marie de Médicis, negotiated the marriage of ten-year-old Anne of Austria, a Spanish member of the Habsburg family, with Louis, creating a Spanish alliance and a pledge of peace between the two great Catholic powers. Anne's father, King Philip III of Spain, had great hopes that his daughter's presence at the French court would support the interests of Spain.

Anne married Louis XIII, king of France and Navarre, by proxy in Burgos, Spain, on November 24, 1615. Although the newlyweds were only fourteen years old, Marie de Médicis, then regent, did not want this union to be questioned, so she endeavored to ensure that the marriage was immediately consummated for political reasons. However, the wedding night appeared to have been a disaster, partly due to the newlyweds' inexperience.

Moreover, according to historian J. M. Guardia, Louis XIII "never loved a woman, not even his own." And as for the wedding night, he may have been asked to fulfill an act of manhood—before being a man. The story of what happened that evening was documented by journalist Armand Bashet.

After the wedding ceremony at about seven o'clock in the evening, Louis and Anne made their way to the archbishop's palace for the nuptial to be blessed. Louis then went to lie down in his room and in his usual bed, according to custom, and Anne was directed to another chamber. The queen mother then went to Louis at eight o'clock, sending all the guards and persons away in the hallways.

"My son," she said, "it is not enough to be married, you must come to see the queen, your wife, who is waiting for you."

"Madame," he replied, "I was only waiting for your command. I'm going, if you please, to find her with you."

Louis removed his robe and his boots and followed his mother to his wife's room, where they entered with two nurses, Louis's governor, his physician Héroard, and his valet carrying the candle.

The queen mother approached Anne's bed: "My daughter, here is your husband whom I bring you, receive him near you, and love him, I beg you."

When Anne replied in Spanish that she had no other intention than to obey and please him, Louis joined his queen in bed. The queen mother then told everyone but the two nurses to leave, allowing the couple to consummate their marriage. It was reported by the nurses that the young king did his duty and did it twice. After sleeping a short while, he woke and called for his nurse to bring his robe and boots, and he was led back to his own chambers.

This story of the royal couple's consummation, however, was pure fantasy. Louis later confessed that he had only painful memories of his wedding night; the consummation was nothing but a charade for political purposes. It is doubtful that Louis XIII actually knew what was required of him because the young king was so humiliated that night that he kept a long grudge against his mother. Several reigns later, the fifteen-year-old dauphin and future king, Louis XVI, would record his experience with his new fourteen-year-old wife, Marie Antoinette of Austria, writing that "nothing" happened—a short "*rien*" in his journal.

Even if Louis had been informed about the task at hand, the public affair of official consummation—with his nurses watching—may have rendered him unable to do his duty. In any case, this first, failed test of virility might well have discouraged or even disgusted the prince. An official onlooker noted that it only produced "pain and fatigue," and the couple would not produce an heir for another twenty-three years. Moreover, Louis's relationships with mistresses, unlike his father's and his son's, would all be chaste.

Most of what we know about Louis XIII's youth can be corroborated with the journals of Héroard, his personal physician, who kept diligent notes of Louis's medical treatment and personal behavior for more than twenty years.

Although Louis would not share Anne's bed for another four years after the wedding night, the king did visit his queen daily in her apartment, following royal protocol, once in the morning and once in the evening. More notable, in the meantime he also visited the Duke de Luynes several times a day. When hunting, he would leave his wife behind and take the Duke de Luynes with him. When he returned, having not seen the queen for some time, he would pay her a short visit before leaving abruptly to have lunch in the duke's apartment, alone with him. The king's passion for the duke was described as an "extreme condition" or "special love," but his mother, Marie de Médicis, described the passion in more detail; she said it was a "demon that haunts the king and makes him deaf, blind, and dumb."

The Duke de Luynes, although not known for his statesmanship, became Louis XIII's adviser partly due to their shared love of the hunt, but the duke also rose in status to become Grand Falconer of France and Constable of France due to other unique talents. He planned, for example, the king's ballets and even cast himself in starring roles at his protégé's side. But the Duke de Luynes would not be the only male favorite; others included the Marquis de Montpouillan, the royal-page-turned-favorite Barradat, and Claude de Saint-Simon, the father of the celebrated biographer, who "lasted the longest but was loved the least."

It is difficult to confirm whether Louis XIII had the same homosexual characteristics as his second son, Philippe, known as Monsieur during the eventual reign of his brother, Louis XIV. However, the biographer Gédéon Tallemant des Réaux reported that Louis XIII's love affairs with men were indeed strange ones in which he spoke like a "half-hearted lover" and was susceptible to "bouts of jealousy."

He also had female favorites. In fact, on many occasions, disputes erupted between Louis XIII and one favorite, Marie de Hautefort, a young woman who knew herself beautiful and noted, with vexation, that Louis "could not resolve himself with a few carnal acts!" The king referred to the young woman as an "inclination" when their relations were good and as "the creature" when anguished. The provocative favorite taunted Louis one day to come and retrieve a note from her bodice. The king complied, but only by using tongs from the chimney.

Louis also paid attention to another courtesan, Louise de La Fayette. He called her "Angelique," but she too was just another chaste pastime.

His most open affair was with Henri Coiffier de Ruzé, the Marquis de Cinq-Mars, a handsome young subject selected as "an amusement" for the king by Cardinal Richelieu.

Louis XIII and the Marquis de Cinq-Mars

The king would summon Cinq-Mars, "adorned like a wife," to his chambers, first covering his hands with kisses before coaxing him into his bed. While Cinq-Mars was at war, the king ordered reports dispatched daily from the battlefield to check on his favorite's well-being. And when the nineteen-year-old fought in the thirty-eight-year-old king's presence on the battlefield, Louis told Marie de Hautefort that "his affections now belonged to Cinq-Mars." One courtier wrote that Louis loved Cinq-Mars "ardemment," or with fervor, but historian Tallemant des Réaux said the king loved him "esperdument," to distraction.

Although there had been efforts to interest Louis XIII in the fairer sex, he would only profess love for women in a chaste manner. When the court poet Boisrobert, himself homosexual, celebrated the king's love for women in verse and, in particular, for Madame Hautefort, the king objected to the words "with desire" in the song; he desired nothing of the sort. The poet then recounted unsurprisingly with a new verse: "Oh, guess what the king needs to do? Have a list of the Musketeers!" This was unsurprising, because Louis was making sojourns to Versailles with his musketeers much more frequently at this time.

In November 1626, Louis invited his mother, Marie de Médicis, and Queen Anne to dine at Versailles. It would be their first visit and their last, because Louis had not furnished a single bedroom for any women in the twenty-six-room château. In fact, Louis designed the twenty-room retreat to exclude accommodations for ladies. There were two bedrooms, a comfortable apartment for himself, and a "large dormitory for men only."

Louis was neither physically nor emotionally attractive; he was known to be a "cruel, petulant, and jealous" man. Although his younger brother, Gaston, Duc d'Anjou (and later Duc d'Orléans), was jovial, social, and well liked, Louis did not love him. His queen did, however, and as a consequence of her husband's coldness and neglect, she openly vied for Gaston's admiration, hoping to "inspire the king with a more just appreciation of her merits."

But the queen's efforts were in vain. The marriage was hardly a happy one, and after twenty years of marriage, the queen still had not given birth to an heir to the throne. Perhaps she and her husband had relinquished all hope for a child.

On the evening of December 5, 1637, however, marital affairs took a turn for the better. The king was forced to seek shelter from a storm at the Louvre on his way to Blois one evening. He immediately proceeded to Queen Anne's apartments to find the queen quite surprised by the impromptu visit. Perhaps she was even more surprised that he remained with her until the next morning. Consequently, in September 1638, after twenty-three years of marriage, Anne finally gave birth to a son, the future Louis XIV, at the court of Saint-Germain-en-Laye.

Anne, having given the king an heir, desired to play a political role in France, but she never won the trust of her husband or his principal minister, Cardinal Richelieu. The situation only worsened when George Villiers, the Duke of Buckingham, a favorite of the English king, fell in love with the French queen. Severely affronted, Louis decreed that henceforth no male would have permission to visit his queen's chambers unless he was present. The royal marriage deteriorated even more as Louis tried to take control of the queen's entourage.

Louis XIII had a pronounced dislike for women, and for years he did not make his queen happy, perhaps even setting the stage for Anne to succumb to Buckingham's charms. However, when Richelieu died, Louis appointed Cardinal Mazarin as his minister, little suspecting that his new minister would become Anne's lover. Richelieu seemed to have foreseen this when he first introduced Mazarin, then his apprentice, to the queen: "He will please you, madame; he's like Buckingham."

The public announcement of the birth of the heir created quite a stir. Louis was equally astonished and immediately hastened to the Louvre to offer the queen his congratulations, despite the rumor at court that the child was the son of Cardinal Mazarin.

The king's subjects praised the birth as a miracle and, to show gratitude for the long-awaited heir to the French throne, Louis and Anne named him

Louis-Dieudonné, or God-given. The birth of the future Louis XIV was followed by that of his brother, Philippe, Duc d'Anjou (later Duc d'Orléans), two years later in 1640.

Louis XIII died in Paris on May 14, 1643, when Louis XIV was but four years old and too young to reign; consequently, his mother served as Regent of France. Until Louis XIV's majority at the age of thirteen in 1651, his court was held at Saint-Germain-en-Laye. Although he would visit his father's château at Versailles for the first time the year of his majority, he would not become impassioned to expand his father's retreat until ten years later, when Louis finally took the reins of his rule on the death of Cardinal Mazarin in 1661.

And it would be a glorified château at Versailles where Louis XIV would continue his father's predisposition for adulterous affairs, but the new king's conquests would be women rather than men.

From the very first stones mortared in place, Versailles was destined to metamorphose into a labyrinth of spaces where forced marriages with foreign princesses would be unconsummated or plagued with adultery, where courtiers would turn a blind eye to homosexuality, where favorites would be lavished with titles and riches for sexual favors, where sexually transmitted diseases would flourish, and where the high levels of court intrigue and scandal would be unsurpassed in France's history.

2

LOUIS XIV'S REIGN OF BOSOMS
AND COCKLES OF THE HEART

Another motive further forced Louis XIV from his capital [to Versailles]. At first, he feared exposing the scandal of his amours in the eyes of the bourgeoisie, the only class in society where the decency of morals exists. But soon he tired of so much circumspection.

—Charles Duclos, "Mémoires secrets"

From the day of his birth, Louis-Dieudonné left his mark on the ladies. The heir to the throne came into the world with two front teeth, with which he used to bite his wet nurse so hard that she finally refused to breastfeed him any longer. When a second nurse was called, she was also bitten and quickly resigned her lucrative post. A third nurse fled the scene at the first chomp.

Finally, a fourth nurse, Perrette Dufour de Poissy, was summoned. Although she was warned about the young prince's unusual habit, she remained strong and resolute: "Good! If that's all, I'm not afraid. Give me the child."

When Louis bit her as hard as he had his previous nurses, she bravely—and at great risk—responded with a rather strong slap on the royal infant's buttocks. From that moment, the child nursed without a single nibble. However, it was said she was only cured of the infant's bites by applying the relic of St. Anne's finger. Perrette became the young heir's official wet nurse and was ennobled by him when he assumed the throne. For years to come, this busty nursemaid greeted the king at his bedside every morning—with a kiss on the forehead.

After Louis XIII's death on May 14, 1643, four-year-old Louis XIV took the throne with his mother Anne of Austria, who acted as regent until his majority on September 7, 1651. Until this time, his court was held at

Louis XIV's first nurse, Madame Longuet de la Giraudière

Saint-Germain-en-Laye, where he quickly developed a voracious sexual appetite by the age of fifteen.

He was known to haunt the rooftops here for nightly visits to *demoiselles'* chambers, accessed by climbing through windows, especially that of Mademoiselle de la Mothe-Houdancourt, an outgoing and sassy young woman who was known for her flirtatious nature. When her governess, the Duchess of Noailles, had Mademoiselle's window secured with metal grating, the young king considered it an attack against his throne. He immediately ordered the duchess to be removed from his court, and the grating was removed.

Although Mademoiselle de la Mothe-Houdancourt's heart belonged to another, her father urged her to answer Louis XIV's call at any time, thus keeping the family in the king's good graces. Such a strategy would be used in the court of his successor, Louis XV, as well; however, by this time it was too late; Louis had already set his eyes upon another conquest.

The year of Louis's majority, 1651, was the same year he first visited his father's Château of Versailles. In 1660 he married the Infanta Maria Theresa of Spain, his "double cousin," and brought her to Versailles.★ When Cardinal Mazarin died in 1661, Louis took control of his court and declared that he would rule his kingdom and rebuild his father's château on a much grander scale.

When Louis established his court at Versailles in 1666, he decided to create a palace for his entire court to complement his majestic rule—or did he have other motives? Having his nobles reside at Versailles certainly enabled him to keep an eye on them: they had been known to conspire against him. On another note, however, he had often frequented Versailles with his mistress, Madame de La Vallière, allowing only a select few of his courtiers to follow them on their walks. "We often went to Versailles," said his cousin, La Grande Mademoiselle, "but no one could follow the king without his orders. This intrigued the court."

This manner of controlling his surroundings for illicit affairs was evident for most of Louis's reign at Versailles, and it was a trait that was passed on to his successors, Louis XV and Louis XVI. The first transformation of the Château of Versailles was followed by uninterrupted construction for more than fifty years, thus magnifying Louis XIII's modest inheritance "to the limits of fancy." Louis XIV preserved the buildings that still stand in the center of the castle and around the marble courtyard out of "piety to the memory of the late King his father."

When Louis XIV took his father's bedroom in the center of the château, he incorporated the *petit et grand levers*, elaborate traditions of etiquette. The petit lever took place in the king's chamber, where only a select group assisted the king to rise and get dressed; the grand lever was attended by the entire court in the gallery outside the king's bedchamber. His apartments included the first antechamber, where he dined with his family, and the second antechamber, L'Oeil-de-Boeuf, where his visitors awaited their audience.

Maria Theresa of Spain, like other queens of France, was wed not for love but for power. Perhaps, if he had had a choice in the matter, Louis

---

★ Louis XIV's father, Louis XIII, was the brother of Maria Theresa's mother; her father was brother to Louis XIV's mother, Anne of Austria.

would have chosen another for his queen. Cardinal Fleury explained to one of his colleagues: "I do, sir, post this from my hand about something secret and important. I was of the opinion that the Infanta's teeth are all rotten and that her hair is red, two things, especially the second, which would inspire disgust in the Dauphin and cause him to be angry."

And indeed, the young prince had acquired a certain taste for the ladies at court. Until his marriage to Maria Theresa, demoiselles competed to "deflower" the young king. In fact, it became a sport at court: "Girls swooned, their mothers shuddered, and their grandmothers were abounding in recommendation. The competition open, they jostled, they shoved to be the first to launch a glare at the king. Their necklines became aggressively lower, they wore stockings the color of the 'rejoicing widow' that could only mean 'f——k me, my darling.'"

Their makeup was "indecent" as well. Young ladies dotted their faces with *mouches*, or beauty marks. The "passionate" spot was placed near the eyes, and the "kiss me" one was positioned near the mouth; the "discreet" spot was fixed just under the lips, and the "majestic" one was placed on the forehead. To tease the young monarch, the ladies also put spots on their necks and breasts. Some dared to open their bodices when the young king passed by, while others pretended to faint to attract his attention.

Not unlike his father, Louis XIV used Versailles as his "plaything and then his passion" to secure privacy for "his amorous and adulterous needs." At an early age, Louis had shown interest in Isabelle de Chatillon: "She had charming ways, but she had some that attracted everyone's scorn. For money and honor, she would have dishonored herself and sacrificed her father, her mother or her lover. With this beauty, lovers were like a hydra whose head was no sooner cut off that another was regrown."

In 1651, it was rumored that the young lady had masturbated the royal member. The queen mother had Isabelle banished from court when the young paramour boasted about it, and verses were recited in the salons:

Beautiful, do not blame our prince at all for any weakness.
He may well, despite his youth, do the duty of a lover.
Kings of stature and fortune pass the common measure,
And if, in the innocent century, Solomon, at the age of ten, lost his virginity,
Louis is no less wise, and he is no less powerful.

It was well documented that, by 1653, Louis had his first favorite, Catherine-Henriette Belier, the wife of Pierre de Beauvais and first chamber lady of the queen mother. In fact, at age forty-five, the one-eyed, small-pocked woman with a vicious reputation was the first to teach the fourteen-year-old king "what he would later practice so well with women." And according to the Abbe de Choisy, she had more than one such liaison with the young king.

The king's promiscuous activities at such a young age were not without risk. He contracted a sexually transmitted disease, *chaude-pisse* (gonorrhea), at the age of seventeen. If not completely cured, he would have suffered from it for many years thereafter—a royal gift that must have certainly been passed on to his other conquests.

The nature of this condition at the time must have embarrassed one of the royal physicians, Antoine Vallot, so much that he refused, at first, to diagnose it for what it really was. He was also satisfied with the young prince's confession of innocence in the matter. He wrote,

> In the beginning of May, in the year 1655, a little earlier than going to war, I was informed that the king's nightshirts were stained with a substance which gave suspicion of something sinful, for which we needed to pay close attention. Those who gave me the first opinion were not well informed about the nature and quality of the evil, believing at first that it was either some infection or venereal disease; but, having thoroughly examined everything, I had other thoughts and persuaded myself that this occurrence was due to a greater problem. I had no doubt, then, of the purity of [the prince's] life, or of his chastity.

Vallot described the excretion as having the "consistency between that of an egg white and pus, and it was attached so strongly to the shirt that the stains could only be removed with detergent or with soap." Its color was yellow mixed with green and it "passed insensibly in greater abundance at night than day." According to these symptoms, Vallot felt the state took precedence over all other considerations and he ascribed the condition, in an inventive manner, as a "weakness of prostate and spermatic vessels."

As for the cause of the problem, Vallot told the prince it was due to too much riding and he had to take great care of the "weakness of those parts which serve the generation." The prince had to stop riding immediately. Furthermore, the prince would submit to bleeding, preceded by an enema and followed by a purgative. As for medicine, the physician administered a tablet every morning, consisting of a concoction of salts, crayfish shells, pearls, and corals. In sum, the therapy put into use by Vallot, as bizarre as it is, was actually in favor of the hypothesis for a venereal disease.

On September 7, Vallot implored Louis to begin his treatments without delay, stressing the "terrible consequences" and infirmities that await him if he procrastinated. The king, deeply moved, followed his physician's advice at once and continued until September 18. On October 30, however, when Louis was bedridden with fevers, Vallot's prognosis was questioned.

On the one hand, a physician concurred with the king's *Premier* physician Vallot, stating, "The king is sober, continent, healthy with all his body, who drinks no wine and is not debauched." Vallot added that the infection did not come from any venom that young debauched people usually come in contact with wayward women, because the king had not slept with any girl or woman."

On the other hand, however, that the king lived in pure chastity was not true. In fact, the court poet Benserade boldly mentioned the king's promiscuity at a ballet in which the king danced in February of the year before he became affected by the nocturnal discharges:

> Under which show for us, / And from where can proceed in us
> The change that we notice? / On what grass did you walk,
> That, such a great monarch / Must become so debauched?
> This is the order that your young people / Attach to pleasant topics,
> And that they only ask to laugh; / But do not be carried away,
> Avoid the debauchery, sire, / Pass for fragility.
> There is no censor, nor Regent / Who is not indulgent enough
> To the wishes of an extravagant youth, / And to embellish your court,
> Who cannot find it even excusable / That you have a little love?
> But to use it like that / And run here and there
> Without stopping for someone, / Who may be everything be good to you,
> The blonde as much as the brunette / Ha! Sire it is a very great evil.

Isn't the last verse significant? Alexandre Bontemps, first valet of the royal bedchamber and devoted servant of Louis XIV, was known as the go-between and interpreter for Louis and his mistresses, often leading them secretly through obscure hallways to the king's chambers.

Among these mistresses was Louise de La Vallière, a faithful friend and ardent lover best known for her sweet and amicable nature. She was the maid of honor for Princess Henrietta of England, the king's brother's wife (with whom Louis also had an affair). When Louis became unfaithful to La Vallière for the haughty Madame de Montespan, he humiliated her by forcing her to share chambers with his new mistress. Ashamed of her affair with the king, La Vallière later wrote, "My crimes were public, my repentance must be public, too." A year later, she took her vows as a Carmelite nun.

Louise de La Vallière bore Louis five children, two of whom survived infancy. Louis de Bourbon, the Comte de Vermandois, was the only surviving son who was legitimized by his father at the age of two and given the

Duchesse Louise de La Vallière and Louis XIV

post of admiral of France. Known to be mild, affable, and polite, he displayed all the courtesies of his mother. He was in his father's good graces until he became involved in a homosexual scandal with his uncle Philippe de France, the king's brother, and Philippe's lover, the Chevalier de Lorraine.

When the Comte de Vermandois's mother left Versailles for the Carmelite convent, the count had been installed at the court of his uncle, Philippe d'Orléans, at the Palais-Royal in Paris. There he became acquainted with, and seduced by, the Chevalier de Lorraine.

The Marquis de Sourches, in his memoirs, recalled the role of Philippe and the chevalier in the scandal:

> These young people had pushed their debauchery horribly to the limits, and the court had become a little Sodom. They had even strongly engaged the Count de Vermandois, Admiral of France, the natural son of the King and of the Duchesse de La Valliere, who was only fourteen years old. They were the ones to lose all because this prince, being pressed by the King, denounced them all.

The details of the escapades of Philippe, the Duke of Orleans, and his favorites were kept under cover, so much so that we would not have a history of them if it were not for historian Busy-Rabutin. In his *La France devenue italienne* (France Became Italian), he revealed,

> The looseness of all the ladies had rendered their charms so despicable that young men could hardly look at them anymore at court. Debauchery

(homosexuality) reigned there more than anywhere in the world even though the king testified several times that he had an inconceivable horror for this kind of pleasure. Wine and this vice, which I don't dare name, were so fashionable one hardly paid any attention to those who spent their time more innocently.

This debauched brotherhood was composed mostly of aristocrats and courtiers, but there were royals as well, which angered Louis XIV. He discovered, after his bedtime one evening, that a group of princes had gone to Paris to commit debaucheries, with many returning drunk in their coaches.

The brotherhood knew it was essential to avoid angering the king, and because one of the groups had revealed its mysteries to a woman, the brotherhood was certain that it was from this woman that the king learned of their activities. Therefore, they decided that everyone in their group had to renounce all women.

The brotherhood grew momentum and elected four chiefs, or grand priors. They also wrote a charter with the following statutes:

I. That no persons would henceforth be received in the order who were not visited by the great masters, to see if all the parts of their bodies were healthy, so that they could bear the rigors of the initiation (sodomy).

II. That they would make a vow of obedience and chastity to women, and that if no one should make a vow, he would be driven out of the fraternity, without being able to return under any pretext whatsoever.

III. That each one would be admitted indifferently in order, without distinction of quality, which would not prevent anyone from submitting to the rigors of the initiation, which would last until the "beard had come to the chin."

IV. That if any of the brothers should marry, he would be obliged to declare that it was only for the good of his affairs, or because his parents obliged him to do so, or because he had to have an heir. That he would swear at the same time never to love his wife, to sleep with a woman until she was his wife, and then only after asking permission from the brotherhood, which could only be granted to him for one day in the week.

V. That the brothers should be divided into four classes, so that each great prior might have one as much as the other. And that with regard to those who would present themselves to enter the order, the four great priors would take turns, so that jealousy could not affect their union.

VI.   That the brothers discuss with one another all that happens, so that if one should need to go, it would be based on merit.

VII.   That, with regard to unaffiliated persons, it would not be permissible to reveal to them the mysteries, and that whoever would do it would be deprived of the brotherhood himself for eight days, and even more, if the great master on whom he depended judged it so.

VIII. Nevertheless, it would be possible to open up to those whom one would hope to attract into the order; but that it should be with so much discretion, that one would be sure of success before taking this step.

IX.   That those who brought brothers to the convent would enjoy the same prerogatives for two days, which the great masters enjoyed; but, of course, that they would let the grandmasters pass before them, and content themselves with having what they would receive.

The young Comte de Vermandois eventually joined the secret group, now called La Sainte Congregation des Glorieux Pédérastes (The Holy Fraternity of Glorious Pederasts), whose members practiced *le vice italien*, the contemporary appellation for homosexual acts or sodomy. The group's activities were documented in a police report:

> A general meeting of La Sainte Congregation des Glorieux Pédérastes was held in the old Petite Rue des Marais where, after the theatre, many resorted under pretext of making water. They ranged themselves along the walls of a vast garden and exposed their podices: bourgeois, richards and nobles came with full purses, touched the part which most attracted them and were duly followed by it.

When Louis XIV discovered his son's membership in the group, he was outraged, had him flogged in his presence, and had him exiled along with the Chevalier de Lorraine and several other nobles who were also involved.

In order to cover up the scandal, it was suggested that the boy be married off as soon as possible; however, the king exiled him to Normandy before such a marriage could occur. In order to smooth things over between father and son, the count's aunt, Elizabeth Charlotte of the

Palatinate, suggested to the king that his son be sent to fight in Flanders, and the king agreed. However, when the count fell ill in battle, he continued to fight despite the royal physician's advice not to do so, hoping to regain his father's love. Consequently, the count died at the age of sixteen.[23]

His sister and aunt were greatly saddened by his death, but Louis XIV shed no tears for his son. When his mother, Louise de La Vallière, heard about his death, she was still haunted by the sin of her previous affair with the king. Her only words were, "I ought to weep for his birth far more than his death."

Louis XIV thus had a homosexual father (Louis XIII), a flamboyantly homosexual—or at least bisexual—brother (Philippe d'Orléans), a homosexual son with La Vallière (Comte de Vermandois), and an uncle, Cesar de Vendôme, whose Parisian Hôtel Vendôme was also known as Hôtel Sodôme. In fact, Vendôme was the first noble who ever dared to take leave of the king's court at Versailles for a certain cure: syphilis had eaten away most of his nose. Other members of the Vendôme family were known homosexuals and bisexuals; one of them, Louis-Joseph de Vendôme, was honored for being courageous on the battlefield and was one of Louis XIV's favorite generals.

Although Philippe, Louis XIV's brother, had two wives, he had an undeniable taste for handsome young men on whom he showered money and attention—especially his favorite, the Chevalier de Lorraine, whom he had met for the first time at the campaign of Flanders, during which Lorraine was wounded slightly. Philippe looked after him "as one treats a mistress, with infinite attentions." The scandal was so public that the king had Lorraine imprisoned in the château de Pierre-Encize in Lyon and then the Château d'If.

Duke Philippe I of Orléans, Philippe of Lorraine (depicted as Ganymede), and the Count of Vermandois

Philippe accused his wife of asking the king for his lover's imprisonment, but she died in 1670, and it was rumored that the Chevalier de Lorraine had her poisoned.

Philippe was a small, fat man with a full face and a long nose but attractive eyes and mouth. He often dressed like a woman with a long, black
powdered wig. He wore rings, bracelets, ribbons, and jewels everywhere
and was fond of perfumes and rouge. The eccentric prince Philippe was also
known to wear such high-heeled shoes that "he always seemed mounted
upon stilts."

And yes, this prince was Marie Antoinette's great-grandfather.

Could Louis XIV have been accused of hypocrisy? He could not accept
the sexuality of his son, and homosexual activity was a capital offense in
seventeenth-century France, but the king did accept the sexual preferences
of his brother, certain members of his court, the Vendôme family, and especially his court composer, Jean-Baptiste Lully. In fact, it was said that Lully
"composed almost all his operas while debauchery exalted his brain."

Moreover, Louis XIV's own adulterous affairs were numerous during
his reign. And it is interesting to note that the king did not take communion during his affairs, especially during that with Françoise-Athénaïs
de Rochechouart, the Marquise de Montespan. Adultery was a mortal
sin, but his sin with the marquise was that of double adultery; they were
both married, causing the Roman Catholic Church to soon become her
adversary. In 1675, Father Lécuyer refused to give her absolution, which
was necessary for her to take Easter communion. He was adamant about
it: "Is this the Madame that scandalizes all France? Go, abandon your
shocking life and then come throw yourself at the feet of the ministers of
Jesus Christ."

Although Louis XIV appealed to the priest's superiors, the church
refused to yield to the king's demands. After a short separation, he and
Madame de Montespan resumed their affair. She bore the king seven
illegitimate children, three of whom were legitimized and given the sur-
name "Bourbon." Curiously, the upbringing of the children was entrusted
to one of the Marquise de Montespan's friends, Madame Scarron, who
would later become the Marquise de Maintenon and Louis XIV's second,
but secret, wife.

Of the six children Louis XIV had with his queen, Maria Theresa, only
one survived. He had many illegitimate children, however, including five
with Louise de La Vallière, seven with Madame de Montespan, and even
more who were never recognized. He was "very anxious" to legitimize most

of them and establish them at court, marrying his daughters to princes of the blood.*

Many found the ambitions of Louis XIV's illegitimate, but legitimized, children scandalous, if not "monstrous." They had been given titles and allowed to marry legitimate heirs. The Marquise de Montespan, for example, was thus an ancestor of the modern *Maison d'Orléans*, the House of Bourbon-Orléans, and her great-great-great-grandson would reign as Louis-Philippe I, King of the French, in 1830.

Racine, the French dramatist, referred to the legitimization by his king as a conflict of "overlapping bodies" that affected the family's honor and continuation but also jeopardized France's future and stability. And, perhaps rightfully, the princes of the blood protested the legitimization of the "bastards," as they were called, thus rendering them equal in rank. In fact, the Edict of Marly granted two of Louis's sons by Madame de Montespan the right to succeed to the French throne.†

Despite the consequences, legitimizing children from illicit affairs was never presented more heartily than at the Château of Versailles during the reign of Louis XIV. Of these affairs, one of the most interesting was that with Marie Angélique de Scorailles, Duchesse de Fontanges, who made her début, like Mademoiselle de La Vallière, as a maid of honor to one of Philippe's wives. She was flamboyant and with extravagant taste: Mademoiselle de La Vallière had only two horses for her carriage, Madame de Montespan had four, but Mademoiselle de Fontanges required a gilded carriage with eight horses.

Madame de Montespan said Mademoiselle de Fontanges was as "beautiful and as stupid as a statue." However, the new mistress did create a fashion trend when losing her cap while hunting with the king one day. When she tied her hair up using a ribbon in a manner that pleased him, the new style was imitated by ladies at court, subsequently spreading across Europe. Despite its courtly origins, the new hairstyle, called the "fontange," was forbidden to be worn at French state occasions.

Mademoiselle de Fontanges did become pregnant with the king's child, but she gave birth prematurely to a stillborn boy and she never recovered from complications of the birth. After losing the king's favor, she was sent away from the court, but he did visit her on her deathbed and was

---

* In the language of the French heralds, the title of "princes of the royal family" was confined to the children or grandchildren of the reigning sovereign. His nephews and cousins were only "princes of the blood."

† This hugely unpopular decision led to a political crisis called the "bastard distortion" and was reversed after Louis XIV's death by the Parliament of Paris in 1717.

brought to tears. "Ah!" said the former mistress, "I die happy, since with my last looks I saw the king weep."

Mademoiselle de Fontanges did not add any illegitimate children to the king's long list, but the growing royal family was putting a strain on the slow expansion of the Château of Versailles. By the time Louis had completed the château's two main wings, it was already considered overcrowded, and rooms were still needed to serve as workplaces for the king's ministers as well as accommodations for his nobles, whose presence at Versailles the king had made obligatory. All were "housed in one teeming hotbed of subservience, scandal and intrigue."

Subsequently, the palace hallways began to fill up with refuse, and the stench was becoming unbearable. The public, too, had free rein to walk through the common rooms of the château and to stroll in the gardens; all a visitor required was a hat, gloves, and a sword—all of which could be rented at the front gate. There were no bathrooms: visitors used the stairs, the corridors, or any out-of-the-way place to relieve themselves, and the odors clung to everyone's "clothes, wigs, and undergarments," wrote historians Marie-Luise Gothein and Walter Wright.

That Louis XIV was a great king throughout his reign can be conceded, but that he was ever a great man is doubtful. The egotistical monarch "never hesitated in compelling the sacrifice of whatsoever opposed or impeded his personal interests, passions, or views." His tedious and sometimes childish observance of etiquette, along with a propensity for scandal, was inherited by successive courts at Versailles. Where his father's prudery was carried to excess, the depravity of Louis XIV's court was carried to "ridiculous excess." These included luxuries, extravagance, gambling, nonpayment of debts, debauchery, and hypocrisy.

The women of Louis XIV's court were just as guilty of these transgressions as the king. Madame de Maintenon, the king's wife in his later years, confided to one of her close friends, "The women of today are unbearable; their absurd and immodest dress, their tobacco, their drinking, their gluttony, their coarseness, their idleness, are all so repugnant to my taste, and even so opposed to reason, that I cannot endure it."

Images of Louis XIV portray a strong and virile king, but he was not as healthy as he appeared. He suffered from diabetes, dental abscesses, gout, and recurring boils, but he reigned for seventy-two years as the king of France, outliving most of his immediate family. In fact, Louis XIV's heir was his five-year-old great-grandson Louis, the Duc d'Anjou.

Although Louis's early years were known for wars and building projects, his death was anything but glamorous. The result of his carnal appetite had also left him riddled with syphilis.

As we shall see, the court of his successor, Louis XV, shared the depravity and debauchery of Louis XIV's reign. Even the character of the docile Louis XVI was tarnished by his ancestors' behavior, and immorality was a major charge raised against his queen, Marie Antoinette, when she was brought before the Revolutionary Tribunal.

3

THE *PARC-AUX-CERFS*

Louis XV's Private Bordello

All the passions at Versailles had an air of debauchery. Delicacy was banished from the court; and the whole scene of sensibility passed in the bed of the prince. The monarch often went to bed with a heart full of love, and the next day he rose with indifference.

—Madame la Marquise de Pompadour

"Le roi est mort! Vive le roi!" the messengers cried from the palace windows when Louis XIV died on September 1, 1715.

Before his death, he had said goodbye to his great-grandson, who would be the next to wear the heavy crown of France. "My dear child," he said, "you are going to be the greatest king in the world. Never forget your obligations to God."

This was spoken by a man who not only had created a modern, strong France but also had been corrupted from birth by flatterers and had mistresses bear him children out of wedlock. His thighs swollen from gangrene and his leg rotten from infections and the gout, syphilis-ridden Louis XIV died wanting everyone to lament his death.

While Louis was on his deathbed, however, many courtiers were already flocking to the court of Philippe II, the Duc d'Orléans, who was the closest living relative of the new five-year-old king. Although the Duke of Bourbon was chosen by Louis XIV to be the new king's regent, Philippe was soon able to have Louis's testament annulled by the *Parlement* of Paris, thus becoming regent himself and abandoning Versailles as the royal court until the new king's majority eight years later.

The young Louis XV, although somewhat intelligent, was opinionated, taciturn, and haughty. His parents had died when he was a child, and his governess, Duchess Charlotte of Ventadour, was like a mother to him.

She had been, in a sense, responsible for the continuation of the House of Bourbon. In 1712, measles struck the royal family, leaving Louis XIV's great-grandson, the Duc d'Anjou, as dauphin. Because his brothers' health was weakened by the royal physicians' bleeding, the duchess vowed that the young heir would not receive the same treatment. She locked herself up with three nursemaids to keep the doctors away, and the dauphin survived.

Charlotte paid a price to become a duchess when she married the Duke of Ventadour, an ugly, debauched hunchback, in 1671. Fortunately, the duke left the court to continue his life of illicit affairs, leaving the duchess at court with her inherited privileges, such as the *tabouret*.★ On one occasion, when a number of ladies were presented to the king, the Duchess of Ventadour had to wait some time before a tabouret was brought to her by the grand master. Madame de Sévigné, sitting nearby, asked him, "Monsieur, why did you not give it to her? It has cost her dear enough."

At the age of seven, the young king became frantic when he was taken from the Duchess of Ventadour's care and placed in the hands of Maréchal de Villeroy, a male selected from the court and responsible for mentoring the child in the art of kingship. The maréchal later fell into disgrace, however, for plotting against the regent Philippe and even further disgrace when two members of his family, the Duc de Retz and the Marquis d'Alincourt, were exiled from court for homosexual activities in the palace gardens.

According to custom, the kings of France had a God-given right to rule, but they were still slaves to traditions that were transmitted from reign to reign. The tradition of placing a dauphin under the care of men at the age of seven became the duty of the regent, and Philippe fulfilled it.

When living with men, the prince not only was under the tutelage of a single governor but also enjoyed the services of a captain of the guard, *maître de la garde-robe, a premier ecuyer* (squire), *a premier maître d'hotel*, an intendant, and a *contrôleur général* of the household—all assisted by additional subordinates. The household of the dauphin, for example, numbered seventy-seven persons. In fact, from the time of Louis XIII, all royal children, legitimate and illegitimate, were provided instructors in various disciplines such as falconry, languages, etiquette, and drawing.

However, the Maréchal de Villeroy's ability and intelligence was mediocre. When Madame de Ventadour advised the maréchal to teach the child to "work for the well-being of his subjects," the maréchal replied that such work was the "affair of ministers."

★ An upholstered stool and symbol of privilege, allowing one to sit in the presence of the royal family.

The court returned to Versailles, but Louis XIV, the "Sun King," and his flock of admirers were no more; yet the strict code of etiquette prevailed. The young king began to enjoy the pleasures of Versailles's sumptuous court life: the hunt, for which the child shared the passion of his ancestors; the royal table, at which he showed a formidable appetite; and the multiple temptations of the pretty young women who displayed their grace at the young king's feet.

The regent Philippe II died in 1723, and there was perhaps a reason Louis XIV had not originally named him regent for the young king. Known for his debauchery and illicit affairs, Philippe hosted intimate dinners and indulged in orgies with his guests. His buxom, fat-cheeked daughter, the Duchess of Berry, also called "Joufflotte," was known to attend these soirees, giving rise to rumors of incest.

During the regency, Philippe arranged an engagement of ten-year-old Louis XV with his cousin, the Infanta Mariana Victoria of Spain. However,

Young Louis XV of France

when Philippe died, the Duke of Bourbon replaced him as regent and ended the engagement by sending the infanta back to Spain. In her place, the duke arranged a marriage between Louis XV and a Polish princess, Marie Leszczinska, in 1725. He was fifteen years old; she was twenty-two and thought to be ugly, dull, and far from elegant.

Marie, however, spoke six languages, danced gracefully, and was well educated. The wedding night was a success, and Louis flaunted his prowess to his minister: "I did well," he said. "Soon I'll have an heir to the throne."

The first years of marriage were said to be happy ones, and the queen gave Louis ten children. But he soon became bored with Marie, who was obviously exhausted from her many pregnancies.

At Versailles, the queen was provided the same apartment in which Louis XIV's queen had resided—the same apartment in which Marie Antoinette would feel claustrophobic in the next reign, calling it the *harnais de cour*, or the "court harness." Marie Leszczinska's new chambers received very little attention or upgrades. She could have complained about being neglected, considering the exorbitant expenses for the lodging of the first official mistress, Madame de Pompadour, and the king's sisters. She certainly could have complained because the young king was no longer a spoiled, bad-mannered child; he had suddenly matured, carrying the weight of his new responsibility as monarch on his shoulders.

However, the timid Marie Leszczinska did not complain but preferred to remain far from the court's prying eyes amid her close circle of friends, where she was most comfortable. The honeymoon over, noble ladies soon forgot their scruples and dreamed of playing the role of a "queen without a crown," much like that of Louise de La Vallière, Madame de Montespan, and Madame de Maintenon in the court of Louis XIV. The timing could not have been better, with Marie Leszczinska restricting her life to ceremonial and religious matters. Louis XV, amicable, effeminate, indolent, and sensual, allowed the country to govern itself. He neglected his queen out of boredom and gave himself up to the companionship of a plethora of mistresses.

One of Louis XV's first loves was Comtesse Louise de Mailly, who apparently was dissatisfied with the relationship, given the fact that she had to share the king's favors with her own sister, Pauline-Félicité de Mailly, the Marquise de Vintimille, who gave the king a son. To the countess's dismay, two more of her sisters were added to the list of Louis XV's mistresses: Diane-Adélaïde de Mailly, the Duchess of Lauraguais, and Madame de la Tournelle, the Duchess of Châteauroux.

When lacking a mistress, Louis enjoyed visiting young women in the early hours of the morning, usually before sunrise, as they lay sleeping in

Louise-Julie, Pauline, Diane, and Marie-Anne de Mailly

their beds at Versailles. He would go from room to room, surprising them before they woke; this was called the *ronde du roi*, the king's round. Sometimes he knocked on their doors and shouted, "Fire! Fire!" Or while the demoiselles were still asleep, he would place a necklace of emeralds around their necks.

The king's round was a favorite pastime until, while hunting in the Sénard forest, the king spotted a young woman in a pink dress. He was dazzled by her beauty, and when he saw her again, she dropped her handkerchief (perhaps on purpose?), which he "eagerly picked up." Charles Philippe d'Albert, Duke de Luynes, court memoirist, must have underestimated the consequences of this meeting when he wrote, "There is talk of a Madame d'Etioles, who is young and pretty; her mother's name was Madame Poisson. It is said that she has been in this area for some time, and that she is the choice which the king has made; if it is true, she would probably only be a gallantry (prostitute) and not a mistress."

The Duke de Luynes considered prostitution a prerogative of the nobility; the court, however, found it scandalous, referring to Madame d'Etioles as a *grisette*, a working-class woman. Nevertheless, the graceful grisette was soon declared the king's new mistress and honored with an official presentation to the court by a princess of the blood, the Princess of Conti, in September 1745. Louis XV honored Madame d'Etioles with the title "Marquise de Pompadour" and in 1749 gave her a plot of land on which to build her own palace, the Château de Bellevue.

At the Château of Versailles, the new mistress preferred not to use the stairs to her *cabinets de l'attique*. She therefore moved to the ground floor of the palace despite the humidity and lack of sunshine in her new chambers, where she could more easily participate in the activities of the court to maintain her relationship with the king and thus increase her power, influence the country's politics, and ensure her place in history. It is interesting to note that this apartment had also belonged to Louis XIV's mistress, Madame de Montespan. However, Madame de Montespan never accumulated the power or wealth of Louis XV's Madame de Pompadour.

With her influence increasing every day, Madame de Pompadour soon became the *premier ministre en jupon*, the prime minister in petticoat. She was flattered and obeyed by the king's ministers, who nevertheless worked hard to see her fail. However, they were the least of her problems—the king's unrelenting boredom posed the greatest threat to her power.

When the king suffered from bouts of extreme ennui, the pleasures of the hunt and the sumptuously prepared meals were less satisfying than the pretty visitors who were discretely brought to his apartments. Madame de Pompadour had known for a long time that the king was fond of adolescent girls. The king's first chamber valet, Dominic Lebel, would pluck these sensuous "flowers" as they were just blossoming from the streets of Paris and pay their mothers for them. He then drove them at night, under some pretext, to an apartment at Versailles, the Trebuchet, where the king would first observe them from an adjoining room by gazing through a small hole in the wall.

To avoid unnecessary embarrassment over the nightly visits of young nymphs to Versailles and to secure her position, Madame de Pompadour approved the establishment of a bordello for housing and hiding the girls in a more obscure area of Versailles for the king's enjoyment. The new maison was called *Le Parc-aux-Cerfs*, or "the stag park."

Only Lebel, however, was responsible for finding beautiful young ladies, who were continuously replaced to provide variety for Louis. These

Liaison dangereuse

ladies were required to be virgins, for fear that one might transmit the *grande vérole*, or venereal disease, to the monarch.

The Parc-aux-Cerfs normally accommodated three or four well-compensated ladies who did not know or communicate with each other, and three domestics and a governess managed the house of ill repute.

By maintaining the Parc-aux-Cerfs, the Marquise de Pompadour could receive the love of the king without ever returning it. Due to the marquise's cold nature, it was said she had the beauty of a statue and required a more "lyrical temperament" for such a jaded monarch. The king had actually once spitefully remarked, "She is as bland as boiled chicken."

Knowing the king's lethargic disposition, the marquise must have understood the danger implied in the word "bland," because she solicited help from a pharmacist. At supper every day, she took a concoction of amber and vanilla to hopefully "electrify her blood."

Whether the potion was successful or not, some historians have argued that Madame de Pompadour was still successful in some of her political pursuits, including her role in arranging the future marriage of the young Marie-Antoinette-Joseph-Jeanne de Lorraine to Louis-Auguste, the Duke of Berry. But the health of the king's mistress of almost twenty years was failing, and she had one wish: if she must die, she wanted to die at Versailles.

Jeanne Antoinette Poisson, Marquise de Pompadour, and Jeanne Bécu, Comtesse du Barry

Although only members of the royal family had the right to die at the Château of Versailles, Madame de Pompadour broke that long-standing tradition on April 15, 1764.

After his favorite's death, Louis XV was left without a mistress and enjoyed the obscure ladies from the Parc-aux-Cerfs less and less. However, the valet Lebel knew his job well: when the casino owner and pimp, Comte Jean-Baptiste du Barry, introduced Lebel to his mistress, Jeanne Bécu,* Lebel was struck by her beauty and did not hesitate to arrange for a meeting with the king. At the first meeting, Louis XV was so captivated by Jeanne's charms that he refused to hear about any woman "other than this creature, the prettiest that two eyes could ever possibly see."

In order to appear at court and fulfill such an important role, Jeanne had to have a title. The Comte du Barry loved Jeanne more for the advantages she could bring him than for herself, and he would have certainly given her his name; however, he was already married. Yet he knew that anyone who married this beauty would profit immensely and be assured a high social position at court. The Comte du Barry thus decided to give Jeanne his name—by forcing his brother to marry her.

Comte William du Barry, the future husband of the king's mistress, was a poor officer in the French Navy who lived in Toulouse with his mother. Upon hearing the proposal, William was as scrupulous as his brother: he accepted the opportunity and left immediately for Paris. As soon as Jeanne became Madame du Barry, her husband returned to Toulouse to live with his mother, and Jeanne took up residence at Versailles in a second-floor apartment located precisely above that of Louis XV.

Keeping the tradition of his predecessor and housing his mistress nearby, Louis XV could visit Jeanne at any time without being seen, either by using a staircase leading to the balcony of the Cour des Cerfs or by passing through the library, one of whose doors led to one of the closets in Madame du Barry's bedroom.

Although Madame du Barry was well situated in the château, the king could not see her at court; for that, she would first have to be officially presented. Despite the obstacles, this presentation was quickly made on April 22, 1769. From that moment, Madame du Barry was recognized as Louis XV's official mistress, and she was surrounded by a crowd of courtiers, who, until her fall, never ceased to seek her favors.

Madame de Pompadour had received a brilliant education; as for her expenditures, she was generous in embellishing the arts, concerts, and theatrical

---

* Depending on the historian, sometimes known as Mademoiselle l'Ange or Jeanne de Vaubernier.

performances. Madame du Barry, on the contrary, had received no education; because she had to rely on her beauty to succeed, all her expenses were the result of her personal toilet, clothing, and intimate apartments.

Madame du Barry possessed a self-confidence that gave her the air of a woman of good society. She invited all the nobles of the court to dine with her, and at the bottom of her invitations, she included an important message: "The king honors me with his company."

The king honored Madame du Barry with much more than his company. He gave her the Château de Louveciennes and Madame de Pompadour's Château de Bellevue. However, she soon grew unpopular at court due to the increasingly extravagant gifts she received from the king. Additionally, she was always in debt, despite a generous monthly allowance from the king's treasury.

Madame du Barry's popularity was soon to be challenged even more by a newcomer. The court awaited the arrival of Marie Antoinette, the daughter of Empress Maria Theresa of Austria, with great anticipation. But little did the future queen of France know that she was about to fall into a viper's nest of intrigue, scandal, and debauchery.

The Austrian chancellor, Prince Kaunitz, must have known his princess Marie Antoinette very well, when he said, "As for our little one, all will be well, provided that no one spoils her."

⚜

À SAVOIR

Marie Antoinette's Handwriting (Vienna, Austria)

Graphology is a scientific method of studying the subconscious.

—Dr. Pierre Menard

Graphology is "the study of the character of the man, his tendencies, and aptitudes, based on that of his writing." It is not an exact science, but it is also not magic or connected in any manner with astrology. Although it cannot be used to foretell the future, it may be used to predict a writer's reaction to various situations.

Because handwriting is intricately linked to psychological and physical states of the writer at the time of writing, its energy, extent, direction, form, and rhythm can be objectively determined to translate the writer's mood. According to Menard, a person can have "different scripts at different moments in life and personal crises often reveal themselves in handwriting."

The goal of analyzing Marie Antoinette's handwriting is to discover new insights into her character during four distinct periods of her life. To accomplish this, texts on graphology from the nineteenth century have been consulted in addition to enlisting the expertise of a professional graphologist. In this section, Marie Antoinette's handwriting before leaving Vienna in 1770 has been analyzed.

When analyzing children's handwriting, basic features to be noted are slope, letter size, spacing, and letter decoration. Analyzing these helps in understanding the child's personality traits. It must be noted, however, that the first sample here was not penned by the archduchess. It was presented, however, to the empress to show the child's progress. It had been traced first in pencil by Marie Antoinette's governess, Countess von Brandis. The archduchess then followed over the penciled lines with a pen. The empress

Traced note to Marie Antoinette's teacher (circa 1768)

was thrilled with her daughter's progress until she finally discovered that the writing samples were not truly penned by her daughter. Countess von Brandis was dismissed for "allowing the princess to trace the note."

According to the graphologist, the script has a good standard of form level and is quite wide. This shows vivacity, and the writer has no inhibitions in personal relationships. The connected nature of the script suggests the writer is a consequential thinker and cooperative. It also reveals over-adaptability in the writer.

The good spacing suggests orderliness in thinking and generosity. The direction of lines is leveled, and the script is regular; this shows harmony and moderation. The slowness of the script shows the writer is cautious. The fullness in the middle zone shows warmth, heartiness, and hospitality. The small *i* with the dot placed high and to the right suggests vivacity. Ornamentation in handwriting generally suggests the writer is unreliable.

Because the original was penned by the governess, the traits outlined from the analysis (consequential thinker, cooperative, and cautious) would not apply to Marie Antoinette. They would also not be applicable because she did not display any of these more mature traits.

Another handwriting sample found, however, was a touching farewell message from Marie Antoinette to one of her ladies-in-waiting, Thérèse Durieux, a few days before she departed for France. It was dated in Vienna on April 19, 1770, on the occasion of Antoine's marriage-by-proxy in Vienna when she became the Dauphine of France: "Be persuaded dear Durieux that I will always think of you and that never forget the pains you took for me. This I assure you. Your very faithful, Antoine Archiduchesse."

The graphologist indicates that the speed, fluency, and good distribution of space of the handwriting in this sample suggest intelligence. The

Note to Thérèse Durieux (April 19, 1770)

script and signature are in agreement, which implies that the writer, for the most part, behaves in private as he or she does in public. However, the writer is more reserved and rational than his or her social persona suggests. This is indicated by the less intense forward lean when compared to the body of the script. The high *i* dots show vision and imagination. The regularity and direction of lines of the signature points to perseverance in the writer's character.

Intelligence is debatable at the archduchess's young age, but she was known to be imaginative and to behave in private as she did in public because the court life at Schönbrunn in Vienna was far less rigid and formal than that at Versailles.

Part II

MARIE ANTOINETTE, DAUPHINE OF FRANCE (1770–1774)

Dauphine Marie Antoinette

4

THE STRAWBERRY
BLONDE ARRIVES

The education of Marie Antoinette was certainly very much neglected.

—Madame Jeanne-Louise-Henriette Campan

The depravities of the Bourbon kings from Louis XIII to Louis XV were all intricately intertwined with the development and ever-expanding social and court ceremony at Versailles. Although Marie Antoinette was a member of the Habsburg-Lorraine dynasty, she was also a direct descendant of Louis XIII through his son, Philippe I, the Duc d'Orléans.

The Austrian princess grew up at the serene, familial Hofburg Palace in Vienna. Life at court was simple: according to Goethe, "The imperial family was nothing more than a large German bourgeoisie." This was an accurate depiction, considering that the imperial family members, who were kind and friendly to all, preferred to live amid their subjects. The large family seemed to be forever growing, with Empress Maria Theresa giving birth to sixteen archdukes and archduchesses.

"Will I have a boy or a girl?" the empress asked the Duke von Tarouca, one of her courtiers, in the midst of a court reception.

"A prince, without a doubt, Madame," replied the duke. "I would stake my head upon it."

"Well, I prefer something more valuable," she said. "I wager this diamond you admire so much to your two ducats that I shall give birth to a girl."

The duke accepted the bet, and when a child was born on November 2, 1755, he sent the empress the gold coins she had won, adding the following verse:

I have lost and the august daughter
Has condemned me to pay.
But if it be true that she resembles you,
Then all the world has won.

The following day, the Archbishop of Vienna christened the new princess, Maria Antonia Josepha Johanna von Habsburg-Lothringen, the fifteenth and second youngest child of the Holy Roman Emperor Francis I and the Empress Maria Theresa of Austria. The king and queen of Portugal, Joseph I and Mariana Victoria, were chosen to serve as the newborn's godparents.

Although the thirty-eight-year-old empress, recuperating from a difficult delivery, was unable to hear Mass in her chapel for six weeks, the birth of the new princess was nevertheless celebrated as tradition required. A solemn *Te Deum* was sung, and full court dress was required for those attending the two days of gala events. Festivities that were more low key were held in Budapest, Prague, and other major cities of the empire.

At the time, however, all the churches in Vienna were decorated in black to celebrate All Saints Day, reminding everyone to pray for souls in Purgatory. Known also as the Day of the Dead (*le jour des morts*) in France, this was hardly a reassuring welcome for the birth of any new princess.

Emperor Francis was obsessed with premonitions, and after having the newborn's horoscope read, he canceled the customary banquet. Superstitious souls shuddered when news arrived that, on the very day of Marie Antoinette's birth, Lisbon had been devastated by an earthquake that took the lives of thirty thousand inhabitants of Portugal's capital. In fact, Marie Antoinette's godparents were fleeing their crumbling palace at the very moment of her birth.

One of ten children still living at the time, the young archduchess received very little attention during her formative years, either at Hofburg or at the summer palace, Schönbrunn. The first notice we find of her describes a merry, lighthearted child dancing to the libretto *Triumph d'Amour* with her two brothers, Ferdinand and Maximilian, at Schönbrunn.

Another mention is that on the eve of a journey, her imperial father delayed his whole train of attendants for a few moments to receive a second kiss from his little pet. Marie Antoinette remembered this endearing moment years later: "I was the youngest of the sisters. My father took me on his knee and, with tears in his eyes, kissed me over and over again. He seemed greatly pained at leaving me, which surprised all those who were present."

Francis was often absent from court, however, for reasons other than his imperial duties. The warm affection that Maria Theresa showed her

Marie Antoinette dancing with her brothers

husband did not preclude him from indulging in more gallant, chivalrous adventures. Supper parties unknown to her from time to time took place, and it was rumored that his shooting expeditions were "not entirely spent in the pursuit of game in field or forest."

Detesting any court etiquette whatsoever at Schönbrunn, the emperor would tell ladies attending court functions, "I shall stay with you till the court is gone. By the court I mean the empress and my children; I am here only as a private person."

In a manner of speaking, Francis was a very private person. He left the wielding of power, other than that pertaining to financial matters, to his well-qualified wife, who had agreed to give up her sovereignty upon the succession of a male heir. Even then, she continued to rule side by side with her son Joseph.

Francis was especially fond of the ladies in his early married life; in fact, he was a serial adulterer who had affairs with the wife of the vice chancellor, Countess Colloredo, as well as with Empress Maria Theresa's maid of honor, Countess Palffy. Although Francis secretly arranged suppers and rendezvous with them and others, his affairs were all well known by his family and the court. Well aware of the emperor's gallant ways, the empress had him followed and spied upon at court. At times the empress's jealousy would compel Francis to restrain himself; whenever she found her husband paying too much attention to any lady, she would "pout insolently" to make her irritation known to him.

Empress Maria Theresa and Emperor Francis I of Austria

When giving advice to his son Leopold about marriage, however, he wrote warmly about the happiness of marriage but said nothing about being faithful. When the empress gave advice to her daughter Marie Christine on marriage, she ironically urged her to allow her husband "maximum freedom and never show suspicion of his relationships with other women."

Francis eventually grew weary of his wife and turned his attention to the seventeen-year-old Maria Wilhelmina von Neipperg, who was thirty years his junior. Under the pretext of going hunting, the emperor arranged extravagant parties for the beautiful maiden, who was received at court the year Marie Antoinette was born. Maria Wilhelmina, having been married to a man twice her age, was already a widower. A year later, she married the Prince von Auersperg. However, she "could not resist the fascination of the Emperor's love" and soon became his unofficial mistress. This relationship, however, did not last long.

Francis died suddenly in his carriage returning from the opera in Innsbruck in 1765, when Marie Antoinette was ten years old. Though the empress did her best to singlehandedly raise her six daughters and four sons in a manner fit for the high positions they were destined to hold in the world, no one can say how much a loving father's care and counsel might have affected the character of Marie Antoinette in her adult years at Versailles.

On the contrary, the question should be asked if her father's well-known infidelity and other amusements could have had an impact on her own psyche. Francis was always cheerful and active, of manly habits, most graceful on horseback, and one of the keenest sportsmen of his age. Hunting was his favorite amusement, and he was a very good shot, preferring the smaller game—hares, pheasants, and partridges. Besides the chase, he enjoyed tennis and billiards, and especially Pharaoh and dice, but at very high stakes. Two of his friends, the Piedmontese brothers Guasco, kept the bank against him. In 1754, Francis lost upward of ten thousand ducats to them. Marie Antoinette will also one day visit the card tables in the salons of Versailles.

Marie Antoinette's father was not the only ancestor who might have influenced the future queen of France. Her grandfather, Leopold, the Duke of Lorraine, had a mistress, the Princess of Craon, whom he encountered while on a hunting excursion on his property. He spotted the young girl, Anne-Marguerite de Ligniville, "poorly clad but matchless in beauty." After discovering that she lived in an ancient château nearby, the duke paid her a visit and, enchanted by her charm, asked the Baron de Ligniville if his daughter could be presented at his court. The baron replied, "My life is at the disposal of my sovereign; but my honor is and shall be in my own keeping. My daughter must never behold the court, unless she makes a marriage befitting our family."

Duke Leopold left but returned within a week, accompanied by Marc de Beauvau, and formally demanded that the lovely recluse become his bride.★ She accepted, but several months passed before the duke could lure her from the "honor and duty" to her new husband. The Prince de Craon and his new princess had fallen in love. The prince, however, realized that he had to cede his rights to his sovereign, and Princess de Craon was soon attending Leopold's court, where the duke was wholly devoted to her. Over the years, the Princess de Craon retained her beauty even though she bore him seventeen illegitimate children.

In 1721, Duke Leopold arranged for his legitimate son and heir, Leopold Clement, to receive an education in Vienna, where he also planned to arrange his marriage with Archduchess Maria Theresa, the heiress of Emperor Charles VI. However, Leopold Clement died shortly afterward, and Duke Leopold sent his younger son, Francis Stephen, in his stead, who became Francis I, Emperor of the Holy Roman Empire, when he married Empress Maria Theresa of Austria.†

During her entire life, the empress, a devout Catholic, showed no tolerance for any signs of immorality. She went so far as to introduce a "chastity

---

★ Marc de Beauvau-Craon, Prince de Craon, married Anne-Marguerite de Ligniville on December 16, 1704.

† Francis I became emperor, and his descendants of the House of Habsburg-Lorraine ruled Austria until 1918.

court," in which prostitutes, adulterers, homosexuals, and even members of different religions who had sexual intercourse were indicted and convicted. Depending on the crime, the sentences included whipping, deportation, or the death penalty. One person, however, who was never charged by this court was her own adulterous husband.

After her husband's death, the empress became a forbidding figure, clad in black mourning attire and absorbed with the administration of her vast empire, and she had little time for maternal obligations. Having been so engaged with the War of Austrian Succession and the Seven Years' War, Maria Theresa asserted that if she had not almost always been with child, "she would certainly have gone into battle herself."

To establish a household for her newest daughter, Antoinette, the empress chose a respectable Viennese housewife and mother, Constance Weber, as wet nurse. She also placed Marie Antoinette under the care of Countess Maria Judith von Brandis, the governess of the imperial children (Gouvernante der kaiserlichen Kinder). Marie Antoinette shared her new "aja"★ with Ferdinand and Maria Carolina, the two siblings closest to her in age. When the sixteenth and final child, Maximilian, arrived a year later, he too was placed under the countess's care.

Ferdinand's and Max's upbringing would not be left up to the rather indulgent governess for long. She taught them manners but otherwise let them enjoy their free time painting, singing, and dancing. At the age of seven, Ferdinand and Max were turned over to male instructors to prepare them for careers that would place them on the throne, in the army, or in the church.

Maria Carolina and Marie Antoinette, meanwhile, would be left under the supervision and control of Governess von Brandis until the time came for Empress Maria Theresa to find husbands for them. In fact, the empress would see her children only every eight to ten days. To fill this nurturing void, the royal physician, Wansvietten, visited the young members of the imperial family daily and reported the minutest details of their health to Maria Theresa.

As soon as any visiting dignitary of rank arrived at Schönbrunn, however, the empress would call her family to gather around her and invite them to her table, thus creating the impression that she herself was supervising her children's education. This was but an illusion.

★ A governess was called "aja," a Portuguese word meaning "Auntie," who would take charge of imperial children. She was often the general-in-chief of a small army of nurses, maids, and wet nurses.

The empress was also unaware of Governess von Brandis's negligence in her duties. Never fearing any inspection by the busy empress, the governess was able to make herself beloved by her pupils by simply being overly indulgent. Perhaps the governess was also very naïve, because Marie Antoinette soon caused her to be dismissed; the princess confessed to the empress that all her exercises and letters had first been traced out in pencil for her by the governess.

The empress immediately removed Governess von Brandis from service. Because the empress noticed that Marie Antoinette and Maria Carolina had become idle and talked nonsense, which began to raise eyebrows at court, she appointed Countess von Lerchenfeld as their new governess. The countess fulfilled her duties with great skill, but the empress discovered she had conferred her daughters' education to the talented countess too late to bring about positive change.

Royal marriages, regarded as affairs of state, were always arranged for political reasons. Because princes and princesses were betrothed to each other at a very early age, it was not unusual that marriage for thirteen-year-old Marie Antoinette was discussed. At the beginning of 1769, the French minister of foreign affairs, the Duc de Choiseul, instructed the Marquis de Durfort, the French ambassador to Vienna, to negotiate Marie's marriage to the heir of the French throne, the Dauphin Louis-Auguste, who was only slightly more than a year older than the princess.

Other than replacing Countess von Brandis with Countess Lerchenfeld, the empress had given very little thought to the education of her younger children—until she discovered that the soon-to-be dauphine of France could write neither German nor French. Moreover, her daughter was lacking in history and other disciplines appropriate for a princess of her age and rank.

That the education of Marie Antoinette was "much neglected" is certainly an understatement. Journalists boasted the superior talents of Maria Theresa's children, and they sometimes noted the answers that the young princess Marie Antoinette gave in Latin; she uttered them, it is true, but without ever understanding them and, in fact, without knowing a single word of the language.

Empress Maria Theresa realized that her daughter had been kept in the background far too long. Her handwriting was poor, and like many other girls her age, she was not fond of studying. Far from speaking her own German well, the future queen of France was less adept in speaking French, which was riddled with grammatical errors. Therefore, Maria Theresa brought two French actors to Vienna: one for pronunciation and one for singing in French. Even the tiniest details were considered, as the empress also acquired draperies, furniture, toys, and clothing from Paris to immerse the child in the French way of life.

Unfortunately, the court of Versailles disapproved of the character of the two actors, calling them "vagabonds," and they were promptly dismissed. Recommended by the Duc de Choiseul, the Abbé de Vermond was brought from France to tutor Marie Antoinette for her new role at Versailles. The abbé did his best to correct the results of von Brandis's permissive curriculum, but curiously, he took more pains to become his pupil's favorite than her instructor.

Did he keep the princess "ignorant" in order to ensure her dependence on him in France? In any event, although Marie Antoinette could not write French well, she did learn to speak it gracefully, at least well enough to take her place at the illustrious court of Versailles.

The incessant social etiquette of Versailles was never practiced at the empress's court in Vienna, where the young Marie Antoinette was often described as "coldhearted," and she was easily excited, which made her appear "hasty and impulsive." She was quick to like (or dislike) something "which she indulged with petulant vehemence." However, among Marie Antoinette's most dangerous qualities was her sarcasm. Though her manner was radiant and gracious with those she liked, there remained a tinge of haughtiness that many found offensive. She had succumbed to the "Habsburg fiber of obstinacy" and was known to be tenacious when pursuing any pet fancy.

The empress was aware of her daughter's stubbornness: "I am more and more convinced that I have not been mistaken in the headstrong and pleasure-seeking character I have long attributed to my daughter."

Accentuating Marie Antoinette's haughtiness was the fact that her very appearance invoked the perception of snobbishness. The eyes of the dauphine were azure blue with a quick, but somewhat bold, expression. She had a prominent nose, a small mouth, thick lips, and a troubling "high forehead." Marie Antoinette walked tall and carried her head high with a bit of arrogance in her countenance. A hairdresser of the day found Marie Antoinette neither pretty nor attractive. Although extremely slender, the princess lacked grace; most disappointingly, her pale strawberry blond hair seemed very "badly arranged."

It was no secret that Maria Theresa was anxious, for political reasons, to secure the hand of the Dauphin Louis for her daughter—the overarching goal was to secure an alliance with France. Yet the question of beauty and youth could not be overlooked in these diplomatic negotiations. It was customary for monarchs to send flattering miniature portraits of their princesses and princes before marriages were arranged, because the future spouses were not given opportunities to meet in person before any engagements were negotiated. The charm, as well as the intelligence of these political pawns, was a factor that could not be ignored if a princess would one day be queen of the realm and, more important, would have to provide an heir to the throne.

As early as 1768, the empress had wished to have her youngest daughter's miniature painted. She would have preferred a life-size portrait but complained that there was "no one in Vienna capable of undertaking such a work." Her own minister in France, Comte Florimond Claude de Mercy, proposed that a painter be sent to Vienna from Paris; little did the empress know that Mercy had other plans as well. He wanted to send along a "friseur" capable of showing off the fair locks of Marie Antoinette while covering up a major defect. He explained, "She has a rather high forehead with the hair growing badly. Her Majesty can assure herself that a man who is perfect at his trade will succeed in correcting, or at least in concealing, this small defect."

This trifling imperfection might have been a considerable setback at a time when high foreheads were no longer in fashion, but negotiations were soon concluded, and by the beginning of July, the French newspapers were authorized to announce the marriage. King Louis XV had also begun building magnificent carriages to receive the new dauphine on French soil.

By spring of the following year, all necessary preparations had been completed. On the evening of April 19, 1770, Emperor Joseph II and his then-widowed mother received French Ambassador de Durfort, who, on behalf of the king of France, formally requested the hand of the Archduchess Marie Antoinette for the Dauphin Louis-Auguste. After the emperor and empress gave their amiable consent, Marie Antoinette was summoned to the hall and informed of her family's approval of the proposal. The ambassador then presented Marie Antoinette with a letter from the dauphin along with his miniature portrait, which she at once hung around her neck.

Farewell to Schönbrunn. There was deep excitement in both the palace and in the city of Vienna on the morning of April 21, 1770, when Marie Antoinette bade her mother, family, and friends goodbye. The avenues and streets were a sea of sad faces. One eyewitness wrote, "The capital of Austria presents the appearance of a city of mourning."

As the procession of fifty-seven carriages rolled through the palace gates, witnesses said Marie Antoinette cried so bitterly that the tears streamed through the slender fingers covering her face, and she kept turning back again and again for a last look. Empress Maria Theresa had no idea that she was thrusting her impetuous and thoughtless young daughter into the vicious atmosphere of the court of Versailles with very little protection.

Marie Antoinette never saw Schönbrunn's long yellow facade with its green shutters—or her imperial mother—again. Little did she know that the new palatial home awaiting her, following the reign of three immoral and licentious kings and their courts, could only be described as a den of iniquity.

5

NEW FRIENDS, NEW ENEMIES, AND THE *PRINCES CHARMANTS*

It is certain that this princess, always closer to her sex than her rank, has indulged too much in the charms of private life.

—Comte Antoine de Rivarol

Marie Antoinette's stunning cavalcade proceeded from Vienna to the border of Austria and France near Kehl, where a magnificent pavilion had been erected, consisting of a salon with chambers at either end. One of these chambers was assigned to the courtiers from Vienna; the other was assigned to the delegation that had come from Paris to receive the new bride. The two courts spared no expense to compete in their display of wealth and magnificence in their respective suites.

Following French tradition on such occasions, a foreign princess would receive her wedding dress from France and retain nothing belonging to her former court. Marie Antoinette was, consequently, brought to the Austrian suite, unrobed of all her garments, except for her body linen and stockings. The doors were then opened, and the "blushing child" entered the salon, where French ladies-in-waiting rushed to meet their new dauphine. Weeping convulsively, she threw herself into the arms of the Comtesse de Noailles, her new *dame d'honneur*.

Unfortunately, the young princess was not aware that she had committed a faux pas; any physical contact with a foreign sovereign was unthinkable, even for someone of the stature of the Comtesse de Noailles.* The princess surely noticed her lady of honor had "nothing agreeable in her

---

* Marie Antoinette was also not aware that she had not respected rank. She should have greeted the Comte de Noailles first.

appearance" and she would soon learn that the demeanor of the "mistress of etiquette" was always stiff and severe.

After a quick rebuke from the comtesse, Marie Antoinette was immediately shown to the French apartment, where the few remaining articles of clothing were removed, and she was re-dressed in the most brilliant attire that the French crown could furnish. And now, after bidding her Austrian friends adieu, the princess stepped into her *berline* at the head of a stately parade of carriages for the journey to her new court at Versailles.

In the meantime, Dauphin Louis-Auguste had traveled from Paris with his grandfather, King Louis XV, and a splendid retinue of courtiers as far as Compiègne to meet his bride. When the king stepped down from the royal carriage, Marie Antoinette scurried up to him and curtseyed. The king, whose experience at the Parc-aux-Cerfs had made him a connoisseur in the matter of a young girl's charms, leaned forward and lifted her up to kiss her on both cheeks.

The king then introduced Marie Antoinette to the lanky young dauphin, who, with sleepy, short-sighted eyes, was looking on with "clumsy embarrassment." The dauphin, in turn, greeted the stranger with cold and distant respect but kissed her on the cheeks as etiquette demanded. Was the princess hurt by her future husband's indifference? Was he setting the tone for their new relationship?

Louis XV, however, was enchanted with the beauty and spiritedness of the young bride. Minutes later, when Marie Antoinette was seated in the carriage between the king and his grandson, the old man seemed more inclined than the young one to "play the role of bridegroom, chattering in a sprightly fashion, and even paying court to the girl."

Three weeks since leaving Vienna on May 15, 1770, Marie Antoinette arrived at the Château de La Muette, where her husband's brothers, the Comtes d'Artois and de Provence, awaited her. Among those invited to dine at the dauphine's table that evening were a number of courtiers and, surprisingly, Louis XV's mistress, Madame du Barry. However, Madame du Barry was no stranger to La Muette, where she often enjoyed the privacy and intimacy of the small château with the king.★

The court returned to Versailles after dinner while Marie Antoinette and her entourage remained at La Muette to spend the night. When Marie Antoinette was asked what she thought of Madame du Barry after her first encounter, she simply answered, "Charming."

★ On one occasion, when Louis XV was preparing breakfast for Madame du Barry at La Muette, it is said that she called out to the king: "France, be careful, the coffee is boiling over." He supposedly answered, "I don't give a damn. After me, the deluge."

The royal party journeyed on to Versailles, where Marie Antoinette was introduced to Louis-Auguste's brothers and sisters, ranging in age from eight to thirteen. In other words, including Marie Antoinette and her husband, they were all still children. Had they been older and wiser, perhaps the abysmal results of many of their foolish acts might have been avoided.

The marriage ceremony was performed the next day in the chapel of Versailles and followed by a wedding dinner in the new opera theater, inaugurated for the special occasion. At the head of the twenty-foot-long table sat the king, facing the stage with an orchestra. On each side of the

The siblings: Comte de Provence, Comte d'Artois, Marie Clotilde, and Elisabeth

table sat the king's three daughters, his grandchildren and the dauphine, and the princes of the blood. Madame du Barry, however, was not seated at the table; according to court etiquette, only members of the royal family were allowed to dine at the king's table on such special occasions.

The table, adorned with twenty-two place settings, was surrounded by a marble balustrade to separate the royal family from the crowd of spectators. The first course was served in golden dishes with the rest in vermeil crockery. The court was gathered in the boxes and the loges of the opera. The superintendent of the King's Music, Monsieur Rebel, with baton in hand, conducted his orchestra, which played without interruption during the two-and-a-half-hour banquet.

Among the royals at this table were Marie Antoinette's soon-to-be favorites or soon-to-be enemies. The Princesse de Lamballe, whom the dauphine had met in Compiègne upon arrival in France, would become one of Marie Antoinette's earliest favorites. She sat at the end of the table across from her father-in-law, the Duke of Penthièvre. Her husband, Louis Alexandre, had died two years earlier, after sixteen months of marriage, of a debilitating venereal disease.

Among the soon-to-be enemies at the table were the king's three daughters, the Duc d'Orléans, the Duc de Chartres, and one of her new brothers-in-law, the Comte de Provence. Soon-to-be favorites who would join the dauphine's most intimate circle, including the Comte de Vaudreuil, the Duke and Duchess of Polignac, and the Duke of Besenval, were scattered among the crowd of onlookers beyond the marble balustrade.

Nineteen years later, another famous dinner, and the last one here, will take place for the Flanders Regiment that was brought to Versailles to protect the royal family. The last occasion would have attracted little notice, but the story of the feast was distorted. The radical press, provoking revolutionary fever, reported that a "royal orgy" had taken place.

Surely all hearts were filled with happiness, except those of the newly married couple. Neither allured nor repelled by his bride, Louis-Auguste appeared tranquil and content as he sat across from Marie Antoinette. It is doubtful that he carried on an interesting conversation with his new bride. Not only was he awkwardly timid, but also it is said he had an enormous appetite, especially at this table. Perhaps apocryphal, but possible, Louis XV jokingly told the dauphin, "Do not load the stomach too much for the night."

"Why is that?" the dauphin replied. "I always sleep better when I have supped well."

And the dauphin Louis probably did sleep well, because the king learned that his grandson had left the conjugal bed very early the next morning to go hunting. And the dauphin made the following entry for his wedding night in his journal: *Rien*, meaning "Nothing."

Louis-Auguste's father, the Duke de Bourgogne, had died in 1765, leaving Louis-Auguste, the eldest of three surviving sons, to inherit his grandfather's crown. However, very little pains had been taken with his education. Due to poor health, the child was forced to move away from court to Bellevue with his governess, the Comtesse de Marsan.

At the age of six, a year earlier than was customary, the young prince passed under the direction of the Duke de la Vauguyon, who was appointed governor by the "cabals of the infamous mistress and parasites" who formed the court of Louis XV. Under such a governor, the young prince had little chance of receiving the education needed for the arduous task ahead of him. And Louis-Auguste was aware of his inferiority. When a courtier once complimented him on his precociousness, the dauphin replied, "You are mistaken. I do not have wit. That's my brother, the Comte de Provence."

Not only was the dauphin's education neglected, but also no care was taken to cultivate his taste or to polish his manners.* The Austrian ambassador, Comte de Mercy-Argenteau, pitied the nearsighted, maladroit, and grossly overweight teenager, saying, "Nature seems to have denied everything to Monsieur le Dauphin. The unfortunate prince had thick-lidded, watery blue eyes, a shambling gait, a nervous bark of a laugh, a hoggish appetite, and, because of that, a corpulent physique."

However, these were the least of the dauphin's problems when the time came to consummate the marriage. The Archbishop of Reims blessed the nuptial bed in a room that was filled with spectators. The future king and queen of France were handed their nightclothes: King Louis XV handed the dauphin his "chemise" while the Duchesse de Chartres handed the dauphine hers.

Once dressed, the newlyweds sat side by side on the bed, exposing themselves to the king, the royal family, and the courtiers. It is said that the groom appeared to be pouting while his wife acted dignified and natural. Finally, the curtain was closed, isolating the couple from the curious onlookers who finally retreated.

A heavy storm broke out that evening, accompanied by intense lightning and loud thunder, causing the château to shake. This might have been an omen because the next morning Marie Antoinette was still a virgin and the marriage would not be consummated for years to come.

---

* A still more unfortunate defect and result of his upbringing was an inability to think or decide for himself, or even to act steadily on the advice of others after he had agreed to adopt it. Such dissimulation would be one of the main reasons for his and his queen's downfall.

Newly arrived princesses to wed the dauphin or king to become queen of France were always of foreign birth for political reasons. That said, they were thus educated and mentored for their roles and comportment at Versailles, normally by the then reigning queen and her household. When Marie Antoinette became dauphine of France, however, Louis XV's queen had long passed away. And his mistress Madame de Pompadour, who could have been instrumental in showing the dauphine the ropes, had also died and been replaced by Madame du Barry.

Unfortunately, the new mistress of the king could not help Marie Antoinette acclimate to the austere codes of court behavior. The born-out-of-wedlock and former prostitute had no upbringing in court and, moreover, Marie Antoinette detested "the silliest and most impertinent creature imaginable."

Marie Antoinette quickly learned that to do and behave as she pleased, it would be necessary to be in Louis XV's good graces. When she asked Madame de Noailles what Madame du Barry's position at court was, the dauphin's lady-in-honor, rather embarrassed, answered, "She is charged with pleasing and amusing the king."

"In that case," replied the dauphine, "tell Madame du Barry that she now has a rival."

Marie Antoinette did indeed please the old king. Her lively spirit and grace rejuvenated him, spreading "a perfume of youth and liberty" at the court of Versailles. She wrote her mother, "The King has a thousand kindnesses for me, and I love him tenderly, but his weakness for Madame du Barry, who is the silliest and most impertinent creature imaginable, is pitiful. She played every night with us at Marly. Twice she sat near me, but she did not speak to me, and I did not try to make any conversation with her."

Madame du Barry was surely jealous of her new rival, calling her "la petite rousse"—carrot-top—behind her back. But Madame du Barry was the least of Marie Antoinette's problems. Several of her husband's closest relations had a personal interest in her downfall at Versailles. If she could not provide the kingdom with an heir, her marriage could be repudiated, and she could be sent back to Austria. This would give her husband's two younger brothers a chance to mount the throne in her husband's place.

Within a month of the wedding, the court was well aware of Louis-Auguste and Marie Antoinette's marital problems. Ambassador Mercy reported to Maria Theresa in July that even the king had spoken of the dauphin's coldness toward his new wife: "It's necessary to let him be," said the king. "He's extremely timid and unsociable to the point of not being like other men."

One evening at the theater, the dauphin was impatient and did call it an evening early to take his bride to bed. However, to the dauphine's dismay, he only went to bed early so he could rise early to go hunting. Could Louis-Auguste have also been intimidated by Marie Antoinette at social events? It was noted how beautifully she danced in comparison with her heavy-footed husband. Or could he have been jealous that the dauphine was always the center of attention?

The dauphin may not have been totally at fault for their bedroom woes. According to Comte de Mercy, Marie Antoinette preferred to go on the short weekly trips that the king regularly took rather than to remain at Versailles to consummate her marriage. Also, the Comtesse de Noailles complained that the dauphine refused to wear a corset or clean her teeth regularly. And Madame du Barry reported that the dauphine had simply "neglected her toilette."

But Marie Antoinette was also sharp-tongued. For example, she was known to chastise the gluttonous dauphin for severe bouts of indigestion,★ most often caused by overeating pastries. In fact, on one occasion, she had all such dishes removed from the table and she forbade them to be served for some time afterward. Overall, the dauphin was healthy and, according to his journal, hardly ever ill—except for his indigestion, which was frequent.

"Mariée et sans mari," or married and without a husband, was whispered by those at court who disliked Marie Antoinette. Fortunately, Marie Antoinette found comfort in her miserable position at court in new friends, especially the Princesse Marie-Louise Thérèse de Lamballe, the daughter of the Prince de Carignan of Savoy. Although only twenty years of age, the Princesse de Lamballe had already become a widow, losing her husband, Prince Alexandre de Lamballe, to a *maladie galante*† just two years earlier.

The prince had frequented the parties of the Duc d'Orléans where he contracted venereal disease from a "hussy in the orgy room" at the duke's palace. The prince had to be castrated due to his affliction and was nicknamed the "prince sans (without) balls."

The Princesse de Lamballe, however, was "sweet and amiable," winning the esteem of everyone at court—except for one courtier.[26] Because a marriage between Louis XV and the princess had been considered, the mere presence of the widowed princess struck fear in the heart of Madame

---

★ Indigestion, sometimes referred to as the "vapors," was extremely common and almost always the result of overeating.

†Venereal disease was called *maladie galante*, or gallant sickness, because courtiers considered it a symbol of their conquests.

du Barry, which only created a stronger bond of friendship between the princess and Marie Antoinette.

By the end of 1770, the Princesse de Lamballe suffered from "violent" headaches and would fall into a swoon from nervousness. Madame de Genlis, a lady-in-waiting at the Duc d'Orléans' court, accused the princess of staging the fainting spells to bring attention upon herself. On one occasion, when the princess heard a valet-de-chambre yawn loudly in an adjoining room, she was so alarmed that she fainted in her canape. She was brought around after physicians bled her,* and the fainting spell was attributed to not having eaten dinner. Such scenes occurred, however, several times a week—to the point of becoming fashionable at court.

However, as we shall see, her illness was possibly more serious than the physician's diagnosis.

By the end of 1770, Madame du Barry had scored another victory. She had secured the dismissal of the Duc de Choiseul, France's foreign minister. Supported by Madame de Pompadour, the duke had negotiated Marie Antoinette's marriage contract between Empress Maria Theresa and Louis XV, and Marie Antoinette had considered Choiseul her guide and trusted counselor and thus sided with Choiseul's pro-Austrian faction at court, but the court became anti–du Barry. On December 24, Madame du Barry triumphed over her old enemy and the duke was sent into exile by Louis XV.

With fuel added to the fire, the feud between Marie Antoinette and Madame du Barry would continue into the new year. On the other hand, the dauphine's friendship with Lamballe would become as strong as ever. Or perhaps too strong? The Comte de Mercy reported to Empress Maria Theresa on March 17, "For some time past the Dauphiness has shown a great affection for the Princess de Lamballe."

Because the princess was a princess of the royal blood, she had close contact with the dauphine, and they shared common tastes for the countryside, solitude, and simplicity.† As the dauphine's favorite, the princess consented to increase the opportunities to see her and entertain her. When apart, Marie Antoinette would "draw images of the princess and weep about missing her."

The Comtesse de Noailles hosted a ball every week for the dauphine. Because the countess's apartment at Versailles was small, she could only invite the

---

* When ill, patients were expected to be bled. Even children were not spared—a practice that helped to account for the high rate of infant mortality in the eighteenth century.

† The Princesse de Lamballe owed her position at the dauphine's court to the fact that her husband's grandfather was the third son of Madame de Montespan and Louis XIV.

Marie Thérèse Louise de Savoie Carignan

princes and princesses of the blood royal and a small number of distinguished courtiers from Paris. The dauphin, Monsieur (the Comte de Provence), the Comte d'Artois, and the princes and princesses of the blood always attended. Madame de Lamballe attended too, and from the very first ball, she was distinguished by the dauphine, who "did not delay treating her with friendship and confidence." It was with the Princesse de Lamballe that the dauphine conversed most often, and "their affair soon became very intimate."

In the spring of 1771, the Comtesse de Brionne proposed that her son, the Prince de Lambesc, marry the Princesse de Lamballe. However, Marie Antoinette was asked to give the princess permission to marry. If the princess had married, she would have lost her rank at court and, in turn, Marie Antoinette would have lost her closest confidante at a time when she was still suffering as a "mariée sans mari." Therefore, Marie Antoinette refused.

Also in the spring of 1771, arrangements were being made for the marriage of the dauphin's fifteen-year-old brother, the Comte de Provence. The count's education had formally concluded in April, when he received his own independent household. A month later he was married by proxy to Princess Joséphine Louise of Savoy and the court journeyed to the Château of Fontainebleau to receive the count's Italian bride. She was also met there by her cousin, the Princesse de Lamballe. On this occasion, Madame du Barry was not invited.

It was rumored that the necessity of leaving Madame du Barry behind "threw the king more into the company of Marie Antoinette than he had been on any previous occasion," and it appeared that her graceful manners made a complete conquest of him. In his dressing gown, he went to the dauphine's apartment for breakfast and spent a great portion of the day there. The courtiers even began to speculate on the possibility of the dauphine bringing down the king's mistress. Although Louis was careful to pay his new daughter-in-law Joséphine the honors and attention that were her due as a new addition to his court, he returned as hastily as he could to spend time with the dauphine.

Marie Antoinette, on the other hand, took special care to distinguish her new sister-in-law on all occasions with "the most marked cordiality and affection," but she remained the center of attention throughout the festivities. There was no comparison between the charming dauphine and the new Comtesse de Provence, who "had no beauty, nor accomplishments, nor graciousness." In fact, the count found his wife so repulsive, tedious, and ignorant of the customs of the court of Versailles that their marriage would remain unconsummated.

The reason for the unhappy marriage was unknown. Some historians believed the count to be impotent; others placed the blame on his wife's poor personal hygiene: "She never brushed her teeth, plucked her eyebrows, or used any perfumes." Her lady-in-waiting, the Duchesse de Valentinois, finally confided with her that she must use rouge in order to please her spouse, and the countess agreed she would make a special effort to adjust to French customs.

However, the Comte de Provence had little right to complain. At the time of his marriage, he was already obese and "waddled instead of walked." He never exercised and continued to eat enormous amounts of food. Although the Comte de Provence was not infatuated with his wife, he still boasted that the two enjoyed vigorous conjugal relations—even though such declarations were held in low esteem by courtiers at Versailles. He also proclaimed his wife to be pregnant merely to spite Louis-Auguste and his wife, Marie Antoinette, who had not yet consummated their marriage.

Eventually living mostly separate lives, the Comte de Provence was reputed to have a romantic relationship with his favorite courtier, the Duc d'Avaray; his wife, Marie Joséphine, on the other hand, was reputed to have a romantic relationship with her favorite lady-in-waiting and reader, Marguerite de Gourbillon.★ Marie Joséphine, turning to the bottle in her despair at court, showered Madame de Gourbillon with favors, gifts, and affection. Because Madame de Gourbillon was accused of perverting Marie Joséphine by supplying her with alcohol, she was exiled from court. This scandal was confirmed by François de Lescure in his memoirs.[35]

The Comte de Provence did, however, convince his wife to side with Madame du Barry against Marie Antoinette. He even allowed, if he did not encourage, Madame du Barry and her followers to speak "slightingly" of the dauphine in his presence. The dauphine soon learned that the count could not be trusted. On one occasion, the Comte de Provence imprudently discussed some of his schemes with the door open while the dauphine was in the next room. She confronted him, telling him she had heard all that he said, and reproached him "for his duplicity."

The dauphine soon discovered that the Comtesse de Provence was as little to be trusted as her husband, and the only member of the family whom she really liked was the energetic young Comte d'Artois. She told her mother, "Although still being educated, he shows feelings of honesty, that one cannot believe that his governor is not aware of them."

The dauphine was also swayed by the young count's adventurous spirit and taste for pleasure, which would be detrimental to the dauphine's reputation, by enticing her to attend the horse races, the balls at the Opéra, and parties to which her husband was not invited—all activities that were not befitting of a future queen and the cause of irreparable slander.

The Comte d'Artois was also rumored to be one of Marie Antoinette's lovers. Known for debauchery, the comte, although married, would later meet the love of his lifetime through one of Marie Antoinette's favorites, also a married woman.

The Comtes d'Artois and Provence were still only boys, and Marie Antoinette knew them to be selfish and untrustworthy. She therefore turned

---

★ Although Louis became king in 1814 after years in exile during the French Revolution and Napoleon's empire, Marie Joséphine never became queen. She had died in 1810.

to her husband's aunts for friendship and advice. However, the three aunts at court were not only jealous of the dauphine but also "narrow-minded, intriguing, and malicious."

These aunts were known as *Mesdames Tantes*, all unmarried daughters of Louis XV. Clumsy and plump like the dauphin, they were also described as "old wenches [who never] knew what they wanted to say and always wriggled as if they wanted to make water."

Madame Campan, the dauphine's reader, recollected in her memoirs that thirty-eight-year-old Princess Victoire was so chubby that the king called her "Piggy." Her sister, Princess Sophie, was "remarkably clean but horribly ugly, and therefore known as 'Grub.'" The eldest, Princess Adélaïde, was strong-willed but "shabby with slovenly personal grooming" habits. She was known as "Rag" to her father and never married to keep her high rank at court. Victoire and Sophie did likewise and remained unmarried for the rest of their lives.

The youngest daughter, Louise, had taken up the veil at the convent at Saint-Denis after the arrival of Madame du Barry. The words "Moi, Carmelite, et le roi tout à Dieu" (I Carmelite, and the King all to God) reflected Louise's willingness, with her sacrifice, to redeem the soul of her father and atone for his sins.

With the ascension of the favorite du Barry, the Mesdames Tantes retired from many court activities, devoting most of their time to music and harp lessons, but remaining resolutely hostile to their father's mistress.

The aunts were all painfully jealous of Marie Antoinette's relationship with the king. She had gained a "general popularity" such as the sisters had never won in their whole lives from their father. Pretending to be caring advisers to the dauphine, they put ideas into her head about Madame du Barry, using her to "serve as an instrument to manifest a hate that one does not dare to display oneself."

Mesdames Tantes Victoire, Adélaïde, and Sophie

The king's sisters were not strangers to scandal. When the health of Madame de Pompadour was deteriorating in the 1750s, Adélaïde became such a close companion of her father for a time that it caused rumors of an incestuous relationship. It was also rumored that Adélaïde was the true mother of Louis de Narbonne, born in 1755 by her father. The child was brought up by the Mesdames Tantes, and courtiers always whispered about the physical similarities between him and the king.

Whether the accusations of incest were true or not, Adélaïde was known for her beauty, and the king was jealous of any of her admirers. On one occasion, when a courtier was caught staring at Adélaïde's figure, the king was so enraged that the courtier was banished from court. And when Adélaïde sent a young guard a gold *tabatière*, a snuffbox, with a note saying, "This will be precious to you; you will soon be informed from whose hands it comes," the king, when he learned of the gift, sent the guard into exile to "the end of the French realm."

Incest was not unknown at the court of Versailles. M. de Choiseul had married his sister, Beatrix. Although giving her a nominal husband, M. de Grammont, she remained constantly by her brother's side, to the despair of the seventeen-year-old Madame de Choiseul. Finding his sister "more spirited and amusing than his wife," he did nothing without his sister, even attending the king's suppers with her.

Choiseul considered the marriage between Marie Antoinette and the dauphin in 1770 a personal triumph, and he had always been supported by Louis XV's mistress, Madame de Pompadour, but he was strongly opposed by the faction grouped around Madame du Barry after Pompadour's death. Marie Antoinette, one of the duke's ardent supporters, will one day lose a battle with Madame du Barry, when Choiseul is replaced by the Duc d'Aiguillon, a member of du Barry's clan.

6

FANS AND THE ART OF SEDUCTION

*It is not necessary for a queen, who must live and die on a real throne,
to taste this fictitious empire, which gives grace and beauty to ordinary
women and makes them queens for a moment.*

—Comte Antoine de Rivarol

Before Marie Antoinette arrived in France, a *corbeille de mariage* (wedding basket) had been prepared for her. On the eve of her wedding at the Château de Muette, King Louis XV presented her with jewels from the basket that belonged to his late queen Marie Leszczinska and a string of pearls from Louis XIV's queen, Anne of Austria. On the day of the wedding, the king presented her with diamonds and pearls belonging to the dauphin's mother, Marie-Josèphe de Saxe. The wedding basket also included a blue medallion on a diamond chain, a pocket case, gloves, shawls, laces, and an exquisite fan bordered by diamonds.

The most important accessory in the basket was the fan. The culture of Versailles mingled flirtation with concealment, and fans were used to send flirtatious signals as part of a "complex, gestural language of seduction."

Many ladies' hand fans, during most of Louis XV's reign, were imported from China with designs painted on white silk with gold-threaded embroidery. In the late 1760s, fans crafted in France became popular, which highlighted personal scenes, symbols of love and weddings, or current events such as comets, eccentric fashions, or the first balloon flights. The fan became a social object with its use highly regulated at court. For example, it was forbidden to open a fan in front of the queen, unless you were using it as a tray to present her with a small item. Moreover, according to the "Academy of the Fan," there were a number of ways to flutter a fan: "There is the angry flutter, the modest flutter, the fearful flutter, the confused flutter, the cheerful flutter, and the amorous flutter; in a word, there is almost no passion of the soul, in a fan, that has no analogous flutter."

A great scandal ensued when the Countess of Egmont opened her fan in defiance of the tradition and covered her face. It is not known why she opened it, but the ladies at court began to whisper, and her husband and father, very formal gentlemen at court, were deeply humiliated even though Louis XV and his queen were unaware of the event.

Marie Antoinette signaling with her hand fan?

Marie Antoinette often used the fan to hide her emotions from those at court. When the Marquise de Clermont-Tonnerre, tired of standing, sat on the parquet floor, hiding behind the lacy barricade of Marie Antoinette and her ladies' dresses, she began to mischievously tug on the ladies' skirts to attract attention to herself. When Marie Antoinette hid her grin behind her fan, the older ladies, feeling ridiculed, were incensed by such disrespect. They complained that she lacked decorum, and they would never attend her court again.

Marie Antoinette appeared rather sad one evening while gambling, when a rare accident brightened the scene. The Marquis du Lau, who was also playing cards, let out a noisy wind that amazed all those in attendance. The ladies all opened their fans to hide their laughter. Marie Antoinette, too, could not help but burst out laughing behind hers.

Other courtiers used the fan to cover their face but for reasons of hygiene; they often used the fan to hide their rotting teeth or divert their bad breath. But the fan had many other uses and meanings. When the fan was opened, a courtier could reveal her social status by the quality of the fan or her personal and political ideals by the choice of images on the face of the fan.

As for the art of seduction, the language of the fan was imperative. Studying the fan's intrinsic symbolism was required:

> Yawning behind the fan: Leave, you bore me.
> Holding it up to the right shoulder: I hate you.
> Lowering it close to the ground: I despise you.
> Closing it to touch the right eye: When will I see you?
> Motioning closer from a close range: I want to be with you all the time.
> Closing it at close range: Do not be too daring.
> Raising it with the right hand: Are you faithful to me?
> Hiding eyes behind the fan: I love you.
> Submitting a fan: I like you.
> Concealing the left ear at close range: Do not reveal our secret.
> Holding the fan close to the heart: I am yours for life.
> Slowly closing the fan: I accept all.

Presenting the dauphine gifts at court was not customary and would be seen as improper, but the Princesse de Lamballe presented a bouquet of artificial flowers, having just been invented, to the dauphine in 1772. She used the flat side of her fan to present them to her. However, when the Duc de Lauzun presents Marie Antoinette a gift one day, a court scandal will ensue.

When the dauphine visited the gardens of Marechal de Biron and met his nephew, Armand Louis de Gontaut, Duc de Lauzun, she found him to be witty and chivalrous, and he was soon received by Marie Antoinette at Versailles. A supporter of the Duc de Choiseul and the anti–du Barry clan, he soon became one of the darlings of her court.

Marie Antoinette always demanded the respect due her at court, but she was prone to being too familiar at times. When she was walking in the Trianon gardens with the Duchess of Devonshire one afternoon, she noticed that the Duc de Lauzun was approaching on horseback in tight *culottes*, or breeches. She also knew that her friend, being English, did not find it proper to discuss such items of clothing.

"What do you call *culottes* in English?" asked Marie Antoinette.

The duchess was surprised and blushed: "Small clothes."

"Oh, but I read 'breeches' in the dictionary," she said.

"But one does not pronounce such words, Madame. They are inexpressible."

When Lauzun arrived, Marie Antoinette said with a grin, "I love these irresistible culottes."

"I said inexpressible," snapped the duchess.

"Oh, pardon me, my dear. I misunderstood you," she said. "From now on I will say 'small clothes irresistible' even if a giant like monsieur wears them."

Marie Antoinette's entourage was as ecstatic as the duchess was confused.

When Choiseul was exiled from court, he returned to his Château of Chanteloup but "refused to fade into genteel obscurity." The Duc de Lauzun, now more known for his "rakish excesses," decided to follow Choiseul into exile. Because he did not seek permission from the king to leave court, there were rumors of his arrest, but the king had not given the orders. Lauzun was welcomed back at court, and many courtiers, as well as the dauphine, asked him about Choiseul.

In 1772, Lauzun traveled to England, to attend the horse races, win trophies, and pursue women. He had fallen in love with Lady Sarah Bunbary and Princess Isabelle Czartoryska, both known for notorious affairs. Lady Sarah was divorced for her adultery and for having illegitimate children, and Lauzun claimed he was the father of Princess Isabelle's second son.

When Lauzun returns to Versailles, however, Marie Antoinette will be queen and the Princesse de Guéménée will invite him to her infamous soirees attended by the queen, knowing that the queen liked men in uniform. Even the married Princesse de Guéménée will have a scandalous fling with the "handsome Lauzun."

Louis XV had been lenient with Lauzun's escapades, but he, too, was the source of new whisperings. There were rumors that Madame du Barry was losing the king's interest, and he might therefore remarry. They were, however, without foundation and the king took an opportunity to disprove them. On November 16, 1773, when his grandson, the Comte d'Artois, married Marie Thérèse of Savoy, he broke with tradition and invited Madame du Barry to the wedding banquet, normally confined to the royal family and the princes and princesses of the blood. To everyone's astonishment, the mistress appeared "radiant as the sun, wearing five million livres worth of jewels on her person."

The Comte d'Artois was unhappy about the surprise guest at the banquet, but he was perhaps even more disappointed by his wife, the new princess at court, who was even less attractive than her sister, Madame de Provence. According to Ambassador Mercy, she was "pale and thin, had a long nose and a wide mouth, danced badly, and was very awkward in manner." So awkward that even Louis XV himself, though usually very punctilious in his courtesies to those in her position, was quite obvious in showing how little he admired her.

One would presume that the Comte d'Artois would "settle down" once he married, but that was fanciful thinking. The prince devoted himself formally to his conjugal duty at his Château of Saint-Cloud, but soon his gallant adventures with Lauzun and the Duc de Chartres led him from his château to "several discreet little houses in the capital" of ill repute. Among his conquests, the actress Louise Contat will give him a son, shortly before receiving, as a gift of separation, a mansion in Chaillot. There would be more mistresses and more illegitimate children to come.

Soon after the Comte d'Artois's wedding at Versailles, a handsome, self-confident Swedish noble, Comte Axel von Fersen, arrived in France after traveling across Europe for four years with his mentor, Bolémany. In January 1774, the Comte de Creutz, the Swedish ambassador, escorted Fersen to Versailles, where he met the royal family and paid court to Madame du Barry. Fersen wrote in his journal on New Year's Day:

> It was necessary to go to Versailles to pay court to the King and to see the ceremony of the order of the Holy Ghost. I had ordered my coach at eight o'clock but, cursing like a mad man, I was obliged to wait until half past eight when the tailor brought me a fur coat I had ordered the morning before. At ten o'clock I was at Versailles. The ceremony was only a mass where the King and all the knights attend in ceremonial dress and, after having dined, I went with Count Creutz to visit Madame

du Barry. She spoke to me then for the first time. Afterward, we went back to Paris and I went home to sleep being quite tired.

Fersen never mentioned the dauphine in his daily journal during his first days in France, but he did describe a conversation with her at a masked ball on January 30 at the Opéra: "I spoke to the dauphine for some time without knowing it was her. When she was recognized and everyone crowded around her, she retired to the [royal] balcony. I left the ball at three o'clock in the morning."

Hans Axel von Fersen

Fersen was not just handsome, as his miniatures portrayed. Historians wrote of his sensual mouth that already spoke of a formed character with some disdain, but without bitterness. His brown (some said blue) eyes, velvety and tender, were seductive yet naïve, but the flame of his gaze belied the calmness of his conversation. He was slender with the benevolent air of a grand seigneur free of arrogance. All these traits were pleasing to women, so the question remained: had Marie Antoinette not been taken aback by the dashing young count?

Perhaps not. Marie Antoinette was self-indulgent: attending balls, gambling, and reveling in late-night activities to overcompensate for the pervasive, boring etiquette at the court of Versailles. For four years, too, she had been humiliated on a daily basis by the coldness of her husband and his inability to consummate their marriage. And moreover, she was surrounded by jealous brothers and sisters-in-law, aunts, and her rival, the king's haughty mistress. She might have noticed Fersen, but there appeared to be no *coup de foudre*, or love at first sight.

Fersen resumed his journey through Europe in May but returned to Paris on May 10 when he heard that Louis XV had passed away. Two days later, he continued his journey and at the end of the year returned to Stockholm, where his gay king, Gustave III, anxiously awaited him.

Louis XV became ill in April 27, 1774, at Trianon. He woke with pain in his legs, a migraine, and shivers. He had little breakfast and went hunting but stayed in his coach, complaining of the cold. His doctor diagnosed a dangerous fever and insisted that the king return to Versailles. If the physicians should bleed three times, the king knew that he would need to receive the last sacraments, so they only bled him twice to keep from alarming him. Madame du Barry certainly feared the king receiving the sacraments, because she would then have to be sent away, as tradition dictated.

The physicians could not name Louis XV's ailment until, on April 28, red pustules appeared on the king's face. The royal family was immediately informed and begged not to approach the king—he had *la variole*, better known as smallpox or *la petite vérole*.

❧

À SAVOIR

Marie Antoinette's Handwriting (1770–1774)

Louis-Auguste and Marie Antoinette were married at Versailles on May 16, 1770, and after the religious ceremony was concluded, Louis XV signed the marriage contract, followed by his blood relations in order of precedence.

Louis XV's signature was large and well practiced. Dauphin Louis-Auguste signed next in a thin but accurate manner and then handed the pen to his new wife, who was to sign third. She was able to get through "Marie" with no problem, but from that point onward the writing became awkward and skewed. The "J" in *Josepha* became a huge blot, and she wrote her name *Jeanne* without an *e* as *Janne*. She was no doubt relieved to hand the pen to her new brother-in-law, the Comte de Provence.

According to the graphologist, Marie Antoinette's signature on the marriage contract was written hastily. The script size is small, and the left tendencies of the lower zone show passive sympathy and a bit of narcissism. The signature is rather disconnected and may show self-reliance and

Marie Antoinette and Louis-Auguste's signatures on their marriage contract (May 16, 1770)

individualism. The leanness in the upper zone may also suggest mental clarity and an analytical mind.

A "bit of narcissism" would certainly have been possible, considering the venue of Marie Antoinette's wedding. It was a private affair in Louis XIV's chapel at Versailles, where only nobles of high descent were granted access and spring sunshine "pierced the stained-glass windows, embroidered brocades, and shimmering silks, all the glories of those set apart by privilege and wealth."

After living at Versailles for almost two months, Marie Antoinette wrote to her mother, signing "La plus soumise fille Antoinette" or "The most obedient daughter Antoinette."

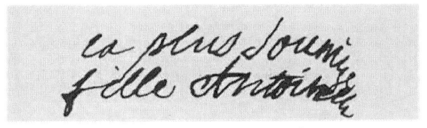

From the dauphine's letter to Maria Theresa (July 12, 1770)

According to the graphologist's analysis of this letter,

- This signature has a garland nature and leans slightly to the right. The initial enrollment in the letter "A" coupled with the lower loop in the letter "F" indicates shrewdness and opportunism.
- This signature has qualities that indicate the Szondian factor "hy" due to its garland connections, uneven base line, and its over-connected nature. These factors suggest the writer enjoys the finer things in life.
- The signature started out with good spacing, but the letters were soon meshed together towards the end. This may have simply been due to the writer running out of space. However, the direction of lines remained consistent (descending nature). This points to pessimism in the writer's outlook on life.

Whether Marie Antoinette was shrewd and opportunistic at such a young age is debatable, but after two months in the etiquette-ridden chambers of Versailles, it might have been possible for her outlook to be pessimistic, especially considering the inability of her husband to "please" her.

A year later, the royal family attended the wedding of Duke Louis-Alexandre-Céleste d'Aumont and Antoinette Marguerite de Mazade. King

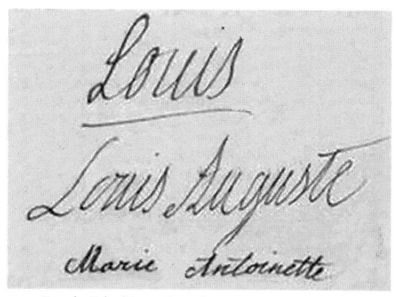

From the Duke d'Aumont's marriage contract (August 19, 1771)

Louis XV, Louis-Auguste, and Marie Antoinette served as witnesses and signed the marriage contract.

According to the graphologist, Marie Antoinette's signature on the Duke d'Aumont's marriage contract shows her to be cooperative, intelligent, and a consequential thinker. Her signature is also simple, showing her to be orderly but insecure when it suits her.

After a year at Versailles, Marie Antoinette would have been subjected to a very orderly routine governed by court etiquette, which she detailed in her first letters to her mother in Austria. However, she detested the court tradition and especially the Comtesse de Noailles, a "stickler for old ideas," whom the dauphine nicknamed "Madame Etiquette."

The young dauphine was certainly capable of being shrewd, especially in her relationship with Madame du Barry, for whom she made no attempt to hide her contempt. In fact, she humiliated the king's favorite by not speaking to her despite warnings from her empress mother. Exasperated by Marie Antoinette's stubbornness, Louis XV finally sent her a message (via the Austrian ambassador) to at least speak a few words—in public—to Madame du Barry.

Interestingly, the graphologist found Louis-Auguste's signature to be lean in the middle and lower zone, suggesting that he was business minded and a realist, pointing to sexual sublimation as well. She added, "This person is a matter of fact person and comes off as cold and rigid sometimes."

A page at the court of Versailles would have agreed with this characterization of Louis-Auguste. He wrote that Louis "was very far from spending his life in debauchery; all his time that could be spared from business and audiences was employed in hunting or devoted to study."

Three years later, on May 10, 1774, Marie Antoinette wrote to her mother about the death of Louis XV: "My God, what are we going to become!" she wrote. "M. Dauphin and I are terrified to reign so young."

Professional analysis of Marie Antoinette's letter to her mother reveals not only a sense of humility but also, at the time, a sense of perseverance:

- The handwriting extends significantly into the upper and lower zones, this along with its direction of script (forward sloping) shows spontaneity, relaxation, and sociality. The writer wants to make an impression on people.
- The small script size shows humility and tolerance, which can translate to a lack of self-confidence in some situations.
- The vertical style of writing shows expressiveness and sociability and a bit of haste in the writer's character.
- The script is disconnected. This points to productive observation and, sometimes, loneliness. The script suggests impulsiveness.
- The narrow script shows inhibition in personal relationships. This, coupled with the disconnected script style, shows the writer to be persistent, intuitive, and self-reliant.
- The narrow distribution of the script reinforces the fact that the writer is spontaneous and impulsive in nature.
- The direction of lines on the script is straight; this can be interpreted as perseverance. The writer can also be seen as being methodical and consistent. This is reinforced by the regularity of the script.
- The high pressure of the script shows the writer to be an idealist and impressionable. The script is speedy, pointing to spontaneity.

After four years at Versailles, the eighteen-year-old dauphine would become queen of France on the death of King Louis XV. The most interesting traits discovered by this handwriting analysis are those with respect to spontaneity and sociality. The dauphine's antics had already included incognito trips to Paris, horseback riding despite her mother's disapproval, and a love for playacting with her brothers-in-law, all activities inappropriate for a princess of her rank. She was also persistent; her mother had long complained about Marie Antoinette's "headstrong and pleasure-seeking character" when she was a child.

Part III

THE BARREN QUEEN'S TEMPTATIONS (1774–1778)

Peace Bringing Back Abundance

7

GALLANT PURSUERS

Every day she supplies the wicked all their weapons against her.

—Prince of Kaunitz-Rietberg to Comte de Mercy, 1775

Smallpox was the dreaded scourge of Versailles, and many fled the court for fear of contagion. However, Mesdames Tantes, the daughters the king had often "scolded and snubbed," remained at their father's bedside at great risk to their lives until the end, which occurred on May 10, 1774. The palace clock was stopped, as was custom, at a quarter past three in the afternoon when Louis XV took his last breath.

Tradition also dictated that a surgeon remove the heart from the royal cadaver and depose it in a Parisian church. However, no one dared approach his remains, let alone cut open the rapidly decomposing body. The dead king's putrefying flesh was emitting a foul odor throughout the palace before he was finally transferred to his crypt in the Basilica of Saint-Denis, the burial place for nearly every king of France. Louis XV would be the only king to be interred here with a heart.

When the physicians had finally diagnosed the king's illness as smallpox, there was little doubt how the king was exposed to the disease. A thirteen- or fourteen-year-old girl in Versailles had the same severe symptoms—the same girl whom Madame du Barry had procured for the king's bed weeks before his illness. She had "found the child, brought her to Trianon, cleaned her up, perfumed her, and presented her to the king." Unfortunately, Madame du Barry was not aware of the condition of the gardener's daughter, who had the *petite vérole*.

Courtiers whispered that Louis XV caught the disease from the innocent victim as his "punishment from Heaven." However, it was also rumored that he purposely gave the young lady the *grande vérole*, syphilis, in return, thinking he could thus rid himself of his venereal disease by giving it to others. That courtiers could espouse such a horrific claim only speaks to the king's depraved reputation at court. A chronicler wrote, "The gift of the King's illness to young, robust persons, lively and in good health, appeared the only appropriate means for enticing His Majesty's morbific humors out of him, thus rejuvenating his person."

Learning of the king's illness, those courtiers allied with the du Barry clan had reason to worry. A few days before the king's death, Madame du Barry had already been exiled from Versailles to the Duc d'Aiguillon's estate near Rueil.

Other courtiers, however, rushed to announce the tidings to the new monarchs amid shouts of "Vive le roi," but nineteen-year-old Louis XVI and eighteen-year-old Marie Antoinette had tearfully fallen to their knees, praying in awe of the great responsibility they had just inherited. Nevertheless, they wasted no time in fulfilling their new roles. The first act of the royal couple was to remove any trace of the scandal that had plagued the last years of late king's reign.

On the very day of Louis XV's death, Louis XVI and his queen sent the Due de la Vrilliere to Rueil to present Madame du Barry with a *lettre de cachet*, ordering her immediate exile to the convent of Pont-aux-Dames, near Meaux. The rest of the court retired to the Château de Choisy for quarantine, except for Mesdames Tantes, who had been infected by their father with smallpox. They were kept in quarantine in a small manor near Choisy, where they recovered.

Mesdames Tantes did return to Versailles, where the queen welcomed them, but she no longer turned to them for advice. She wrote to her empress mother, "As for my aunts, one can no longer say that they lead me." Losing their influence at court, the three spinsters sought refuge at the Château de Bellevue, which once belonged to their father's mistress, Madame de Pompadour. They never returned to Versailles except when etiquette required them to make an appearance, preferring their pastimes of knitting and gossiping at Bellevue.

On May 24, 1774, not long after the king's death, Louis XVI gave his new queen the Petit Trianon, which had once belonged to Madame de Pompadour as well as Madame du Barry. It was ironic that the pavilion that had always been associated with the former king's illicit affairs now belonged to the new queen, who would deny entrance to any guests without an invitation—including her husband. "Tactful and complaisant as ever," wrote Zweig, "he was careful not to turn up uninvited or at inconvenient times, strictly respecting the domestic privacies of his wife."

The courtiers of Versailles were also enraged when the queen would spend weeks at a time there with her inner circle because the courtiers were never invited. The king's brother, the Comte d'Artois, however, was permitted free access to Petit Trianon, even making midnight excursions there with his servant and not leaving until the next morning, looking "very fatigued." Rumors spread quickly that the count was having a sexual relationship with the queen, and when the rumors reached the king, the king had his brother followed one night.

The king's spy reported the next day that the Comte d'Artois had sneaked out of his chambers "dressed in white tights, a sweater, a pink belt, a small cap with feathers on his head, [and] a balancing pole in his hand." On this occasion, the count supposedly had tightrope lessons, and upon hearing the news, the king was undoubtedly dumbfounded: "Well," he said, "my brother is certainly mad."

Indeed, the Comte d'Artois was less reserved than his two older brothers. He was handsome with a compassionate air—until he opened his mouth. And when he did, he could be harsh and blunt, and in front of the ladies, he talked so grossly that they blushed. He loved women, but he also loved to gamble and drink, especially with his debauched sidekick, the Duc de Chartres.

Like Marie Antoinette, the Comte d'Artois enjoyed the lack of formality and etiquette at Petit Trianon, where everyone disregarded titles when addressing each other. Known as a retreat for intimacy and pleasure, Louis XV had the manor designed with the least interaction between guests and servants possible. Even the dining room table was conceived, but never built, to be lowered and raised through the floor so servants could set the table below, allowing the king to dine above with his mistress unseen.

Curiously, Marie Antoinette took the privacy a step further. She added mirrored panels that, by turning a crank, could be raised or lowered to obscure the windows and reflect the candlelight. We know that Louis XV had something to hide, but what was she trying to hide?

All the while, Marie Antoinette's marriage remained unconsummated with no heir to the throne in sight. This became especially painful when the Comte d'Artois and his wife announced the birth of a boy, Louis Antoine, on August 6, 1775. Because Louis XVI and the Comte de Provence had not fathered any children, Louis Antoine would be the first of the next generation of Bourbons. Moreover, the birth of the prince gave the pamphleteers of Paris plenty of fodder to lampoon the king's alleged impotence.★

Because Queen Marie Antoinette was spending much time either at the Petit Trianon or attending events such as the Opéra in Paris, she was shirking her duties of holding court at Versailles. Consequently, many noble ladies were embittered, waiting for hours in vain at Versailles to pay court to her majesty. Some finally left the court for good, including Marie Louise de Rohan, better known as Madame de Marsan, a longtime governess to the royal children, including the young Comtes d'Artois and de Provence.

At the court of Louis XV, Madame de Marsan was known as a clever and extravagant princess who was "too fond" of gambling. A wealthy princess of the Rohan family, she hosted amazing balls where she wore magnificent gowns and lost thousands at the card tables. It was not a secret, too, that Madame de Marsan was never one of Marie Antoinette's admirers. In fact, she had preferred another match for the dauphin Louis.

In 1776, Madame de Marsan resigned her hereditary post as governess to the royal children in favor of her niece, Victoire de Rohan. Better known as Madame de Guéménée, the new governess became an influential friend of the queen. Not only did she introduce the queen to expensive habits such as illegal gambling with high stakes at her salon at Versailles, but she also interested the queen in the new English fashion of horse races. Subsequently, the queen soon accumulated huge gambling debts at court.

There was good reason that the Abbé de Vermond chastised the queen for socializing with Madame de Guéménée. Not only did Madame de Guéménée have an affair with the Duc de Coigny, but also her husband, the Prince de Guéménée, was having an affair with her friend, the Comtesse de Dillon. The abbé considered both Madame de Guéménée and the Comtesse de Dillon "women of ill repute."

Another member of Madame de Guéménée's circle was the witty and chivalrous Duc de Lauzun. Marie Antoinette, as dauphine, was accustomed to seeing him at the king's suppers, but now, as queen, she showed him considerable attention when he attended Madame de Guéménée's soirees. It was well known that the queen was especially keen on men in uniform, and one evening Lauzun appeared in uniform with the "most magnificent plume of white heron's feathers that was possible to behold."

Madame Campan wrote in her memoirs that when Lauzun discovered the queen admired the plume, he offered it to her through Madame de

---

★ When his father abdicates the throne in 1830, Louis Antoine will technically be king of France for twenty minutes until he himself abdicates.

Guéménée, not being able to give the queen a gift himself due to court etiquette. The queen had never imagined that he could think of giving the plume to her, and when it was offered, she was embarrassed because she dared not refuse it, nor did she know if she should offer a gift in return.

She decided to wear the plume once, as a matter of *politesse*, letting Lauzun see her hair adorned with the present. In doing so, Lauzun's vanity might have gotten the best of him. Madame Campan explains:

> His vanity magnified the value of the favour done him. A short time after the present of the heron plume, he solicited an audience; the Queen granted it, as she would have done to any other nobleman of equal rank. I was in the room adjoining that in which he was received; a few minutes after his arrival, the Queen opened the door, and said aloud, in an angry tone of voice, "Go, sir."

The Duc de Lauzun bowed low and withdrew, but the queen was very agitated, saying to Madame Campan, "That man shall never again come within my doors." However, Lauzun told the story differently in his memoires. When the queen asked him what he thought of her headdress, he replied that he liked it very much. The queen replied, "I never saw myself so becomingly dressed before."

According to Lauzun's memoirs, one of his rivals for the queen's favor, the Duc de Coigny, had noticed the feather that evening and asked the queen about it. She was somewhat embarrassed and answered that Lauzun had brought it to Madame de Guéménée from his travels, and she had given it to her. Lauzun wrote that the Duc de Coigny spoke severely about it to Madame de Guéménée the same evening and told her that nothing could be more ridiculous or inappropriate than the footing Lauzun was on with the queen. Moreover, Coigny told Madame de Guéménée that he found Lauzun's "acting the lover so publicly" was unprecedented and that it was incredible that the queen "should look as if she approved of it."

Lauzun also suggested that his rival's comments were not well received and that it was obvious that the Duc de Coigny was just trying to get him out of the way.

After the incident, the Abbé de Vermond and Comte de Mercy were no doubt relieved that Lauzun was no longer in the picture, but they were still concerned about the queen's attraction to Madame de Guéménée's circle. Mercy wrote Empress Maria Theresa,

> We've managed to unmask the Duc de Lauzun, who is one of the most dangerous personages, and in whom the queen has lost all confidence.

He has succeeded in destroying the pernicious credit of the princess of Guéméné, but the queen, knowing it for what it is worth, still goes from time to time to spend hours of the evening with the princess who brings together the youth of Versailles.

The "youth of Versailles" was not an understatement. The queen had been known to hide her grins behind her fan when older dames of the court were ridiculed. In fact, she preferred mostly young—and attractive—people in her inner circle:

> With her ladies at the palace, the queen led a conduct not very suited to deserve the respect of the French. She had found in charge . . . ladies of the late Queen who were still counted among the remains of the old court with decency and the dignity of their rank, such as the ladies Talleyrand, Grammont, Tavannes, Adhemard, Chaulnes, and Duras, whom the queen found old and troublesome. She laughed in their face and was pleased to rattle them, to the point that many of them preferred a retreat from such an unpleasant service.

Moreover, she could not understand how anyone past the age of thirty could dare attend court, even referring to elderly ladies at court as "siècles," or "centuries." Marie Antoinette was queen of France, yet she was still but a teenager.

The queen's intimate circle also included many young, attractive men who were known as her favorites. One in particular, Édouard Dillon, who had been the Comte d'Artois's gentleman-in-waiting, was also known as "le beau Dillon," or the handsome Dillon. One day, when he was practicing the quadrille,★ which would be danced at the next ball at Versailles, he turned pale and fainted. He was moved to a sofa and the queen placed her hand on his heart to feel if it was still beating. This imprudent act on the part of a queen was shocking to the court.

When Dillon recovered, he apologized and explained he had left Paris without eating breakfast in order not to be late for his rendezvous with the queen.† The queen ordered some soup for him, and the courtiers, jealous of the queen's attention, spread the rumor that he was intimate with her. This rumor dissipated at court but was later confirmed when Dillon was seen riding across Paris in the queen's coach on St. Hubert's Day. He had fallen from his horse while hunting and broke his arm. The queen ordered that

---

★ Fashionable eighteenth-century dance for four couples in square formation.
† Dillon had been known to faint whenever he fasted due to a battle wound he had received at the capture of Grenada.

Dillon be taken home in her own coach—which was unspeakable—and she returned to Versailles in the king's coach.

The king and queen asked to be present when Dillon's injury was dressed, but the tearful queen was devastated by the accident. Later, it was rumored, the queen and one of her ladies wrapped in cloaks secretly visited the handsome Dillon. This act of kindness appeared to all the courtiers as "overstepping the bounds of ordinary compassion."

Dillon was also admitted to the games at the queen's Petit Trianon, where he played the *garde champêtre*, the pasture guard, and Marie Antoinette was the *bergère*, the shepherdess. Dillon was just one of the rivals for the queen's favor who would visit Trianon unchaperoned, join the nocturnal walks at Versailles, and accompany her to the balls and the Opéra in Paris. He was just one of the rivals would also share intimate connections with men and women of "unworthy" reputations at the court of Versailles. And such connections were becoming of interest to pamphleteers.

In 1777, the British government assisted its French counterparts in seizing copies of a new libelous pamphlet, *La Guerlichon femelle*, penned in the same year but suppressed before publication. The defamatory work accused the queen of being in a lesbian relationship with the Princesse de Lamballe. When information was secretly communicated that the work was about to be printed, the lieutenant of the police commissioned his inspector, Étienne Goupil, to make inquiries and discover the author of the pamphlet.

Within days, Goupil returned with two printed sheets of the pamphlet obtained from a printing house near Yverdon, and for a considerable sum of money, he could retrieve the entire work before it could be printed and distributed. After receiving one thousand gold coins as a reward, he was in line for a promotion when another spy, envious of Goupil's good fortune, disclosed that it was Goupil himself who had authored the illicit pamphlet.

In fact, the Abbé Véri, one of the king's confidants, described the pamphlet as just one of many attacks against the queen for her suspiciously close friendships with women. The accusations seemed to ring true when the queen asked the king to buy up the entire edition, which he did, and have it stored under seal in the Bastille.

Ever since Madame de Noailles's Monday evening balls in 1771 in honor of the dauphine, Marie Antoinette had been very close to the Princesse de Lamballe. Like the princess, Marie Antoinette, too, was a princess on foreign soil, but Marie Antoinette was also drawn to the melancholic princess who was a widow at nineteen years of age. Although the princess was six years older, the two were said to be "inseparable," and the dauphine tearfully grieved whenever the princess was absent from court. And the dauphine would dismiss everyone in order to be alone with the princess for long walks and to dine privately far from the eyes of the court.

On September 18, 1777, Queen Marie Antoinette appointed the Princesse de Lamballe as the Superintendent of the Queen's Household, the highest rank possible for a lady-in-waiting at Versailles. Unfortunately, the new appointment for the princess required the resignation of the Comtesse de Noailles, who would never have retired from this hereditary post. To smooth the family's ruffled feathers, however, the Comte de Noailles was promoted to the post of Marshal of France.

A year later, the busy schedule of balls and quadrilles gave rise to the intimacy of the queen with a newcomer at court, and in time, the Princesse de Lamballe, being too reserved for Marie Antoinette's frivolous taste, fell out of the queen's favor, yet keeping her rank and duties at court.

The newcomer was the Comtesse Jules de Polignac. At one of her winter receptions, Marie Antoinette spotted a pretty, somewhat demure, young lady in a simple white frock in stark contrast to the magnificent gowns of the other ladies at court. She discovered the lady was the Comtesse Jules de Polignac and, very interested in her, sent for her. When the queen asked why she had never seen her at court before, the countess answered that her husband lacked the means to attend court; she could not afford it.

"My heart reminds me," she said, lowering her eyes, "that the mediocrity of our fortune keeps me on our estate at Claye."

"Truly?" said the queen in a concerned tone.

The queen asked other questions and was so impressed with Madame de Polignac's answers that she sent for her the next day and called her an "angel," promising to remedy her poverty at once. Accordingly, the Polignacs' debts were soon paid. Moreover, the family was given apartments at Versailles, leaving the new favorite at the queen's beck and call.

After the long conversation, Madame de Polignac appeared very emotional when she left the queen's chambers, and courtiers attributed it to "disgraceful" conduct on the part of the queen. Obviously jealous of the attention that the queen had also paid to Madame de Polignac the night before, the courtiers now named Madame de Polignac the new favorite.

The Princesse de Lamballe, still the queen's superintendent, was not the last to notice Madame de Polignac's effect on the queen, who in spite of the severe etiquette at court, spoke more often and longer with the new favorite than normal. And the princess was undoubtedly jealous and might have worried about the influence of Madame de Polignac on the queen's lighthearted and frivolous nature. She might also have worried about the loss of her envied place at court that had given her such self-esteem after the disgraceful death of her sexual-disease-ridden husband.

Wanting to keep the Princesse de Lamballe and Madame de Polignac in her intimate circle, the queen said, "I will receive them in my cabinet, or at Trianon. I will enjoy the comforts of private life, which exist not for us, unless we have the good sense to secure them for ourselves."

However, the Princesse de Lamballe could not fathom joining the intimate circle with Madame de Polignac. She was now destined to the shadows of the new favorite. Other courtiers, too, who were not admitted to this circle were just as jealous and even vindictive.

Comtesse Diane de Polignac, Madame de Polignac's sister-in-law and lady-in-waiting to the Comtesse d'Artois, and M. Vaudreuil, a friend of the family, understood Madame de Polignac's character, one that made it difficult for her to ask the queen for financial assistance. To improve Madame de Polignac's favor at court, they penned a farewell letter for her that expressed her sadness at the need to leave court, but her financial situation was too dire to remain. Moreover, the queen's favoritism for her had already created new enemies for her at court.

The Comtesse Diane and M. de Vaudreuil's letter produced exactly the effect they had desired, knowing that Marie Antoinette was "brash, impetuous, and would not tolerate being contradicted." To the queen, the charming Madame de Polignac had provided a degree of consolation and tender amity that she had not experienced at court. She wasted no time in sending her favorite a letter, which denied the favorite permission to retire to her manor at Claye by giving her the hereditary title of *premier écuyer*, master of the stable, at Versailles. The title included a beautiful apartment at the top of the marble staircase at Versailles and a hefty pension.

One could imagine the jealousy at court when hearing of Madame de Polignac's rise in stature. The Princesse de Lamballe was livid, especially when the queen became absent in her salon and preferred that of her new favorite, where many courtiers were refused admittance. It is unlikely, however, that the princess ever confronted the queen about her displeasure, but the Noailles family would have certainly been displeased upon losing the post of stable master, especially after having lost the post of superintendent of the queen's household too.

The Princesse de Lamballe was still superintendent of the queen's household but no longer a member of the queen's intimate circle, where Madame de Polignac now admitted new members such as the Comtesses Diane de Polignac and de Chalon; Messieurs de Guînes, de Coigny, d'Adhemar, de Besenval, de Polignac, de Vaudreuil, and de Guiche; and the Prince de Ligne.

Yolande Martine Gabrielle de Polastron, Duchesse de Polignac

Madame la Comtesse Jules de Polignac was a charming, beautiful, and extremely fascinating woman, who had great talents for intrigue. Because she came from an obscure estate where she lived on a meager income, she would not have made an impression on Marie Antoinette if it were not for that accidental meeting at court.

Madame de Polignac was a gentle soul, much unlike her haughty and sometimes violent-acting sister-in-law, Diane de Polignac, who was already established at the queen's court as well as a "ruling" member of the queen's private circle. Diane, in spite of her "depravity of manners," was also the rather despotic lady-of-honor of the king's sister, Madame Élisabeth.

Curiously, Élisabeth often struggled with Diane's violent streak to the point of requesting a retreat to a nearby chateau, but the king persuaded her otherwise. He, too, looked upon the lady-of-honor with fear. Diane had thus a position of authority in Élisabeth's and the queen's household, displaying talents for ordering, arranging, intriguing, and above all, advancing the interests of the house of Polignac.

News of the queen's excessive favoritism for Madame de Polignac soon reached the Empress Maria Theresa in Vienna. Ambassador Mercy-Argenteau wrote to the queen's mother that Madame de Polignac "has neither the wit, nor the judgment, nor even the character to enjoy the confidence of a great princess." This relationship did not escape the secret, but suspect, memoirs of courtiers, especially those of Bachaumont:

> Everyone knows the affection of the Queen for Madame Jules de Polignac; we know that it was from her that Her Majesty caught the measles, the reason why they had not seen each other for a long time. Madame Jules wrote the Queen from Claye, where she was recovering, that she would have the honor of going to court at Marly on Monday, the day after her arrival. Her Majesty replied: "Undoubtedly, the most eager for us to embrace is me, since I will go Sunday to dine with you in Paris."

In fact, on Sunday at one o'clock, the queen went to her favorite's house on the rue de Bourbon and dined privately with her, remaining together until five o'clock, when she left. Her lady-in-waiting Mademoiselle de Chimay, who had accompanied her, was not admitted and ordered to depart.

All of Paris, informed of the arrival of Her Majesty at Madame Jules's house, flooded the street to await the moment of her departure, and "thousands of conjectures" were formed about this secret tête-à-tête.

Mercy-Argenteau wrote to Maria Theresa that the queen continued such visits to Madame de Polignac at Claye, adding that the queen wanted to sleep there too, but the king would not permit it. On one occasion, she didn't return until four in the morning, and when her coach broke down, she was obliged to continue her journey on foot to Versailles. The ambassador was well aware of the scandalous rumors that were flooding Versailles and Paris about such indiscretions: "The Queen can no longer do without the society of this young woman, with whom she shares all her feelings, and I very much doubt that there are any exceptions to this boundless trust."

Pamphlets and secret memoirs written about Queen Marie Antoinette's lesbian relationships with Madame de Polignac and the Princesse de Lamballe were not uncommon at this time. Furthermore, lesbianism was not unknown to Marie Antoinette or her family. In fact, her older sister, Maria Christina, governor of Austrian Netherlands, had an intense love affair with her sister-in-law, Princess Isabella of Parma, a granddaughter of Louis XV.

More astonishing was Marie Antoinette's relationship with her sister and closest sibling, Maria Carolina, later queen of Naples and Sicily by marriage. The girls shared the same governess, Countess von Lerchenfeld, and were said to be so close that they would be sick at the same time.

However, the girls "behaved very badly together," and Empress Maria Theresa, very displeased with certain questionable actions, separated the girls in August 1767. After Maria Carolina left Vienna for Naples, she wrote to Countess Lerchenfeld, "Write to me everything you know about my sister Antoine, down to the tiniest detail, what she says and does and even what she thinks. . . . Beg her to love me, because I am so passionately concerned for her."

The Comte de Mercy actually chastised the queen, albeit with a tone of gentleness, about her relationships with women: "Madame," he said, "within your circle and with your friends, you have become very indulgent in morals and reputation. I could prove that at your age this indulgence, especially for women, has a bad effect."

There is no proof, however, of an illicit affair between Marie Antoinette and Madame de Polignac, but the new favorite had an enormous influence on the queen. Moreover, according to Comte de Mercy, the new favorite had an entourage of supporters of young men and the older Baron de Besenval, all with bad reputations and "equally dangerous."

The vain and intriguing Swiss Baron de Besenval, although nearly fifty years old, was as seductive as he was witty. His lively, cheery air pleased the ladies at court. The Prince de Ligne described him as "the gayest man" and one of the most amiable men he had ever known.

However, the baron's memoirs painted a portrait that was not very flattering. The style of his work was crude and included obscene epigrams, and most of the court at Versailles did not approve of his conduct or of his rumormongering, which often included the king's attempts to consummate his marriage or the king's need for the "famous operation" to correct his possible phimosis.* One of the baron's epigrams discussed the problem of the king's alleged impotence:

> The queen said impudently
> to her confident Besenval,
> "My husband is a poor sire!"
> He responded in a light tone,
> "Each thinks it without saying it,
> You say it without thinking it."

Another of Madame de Polignac's followers was the Duc de Coigny, who was thirty-eight years old at the time and no less debauched as the Baron de Besenval. The king's first lieutenant in 1774 and lieutenant-general in 1780, the Duc de Coigny became a frequent visitor to the Petit Trianon or Madame de Polignac's house by 1788. It was soon rumored that he was the father of the queen's first child, Madame Royale.

---

* A condition when the foreskin of the penis is unable to be fully retracted.

The queen spent most of her time at Madame de Polignac's house about this time, but whether she held court there or at Trianon, it was most often composed of the Coigny, Polignac, and Vaudreuil families. Wherever she held court, however, she was confronted with annoyance, calculation, and greed.

No one paid much attention at first to Madame de Polignac, nor dreamed that her influence over the queen would ever surpass that of the Princesse de Lamballe. However, Madame de Polignac had powerful friends for support, and perhaps more powerful was her own indifference. Unlike the Princesse de Lamballe, Madame de Polignac never appeared to have had the least personal feeling for the queen.

This indifference was best illustrated when Marie Antoinette once complained to Madame de Polignac that she no longer found the company of Madame de Polignac's circle suitable. Forgetting the kindnesses, and fortune, she had received from the queen, Madame de Polignac replied that if the queen did not care about her guests, she would not have to honor her parties.

The Princesse de Lamballe was not known for her wit or for any talent, but when Madame de Polignac was sent away from court after the storming of the Bastille, Marie Antoinette understood that the princess was more than just a favorite; she was a true friend. During one of the Princesse de Lamballe's short absences from the court then held at the Tuileries, the queen wrote on November 7, 1789,

> You will not take care of yourself, and I am quite worried about you. Listen to me, my dear Lamballe, I shall be really angry with you. My health is fairly good, and my children's excellent. . . . My daughter longs to see you again. . . . The Dauphin has asked for you many times to help him with his garden; he tells me in his baby language that he wants to give you breakfast with Mama Queen.

8

DÉCAMPATIVOS AND
RISKY DIVERSIONS

*They introduced a taste for trifling games, such as question and an-
swer, blindman's buff, and especially the game déscampativos.*

—Madame Campan, First Lady in Waiting to the Queen

After Louis XVI was crowned king, Queen Marie Antoinette's intimate
friendship with her brothers and sisters-in-law soon dissipated, especially after the Comtesse d'Artois gave birth to a possible heir to the throne
in September 1775.

It was understandable that the queen was not close to the Comtesse
d'Artois. She was clumsy and was not regarded as beautiful. Although she
was the only royal to give birth to any children, she was "in all other aspects
a complete idiot."

The winter following the birth of the countess's son was severely cold,
which reminded Marie Antoinette of her sleigh rides when she was a child
in Austria, and she wanted to re-create them in France. Some sleighs, found
in the stables that had been used by the king's father when he was a child,
were reconstructed and modernized for the queen.

With six weeks of snow, the queen and her entourage used the
sleighs, even extending their rides as far at the Champs-Élysées. Although
the ladies were masked, all of Paris knew that the sleighs belonged to the
queen by the abundance of gold accessories, billowing white plumes, and
ladies' furs. Parisians, suffering from the severe cold and many dying of
hunger, were insulted by the queen's winter festivities and the absence of
any charitable works.

The sleigh rides were not the only activities harming the queen's
reputation. Before she began attending Madame de Polignac's salon, she

had spent evenings with the Duc and Duchesse de Duras, who entertained young courtiers with trifling games such as blindman's bluff and *décampativos*. Whether these games were played at the court of Versailles or in the gardens of Trianon, Parisians imitated the court, especially to the dismay of parents with young daughters.

By this time, the Comte de Vaudreuil was known to be Madame de Polignac's lover and attended her salon and parties, where the queen was always present. However, because the queen enjoyed his company, he was also known to attend the queen's parties in the gardens of Versailles, which soon raised eyebrows at court. The queen normally invited about forty guests, in equal numbers of both sexes, to these events to play décampativos in the gardens at a spot sheltered from view from the château by lofty woods.

An altar of turf being erected, the election of a high priest followed— who, by virtue of his office, possessed the power of pairing the different couples for the duration of one hour, at his arbitrary pleasure. On pronouncing the word "décampativos," the couples all scampered off in different directions, but they were bound by the rules to reassemble at the same place when the hour had expired.

Those persons who maintained that the amusement was altogether innocent, as far as Marie Antoinette had any participation in it, also reported that the king repeatedly sanctioned it by his presence. They added that he appeared to enjoy the diversion no less than any other players, and he was himself repeatedly paired with different ladies.

However, the Comte de Vaudreuil generally played the role of "pontiff" and, being the most powerful player, chose everyone's partner. He could also choose his own, who was almost always the queen. Unfortunately, rumors flouted the queen's obsession with the risqué game. It was an opportunity to compensate for the king's boring nature and, more important, for his inability to perform in the royal bed.

Sir Nathaniel Wraxall, an English author visiting Versailles, who observed or participated in the déscampativos, was well aware of the lewd behavior during such games, claiming that if Marie Antoinette "ever violated her nuptial vow," Monsieur de Vaudreuil would be one of the "favored individuals." However, Vaudreuil was just one of the queen's favorites who had opportunities for private audiences with her.

When the queen contracted the measles, she enlisted four courtiers to stay all day by her side at Trianon while she convalesced. Messieurs Coigny, Guînes, Esterhazy, and Besenval watched over her from seven o'clock in the morning until eleven o'clock in the evening, "only taking leave from her majesty for their meals."

Ambassador Mercy reported little of this strange arrangement to Empress Maria Theresa, but he wrote in a secret report, "It is very true that the king, accustomed to denying himself anything that may please his august wife, had approved that the Dukes of Coigny and Guînes, Count Esterhazy, and Baron de Besenval could stay with the queen, but his consent had been provoked by this princess."

Marie Antoinette was not aware of the gravity of the situation, which resulted in all sorts of very unpleasant remarks and bad jokes at court. For example, courtiers jested about which four ladies would be chosen to keep company with the king should he ever fall ill. Most damaging, however, was the fact that the queen had forbidden the king to enter the premises of the Petit Trianon while she was recuperating. Even the ladies of her household were excluded.

Curiously, one of those caring for the queen, the Duc de Coigny, had a year earlier imprudently professed his love for the queen. The queen had supposedly lamented her unconsummated marriage with him in a private setting and, subsequently, the duke fell to her feet with a declaration of love. After such an imprudence, why would she, a year later, allow him to care for her at Trianon unchaperoned contrary to court etiquette? Had the queen since blamed herself for the duke's impropriety? Or had she perhaps invited it?

"Thank Heaven," wrote Mercy when the queen recovered, "that this aggravating epoch is at end." However, the balls, the operas, the horseracing, the sleigh rides, the games, and foolish nocturnal walks in the gardens of Versailles—often without the king—would still continue in the first years of the queen's reign. Historian Thomas Wright reported on the nocturnal walks:

> Writers like Madame Campan, who were least likely to speak harshly of the queen, and of whose truthfulness we can have no doubt, assure us that these parties were held after king had retired to bed, and that Marie Antoinette mixed in them with so little reserve, that she was at times accosted by guards or by strangers, who whispered bold proposals in her ear. These night parties on the terrace became soon known by a name which was calculated to produce an unfortunate impression on the imagination: they were called the *Nocturnals of Versailles*.

Gambling, a pastime enjoyed in the past by kings' mistresses, not their queens, was another vice that damaged the queen's reputation. Marie Antoinette wagered gold coins at the salons of Princesse de Guéménée and the Duchesse de Chartres, Princesse de Lamballe's sister-in-law, where lans-quenet* or pharaoh† was played with high stakes.

These games were also played during the sojourns at the courts of Compiègne and Fontainebleau, even though the king had prohibited them. Toward the end of 1776, the queen went so far as to ask the king to permit bankers to attend the games of pharaoh. The king thought admitting them to court was a bad example to set for the errant princes of the blood, but with his usual kindness, he conceded, although for only one evening.

The bankers arrived on the evening of October 30 and dealt cards the whole night. The queen remained until five o'clock in the morning, returning that evening and playing until nearly three o'clock in the morning on November 1, which caused a public uproar because the games ended on All Saints' Day. The queen countered the discontent by jesting that the king had allowed the gambling without specifying its duration. She thus had the right to prolong it for thirty-six hours. The king laughed: "Go! You are all worthless!"

Marie Antoinette lost more than five hundred gold coins one evening and, to repay the debt the next day, had to ask help from the king, who, without any reproach, paid it from his own purse. Disreputable courtiers attended the games at which Marie Antoinette was treated and addressed as a commoner. Cheating, too, was a problem, and news of it spread across Europe. On one occasion at the queen's game at the Château of Fontainebleau, a suspicious Englishman named Smith won more than 1,500,000 pounds of the princes' money. These rumors reached Maria Theresa in Vienna. The queen's brother Emperor Joseph II, who visited Versailles in April 1777, wrote that he did not know how to stop the queen's behavior and warned that if it took a revolution, it would be a "cruel" one.

Marie Antoinette's imperial brother was shocked by the debauchery and *l'air de licence* that ruled Princesse de Guéménée's salon, which could only be described as a *tripot*, or a dive. During his stay in France, he chastised his sister for frequenting such a "gambling den," where losses of more than 100,000 gold louis were not uncommon. On one Christmas Day, she had lost 700,000 louis.

Empress Maria Theresa warned her daughter that such passion for gambling would be her ruin and must be ended immediately at all cost. If not, she threatened to severely reprimand the king for his permissiveness.

---

* One of the oldest gambling card games, dating back to the sixteenth century, similar to today's blackjack.

† A seventeenth-century gambling game originating in France, also known as faro.

However, a chronicler recollected, "Certainly there was something to worry about, and history has the right to remember. But had Versailles known anything else? The excessive expense under the two previous reigns? Was it not a similar game, that of Madame de Montespan, which made the loss in the coffers blow up to a million?"

Kings had indeed spent a fortune on scandalous gifts for their mistresses. Madame de Pompadour's Château of Bellevue was built for three million louis and then sold to the king for another three million. Is it fair to compare the extravagant lifestyles of Louis XIV and Louis XV with that of the frugal Louis XVI? Moreover, Louis XVI usually paid the queen's debt from his own purse, but did Marie Antoinette have an addiction to gambling? Perhaps not, because she only played for the love of levity, out of idleness, and for fear of boredom.

At the end of his journey to France, Joseph II wrote the following lines: "I left Versailles with difficulty, really attached to my sister. I found a kind of sweetness of life to which I had renounced, but of which I see that the taste had not left me. She is amiable and charming."

However, to fully understand his sister, Joseph took the queen's unhappy marriage into consideration as well as the king's character, writing, "The situation of my sister with the king is singular. This man is a little weak, but not a fool. He has notions, he has judgment, but has an apathy of body and mind. He makes reasonable conversations, but he has no taste for education or curiosity."

In fact, Joseph mentioned that Louis was "rather inert and cold," especially with respect to his journal writing, where he wrote *rien*, or nothing, to describe many of his days as king of France. The king's journal is evidence of his deficient education, the shallowness of his ideas, and his utter incapability to record a single critical reflection. One wonders how this monarch ever reigned at all.

The king's accession to the throne did not deliver the new monarchs from court intrigue. It had only changed the object and those who were the intriguers. The chief enemy was now the prince who should have been their best friend, the Comte de Provence.

Among Louis XV's personal effects, Louis XVI found letters from both the Comte de Provence and his wife to Louis XV that tried to "poison the mind of their grandfather against the dauphiness." The mischief was increasing now since each passing day seemed to diminish the chances of Marie Antoinette becoming a mother. If the current monarchs could not have children, the Comte de Provence would become heir to the throne, and he spoke openly about the probability of his succession.

Despite the need to have an heir, there was a period when Marie Antoinette acted as if she were not interested in sexual relations with the king. As late as November 1777, Mercy wrote about the queen's nocturnal activities: "It is truly deplorable that the queen pays so little attention to such an important point, and what adds to the evil is that the king, out of complacency and weakness, though against his will, seems to applaud all the dissipations."

And the queen's mother appeared at the end of her wits when she replied to Mercy the first week of December. Awaiting news that the queen had become pregnant, she lamented the king's devotion to hunting and her daughter's gambling diversions that, she warned, were bad for her "health and beauty" and only separated her from the king even more: "Do not delude yourself, this gaming only attracts very bad company and consequences in every part of the world. This is recognized. Being too fond of winning, one is always the dupe and cannot win in the long run, if playing honestly. So, my dear daughter, I pray you. No capitulation, you must suddenly tear yourself away from this passion."

It is almost comical, knowing the queen's losses at the card tables, when reading her reply to her mother on December 19, saying she did not wish to bore her "dear mother" about all the "tales and exaggerations" of her gambling that could be heard all the way to Vienna: "I play only in public according to the etiquette of court, and, beginning this week until the end of the carnaval, there will only be gambling twice a week. The balls started this week; but, as I had a very bad cold and was beginning to have the flu, I only walked around when I went to the ball."

The queen continued her busy schedule of balls and gambling throughout carnaval, a time of intrigue and seduction, when women gave themselves totally to the joy of balls and dances. Theaters played the most licentious plays during this period too. But when the carnaval festivities ended, the queen must have given her marriage some attention, because the king finally consummated his marriage. Curiously, Empress Maria Theresa, when hearing of the pregnancy, was not too convinced of the news, writing, "I am almost tempted to doubt it, until the moment that she brings the child of this supposed pregnancy into the world."

The year 1778 was thus looking up: a satisfied queen, an end to the rumors about the king's impotence, and a child on the way. Moreover, an "old acquaintance" with a ballroom friend will soon be welcomed at the queen's court at Versailles again. Since leaving France three years earlier, Axel Fersen had served his king, Gustavus III. He had also been sent by his father to find a wife in London, where a daughter of a wealthy tradesman, Miss Catherine Leyell, refused him.

On August 26, Fersen was presented to the royal family at Versailles. The royal family might have forgotten him. In fact, they didn't acknowledge him at all, and Louis XVI only offered a "solemn nod." Marie Antoinette, however, had not forgotten him: "Ah, here is an old acquaintance." Two weeks later, Fersen wrote to his father: "The queen, who is the prettiest and most amiable princess that I know, has had the kindness to inquire about me often; she asked Creutz why I did not go to her card parties on Sundays; and hearing that I did go one Sunday when there was none, she sent me a sort of excuse."

Parties, balls, and card parties followed until the queen expressed a wish to see Fersen in his Swedish uniform, but not in public: "I am to go Thursday thus dressed," he wrote in his journal, "not to Court, but to the queen's apartments. She is the most amiable princess that I know."

Courtiers were jealous of the queen's attention to the dashing foreigner, especially after the queen apologized to Fersen for his fruitless visit to one of her parties. But when she broke etiquette by allowing him to enter her private apartments, Fersen became the attention of an envious court's eyes. The court had also noticed how Marie Antoinette blushed at the sight of Fersen and how she trembled whenever he entered the room.

On one occasion at court, when the queen was singing an aria from *Dido* at the harpsichord, her eyes lit up and she gazed at Fersen when he entered. She sang, "Oh, how well I am inspired when I receive you in my heart."

Was the queen more brazen now, at the age of twenty-three? After all, the boring and loathsome king had finally fulfilled his duty and produced a possible heir to the throne. She was finally experiencing a romantic affair with the Swedish noble who frequented her private chambers. And the queen had little interest in the court's rumors, what the courtiers thought of her new favorite, or whether they surmised an intimate, adulterous affair.

Fortunately, the court's attention was soon directed to another newcomer, Princess Marie-Thérèse Charlotte of France, the monarchs' daughter, born on December 19. All of France celebrated her birth, inspiring the poet d'Imbert to write,

> For you, France, a dauphin must be born:
> A princess arrives to witness.
> As soon as we see a blessing appear
> Believe that love is not far away.

However, the Duc de Coigny had already been singled out for being Marie Antoinette's lover and the future father of the dauphin, if she had a son:

> Nothing can undo Coigny's work,
> The boyfriend's caresses and his obscene hand,
> Despite nature's offense of the work,
> At Louis's expense arrives a fat dauphin,
> Just after nine months from the time
> When Coigny dove into the royal clam.

Was Louis XVI truly the father of the princess, also called Madame Royale, after all these years? Or as the court speculated, was one of the queen's past favorites, the Duc de Coigny, the father? Among the gossip at court and in Paris salons, it was fashionable to say that the king's first child was the Duc de Coigny's.

In the past, the Duc de Chartres openly boasted that he had rebuffed the queen's advances, and when he heard that the queen was finally pregnant, he insisted that the Duc de Coigny was the prospective father and added that the child of Coigny would never be his king, and he swore it.

Ironically, the Duc de Coigny had an adulterous relationship with the Princesse de Guéménée, who was governess of his niece Aimée and Madame Royale. The Princesse de Guéménée was the personal friend of Marie Antoinette who introduced her to expensive diversions such as illegal card games with high stakes in her salons. Meanwhile, her husband, the Prince de Guéméné, was in the midst of an affair with her friend, the Comtesse de Dillon.

The Duc de Lauzun was also a bad influence on Marie Antoinette. When he brought English horses across the channel, he and the Comte d'Artois enticed Marie Antoinette with enormous wagers on the races. Along with the Duc de Chartres, they set about establishing a racecourse in the Bois de Boulogne. They also had little difficulty in persuading the queen to attend it, and she soon showed such a fancy for the sport and became such a regular visitor to the racecourse that a small stand was built for her. This caused an uproar when the queen gave luncheons in it for some of their racing friends, most of whom were "not of a character deserving to be brought into a royal presence."

The Comte d'Artois had two passions: gambling and the ladies. The court was accustomed to his antics until he wagered 100,000 francs with Marie Antoinette that he could build a new château in the Bois de Boulogne in just six weeks.

When she accepted, the count purchased a small estate from the Prince de Chimay at the edge of the Bois de Boulogne, demolished the existing manor, and ordered plans from architect François Bélanger to build his

"Bagatelle." Nine hundred laborers worked day and night while all of Paris watched the construction. Unfortunately, the count needed materials, especially stone, lime, and plaster, and his deadline was approaching. Therefore, he ordered the Swiss Guards to find the materials on the highways and seize them with payment on the spot. However, because these goods had already been sold to someone else, the public was outraged. The king would have undoubtedly not have permitted such practices, but the queen had given them her protection.

Nevertheless, the Comte d'Artois created his manor for three million livres in the time allotted to win the challenge, and, very pleased with her brother-in-law's success, Marie Antoinette paid her debt and the Château of Bagatelle was opened in her honor with a magnificent fête. Unsurprisingly, the Bagatelle became better known as the rendezvous spot for illicit couples.

It was a stroke of fortune for the Comte d'Artois that the queen acquired a special affection for Madame de Polignac. They formed a circle called the *société*, which included the Duc de Coigny, the Baron de Besenval, the Comte d'Adhémar, and the Comte de Guînes. More prominent were Madame de Polignac's lover, the Comte de Vaudreuil, and her sister-in-law, Diane de Polignac, who became the Comte d'Artois's lifetime mistress.

In 1775, Diane de Polignac served in the Comtesse d'Artois's household until becoming the lady-in-waiting to King Louis XVI's sister, Madame Élisabeth, in 1778. Diane ruled her sister-in-law Madame de Polignac in the société, but she was disliked by the queen. Whereas Madame de Polignac was considered beautiful and graceful, Diane was ugly and spiteful. In any event, Diane was mostly responsible for Madame de Polignac's admission to the queen's circle, but the Comte de Provence saw it otherwise, writing, "It was the queen who was sucked into the circle of Madame de Polignac. Marie Antoinette was wrong to allow herself to be swept along like this, but she loved and saw that her love was returned; the société entertained her."

On one hand, Madame de Polignac captivated all who approached her not only with her beautiful complexion and sparkling eyes but also with her sweet smile and her mild countenance. On the other, however, her liaison with Queen Marie Antoinette would be judged severely by the queen's family in Austria, by King Louis XVI's family, by the nobles and courtiers of Versailles, by her prosecutors at the Revolutionary Tribunal in 1793, and thus by historians of French history.

QUESTIONABLE RELATIONSHIPS WITH WOMEN

You have become very indulgent of morals and reputation. I could prove that at your age this indulgence, especially for women, has a bad effect.

—Abbé de Vermond

Queen Marie Antoinette's favor for Madame de Polignac grew exponentially day by day, which gave rise to rumors of the queen's sexuality. The queen even mentioned the hearsay to her mother: "It is said that I have a taste for women and lovers." But the question whether the queen was a lesbian remains unanswered due to a lack of evidence. The question whether she had any lesbian affairs, however, is not so cut and dry.

The first seven years of Marie Antoinette's marriage at Versailles were fruitless; her husband could not perform his royal duty to please his queen sexually. "Whether she turned to a male or a female," writes historian Stefan Zweig, "she had need of someone who would relieve the spiritual and bodily tensions." However, he added, "Since, for propriety's sake, she would not (or could not) seek it from a man, Marie Antoinette at this juncture involuntarily turned towards a woman friend."

At the court of Versailles, marriages had been arranged for political purposes from which a very permissive extrafamilial social life evolved and one's private life was not defined by conjugal relations. According to historian Elizabeth Susan Wahl,

> Such unofficial alliances and liaisons gave rise to an ethos of "worldliness" that derived partly from medieval notions of courtly love and also from the more recent Renaissance ideas of courtiership. For women, especially, the ties of *amitié* that could be formed with the heterosexual spheres of the

court or salon offered a degree of social and emotional freedom that was often impossible to achieve within the bounds of marriage.

A woman was therefore, according to Wahl, more likely to establish emotional bonds with men and women of her own social circle, and this we have seen to ring true in Marie Antoinette's world. At the same time, she viewed her husband with a formal respect, if not with indifference or even outright contempt because of his lack of attention to her sexual needs. Furthermore, an emotional close relationship between women was socially acceptable at court.

If this was true, then Marie Antoinette's first relationship would most likely have been with the Princesse de Lamballe, until she was replaced by Madame de Polignac as the queen's favorite. The intensity of this new intimacy, however, troubled her counselor and reader, the Abbé de Vermond, who reported to Comte de Mercy a conversation he had with the queen. When he alluded to the confessor of her sister, Queen Maria Carolina of Naples, Marie Antoinette congratulated herself for not having the confessor near her, because he would have liked to "make her devout."

"How would he have done that," replied Vermond. "I have not been able to bring you to a reasonable conduct." The Abbé then took advantage of the moment to express his thoughts: "You have become very indulgent in morals and reputation. I could prove that at your age this indulgence, especially for women, has a bad effect; but, lastly, I think that you do not consider the manners or the reputation of a woman, who you make your friend or include in your society just because she is kind."

He continued to chastise Marie Antoinette, stating that the only qualifications a woman needed to enter the queen's *société* were "misconduct of all kinds, bad morals, and tarnished or lost reputations." The queen listened to his sermon and acknowledged it simply with a smile.

It is interesting that Marie Antoinette would mention her sister, Maria Carolina, when discussing her relationships with other women with Vermond. Maria Carolina's marriage, too, was arranged by Empress Maria Theresa, but Carolina would never forgive her mother for choosing Ferdinand IV, the Duke of Naples, for her husband, whom she found "very ugly."

The feeling was mutual. After their wedding night, Ferdinand reported that Carolina "sleeps like the dead and sweats like a pig."

Carolina wrote to Governess von Lerchenfeld that she could love Ferdinand "only out of duty." Her favorite was John Acton, a brilliant officer of the Spanish navy, who became her prime minister, if not her lover.

"Love-à-la-mode" (Lady Hamilton and Queen Maria Carolina)

Carolina was known to be "a very ambitious woman, unprincipled, spoiled, arrogant, and, like all the daughters of Maria Theresa, prone to corruption."Moreover, Carolina created a stir with her alleged lesbian relationship with Lady Emma Hamilton, an English actress and the mistress of Lord Nelson. It was said that Carolina became so obsessed with Emma that "she wanted no other companion, she shared the same chambers with her, and she slept in the same bed with her."

These rumors spread across Europe about the same time as the accusations that surfaced about Marie Antoinette's relationships with the Princesse de Lamballe and Madame de Polignac. Not only were there reports of Maria Carolina and Marie Antoinette's lesbian affairs with their respective favorites, but also some historians have gone so far as to insinuate a sexual relationship between the two sisters when living at Schönbrunn. Maria Carolina was three years older than Marie Antoinette, and the two were inseparable, "appearing united by an excessive affection," of which the entire court was well aware. On August 19, 1767, due to the heightened rumor-mongering, Empress Maria Theresa sent a note to Maria Carolina.

> I'm letting you know that you will be totally separated from your sister. I forbid you any secrets, intelligence or discourse with her; if the little one starts again, don't pay any attention to it or talk of it to Lerchenfeld or your ladies; all this messing about must end right away. . . . I warn you that you will be closely watched, and that I count on you, as the eldest, and thus the most reasonable, to change your sister's ways. Avoid telling any of these secrets when going to church, at the table, or in your chambers.

Such a stern message from the empress revealed that the children's conduct was far from harmless, and it appears that Marie Antoinette may have been the instigator. Carolina, soon after becoming queen of Naples in April 1768, wrote to the Countess von Lerchenfeld: "Write to me all the little circumstances of my sister Antoine, what she says, what she does, and mostly what she thinks. I swear to you, I pray to love her very much, for I am very interested in her."

A month later, Carolina wrote Lerchenfeld again: "Tell my sister that I love her extraordinarily." When Marie Antoinette became dauphine, she asked her mother if she could write her sister in Naples. Her mother acquiesced—but only if the letters were first sent to Schönbrunn to be scrutinized before being forwarded to Naples.

Marie Antoinette and Maria Carolina

Reports of lesbianism at Schönbrunn were not confined to Marie Antoinette. Marie Antoinette's older sister, Maria Christina, had a documented love affair with Isabella of Parma, Louis XV's granddaughter—despite the fact that Isabella was married to Christina's brother, Emperor Joseph II. Although Christina was Maria Theresa's favorite daughter, it is doubtful that the empress approved of her daughter's relationship with her daughter-in-law, Isabella, because the affair was so "intense." Isabella once wrote to Christina, "I am told that the day begins with God. I, however, begin the day by thinking of my lover, for I think of her incessantly."

Christina and Isabella continued their relationship until Isabella's death in 1763, leaving both Christina and Joseph heartbroken. The empress was perhaps more relieved than grief-stricken, and she quickly set about finding a new bride for her son.

Another older sister of Marie Antoinette was also not free of scandal. Maria Amalia, who was nine years older, was displeased with the marriage the empress had arranged for her with Duke Ferdinand of Parma in 1769. To show her contempt for her new husband, Amalia spent lavish sums for clothing and parties, and replaced her ladies-in-waiting with handsome young men of the Royal Guard. The empress was distraught with Amalia's "gallivanting at the officer's club and gambling away the small fortune that was allotted to her as a duchess." Moreover, she found Amalia's conduct, including cross-dressing, a horrific stain on Marie Antoinette's position as the future queen of France: "She made it a point to break with almost every social etiquette that was expected of a reigning consort. She wandered through city streets late at night unescorted, craving amusements; she openly took to love affairs with her male bodyguards; and even dressed incognito as a man, pretending to be a Spanish prince."

Unlike Marie Antoinette's husband, who was not interested in other women, Ferdinand took mistresses—even among the peasantry. Consequently, both Amalia and her husband were subjected to scandalous rumors throughout Europe. Marie Antoinette was also making waves, but these first whispers of scandal were limited to the court of Versailles. On August 7, 1770, Comte Mercy wrote the empress, "The Dauphine had supper with the King and asked his consent that the wife of the Dauphin's chief valet, Thierry, should be appointed one of her women of the bedchamber, which was granted at once."

Comte Mercy did not approve of the assignment because the Thierry family was part of the du Barry clan, but Marie Antoinette persisted for two reasons: the Mesdames Tantes had suggested it and the Thierrys had a little boy whom she could play with in her chambers. However, Madame Thierry soon became disgusted with Marie Antoinette's conduct, her favorites, her disrespect for the elderly ladies of court, her lightheartedness, her gambling debts, and her illicit escapades.*

The court was shocked when Madame Thierry informed Louis XV that she could no longer fulfill her duties for the dauphine, and His Majesty was certainly taken aback because resigning from the household of the dauphine, the future queen of France, was unprecedented.

Madame Thierry's retirement subsequently gave rise to the most scandalous remarks, and more important, it also gave credibility to other stories floating about the palace. For example, it was said that the Duc de Coigny, the king's first squire, was entering Marie Antoinette's chambers at all hours of the night.

Dauphine Marie Antoinette's acquaintances from the theater also added fuel to the flames of scandal. Mademoiselle de Raucourt was the first to receive the dauphine's favor. Raucourt, baptized Françoise-Marie-Antoinette-Josephe Saucerotte, made her sensational debut at the Comédie Française with the main role of *Dido* at the end of 1772. Because Madame du Barry was enchanted with her performance, she insisted that Louis XV give the actress permission to keep the role for the entire run of the play on January 10, 1773, as well as fifty gold coins. This would be the date that the king introduced the actress, his rumored lover, to Marie Antoinette.

However, Raucourt was better known for her romantic affairs with women than her talents on the stage. Her name became synonymous with

Mademoiselle de Raucourt and Sophie Arnould

---

* It was the aunt Madame Adélaïde who had encouraged the dauphine to take Madame Thierry into her household.

furor amoris antiphisici, or "the madness of anti-physical love, that infected the capital." And her life, both on and off stage, was a hot topic of current newspapers, reviews, and the salons of Paris, including her bankruptcy in 1776. Apparently, she had squandered so much of her money and incurred huge debts due to her sexual persuasion: "Her taste for tribades★ supposedly prevented her from following the example of other actresses and selling herself to male admirers."

In March 1777, matters turned worse when Raucourt was arrested and taken to the For-l'Evêque prison.† But hours later, the actress was ordered released, and it remains unknown who had given the order. It also remains unknown if it might have been a "royal" order; however, Raucourt was presented at the court of Versailles the next day and did not leave until the following day. Rumors gave rise to "shameful attachment" with the queen because Raucourt's miserable situation did not prevent her from receiving the queen's favor.

One might have considered Raucourt to be Marie Antoinette's mistress when, in November 1777, the queen was willing to pay Raucourt's debts of 200,000 livres, but it is unknown whether she actually paid them.

Raucourt returned to the stage as Dido in 1779, to be cheered by her inseparable lesbian companion Jeanne-Francoise-Marie Souck, the lesbian opera singer Sophie Arnould, and "lots of other tribades." Several days later, when Raucourt played Phèdre, the audience jeered the "illustrious sister" with the "masculine manner and coarsened voice." She was expelled from the theater group.

Raucourt, the "young priestess of Lesbos," was not the only actress to be in the queen's entourage. Sophie Arnould, an illustrious singer, who reportedly staged orgies with groups of women, had assisted Marie Antoinette by introducing the queen's childhood music teacher and favorite composer, Christoph Willibald Gluck, to Paris circles.

However, as dissatisfaction with the monarchy increased, so did resentment with anyone associated with it, especially Marie Antoinette's prized musician. When Sophie Arnould appeared in Gluck's *Iphigénie*, audiences booed and hissed until being quieted when the queen attended her performances. But subsequently, the hissing became so loud that Arnould could not be heard.

★ A label for a lesbian who lies on top of her partner and simulates the movements of a male in heterosexual intercourse.

† Complaint delivered on March 27, 1777, by Thomas-Philippe Violet, keeper of seals, against Miss Raucourt and Lady Souck for threats and insults.

Lesbian relationships at the time were referred to as "romantic friend-ships" or "particular friendships," whether platonic or not, and the most famous was that between Raucourt and Arnould. The queen's patronage of these women tended to "reciprocally confirm their bad reputation." Even the famous artist Élisabeth Louise Vigée Le Brun, was subjected to the same sexual suspicion with the queen after painting the famous *Marie Antoinette en chemise.*

Le Brun was the queen's favorite painter, and her first official portrait, or flattery, was completed in 1778, depicting the queen in white satin with her crown on a table next to her and a bust of Louis XVI looking down upon her.

The controversial portrait en chemise was painted and exhibited in 1783. The queen is depicted wearing a simple light dress made from the muslin used for blouses; it was basically an undergarment. This was a far cry from the more structured gowns traditionally worn by queens or noble ladies at Versailles. Although dressing in such intimate apparel was the trend at the queen's Trianon, portraying Marie Antoinette in lingerie in boudoir portraits did nothing to help her already tarnished reputation.

Due to the outrage of a queen being depicted so commonly and in such a vulgar manner, Le Brun quickly withdrew the painting from the exhibit and re-created another to take its place. The pose was the same, but the queen was dressed in a dress more befitting a royal, although the lower-cut neckline was more revealing.

Original painting en chemise (left) and re-creation (right)

Being a woman, as well as the queen's favorite portraitist, Le Brun caused a stir with her relationship with Marie Antoinette that became a topic of scandalous allegations. This was only intensified with the painter's new direction in painting with the depiction of two women in "Peace Bringing Back Abundance," a work suggesting an erotic encounter between the feminine, breast-bearing "Abundance" submitting to the more masculine-dressed "Peace."

Whether fact or fiction, Élisabeth Louise Vigée Le Brun became known as the painter of the "tribades of Versailles." Her painting of the Duchesse de la Guiche as a milkmaid only added fuel to the fire of scandalous stories about the women's intimate manner of dress and bizarre antics at the queen's hideout at Trianon. Le Brun obviously adored the queen, writing in her memoirs,

> But the most remarkable thing about her face was the brilliance of her complexion. I have never seen another to equal it, and brilliant is the right word to use; for her skin was so transparent that it did not take shadow (*elle ne prenait point d'ombre*). I could not render it to my satisfaction: the colors were wanting that could paint that freshness, those tints so fine which belonged only to that charming face and which I have never found again on any other woman.

Marie Antoinette also broke the rules of etiquette with her favorite painter, a woman far below her rank. When Le Brun, in advanced pregnancy, dropped her paintbrush, the queen, who was seated on an armchair at the top of a platform where Madame Vigée Le Brun painted her, rushed to pick up the artist's brush, concerned that she might get hurt. After painting, the queen and Le Brun sang the duets of André Gretry on the harpsichord.

Considering Le Brun's admittance to the queen's private quarters, it was not surprising that there were rumors of an affair. Historians have noted that saphism, or female homosexuality, was recorded more frequently among ladies of the aristocracy, the theater, and prostitutes. One expert during this period wrote, "The saphists have their places of meeting, recognize each other by peculiar glances, carriage, etc. Saphistic pairs like to dress and ornament themselves alike, etc. They are called 'little sisters.'"

Another expert of this time distinguished between tribady and cunnilingus. The former was practiced only by women of "antipathic sexual instinct" as a means of sexual satisfaction, whereby a desire for the opposite sex is present; however, it is "much weaker and is manifested episodically only, while homosexuality is primary, and, in time and intensity, forms the most striking feature of sexual life."

Cunnilingus, on the other hand, was found among women with normal sexual instinct but hypersexual feeling, such as those with no opportunity for coitus, afraid of coitus, pregnant, or married women whose "sexual desires remain unsatisfied in consequence of the husband's impotence."

Such an explanation would give credence that Marie Antoinette, bored with her husband's disappointing performance, may have experimented in this area since it was more common with other upper-class women. Also, as we have seen, Marie Antoinette was not unfamiliar with deviant behavior of her generation.

Perhaps the most peculiar behavior of the time was cross-dressing, even though Marie Antoinette's sister Amalia was known to practice it. Closer to home, Marie Antoinette commissioned her milliner Mademoiselle Rose Bertin to create a wardrobe for a male cross-dresser to be presented at court. Bertin was not the cross-dresser's only fashion designer, however. Being dressed by her was beyond his means—unless the queen paid the bill.

His name was either the Chevalier d'Eon or Mademoiselle de Beaumont, and when the queen took him under her wing, he became a more prominent member of society, and not just a freak. The chevalier was notorious because, having spent the first half of his life as a man and the second as a woman, nobody could determine his gender. However, a medical examination after his death revealed him to be a man.

Even when dressed as female, the chevalier was known to be an astute fencer. He defeated the Chevalier de Saint-George in a contest on April 9, 1787, in the presence of the Prince of Wales.

Marie Antoinette, too, was known to don elements inspired by fashions of the opposite sex. She loved riding horses but was criticized for it, as it was considered very unladylike. Even more controversial was the way she dressed when riding. Instead of riding sidesaddle in skirts, Marie Antoinette took to dressing *en chevalier,* or in the manner of men in breeches.

Marie Antoinette's imperial mother criticized her desire to ride, fearing that it was too risky for a young dauphine whose main role was to provide an heir for the kingdom. When Marie Antoinette appealed to the king, he agreed but only if she rode a donkey, and she was satisfied until the Mesdames Tantes encouraged her to ride a horse so she could join them on hunting.

When the royal family visited Fontainebleau far from the imperial mother's spies, Madame Adélaïde succeeded in obtaining the king's permission of arranging for a horse to be available at a specified spot during the hunt, allowing Marie Antoinette to dismount the donkey and mount the horse. She obviously felt victorious but soon had to explain her stunt to

Fencing match between the Chevaliers de Saint-Georges and d'Eon; Marie Antoinette in redingote

Comte de Mercy with promises to never ride a horse except on the hunt, promises that were often broken. Comte de Mercy and Maria Theresa disapproved but did not make an issue out of the matter; after all, King Louis XV had given his permission. Also, Maria Theresa had told her daughter to obey Mesdames Tantes, and she did just that.

Maria Theresa may not have approved of Marie Antoinette's riding clothes either. Wearing a version of the English redingote (riding coat) and breeches normally worn by men, Marie Antoinette also rode with one leg on either side of the horse, shocking and dismaying the nobility of France.

The redingote illustrated the trend of women adopting masculine styles of dress. Marie Antoinette's redingote was open in the front to reveal her petticoat and buttoned at the top to mimic the style of men's coats, only adding credence to stories of the queen's lesbianism.

À SAVOIR

Marie Antoinette's Handwriting (1774–1778)

Signature (November 16, 1774)

This signature, according to the graphologist, is angular; it shows persistence and stubbornness in the writer. The writer is unreliable and of low intelligence. Keep in mind that the level of unreliability depends on several factors. For this signature, the illegibility, ambiguity in letter execution, slowness, broken letters with missing parts, and impeded flow suggest this. This signature is also very pasty, and this level of pastiness suggests crudeness. The high pressure combined with the irregularity of script implies impulsivity and emotionality. The writer is adaptable and receptive. Negatively, it can be interpreted as aggressiveness, brutality, or irritability.

Letter from Marie Antoinette to Count von Rosenberg (April 17, 1775)

The following notes refer to the handwriting from Marie Antoinette's letter to her mother's gallant minister and friend of the family, Count von Rosenberg:

- This handwriting has a good standard of form level.
- This script size is small as well, showing humility and tolerance.
- The writing angle leans left ever so slightly. This suggests the writer to be self-controlled and neutral, and not being social very often. Some would say the writer is standoffish, but the arcade nature of the script suggests this quality is toned down in the writer.
- The arcade form of connection symbolizes reserve and diplomacy while also reinforcing distance.
- This script is disconnected. This points to productive observation and, sometimes, loneliness and impulsiveness.
- The script has good spacing and is regular. This shows moderation and a bit of indifference.
- The leveled direction of lines on this script shows the writer to be social but holds back a bit. This could come off as being neutral and distant to some people.
- High pressure combined with a regular script symbolizes willpower, tenacity, and self-control.
- The script is at a good balance between being pasty and being sharp. This was produced by holding the writing instrument at just a bit less than 90 degrees. This shows an analytical mind which is balanced out by warmth.
- The fullness in the upper zone suggests the writer is imaginative and has colorful speech.
- The writer has a predominant left tendency in the upper zone suggest the writer has a flexible morality.

It is interesting that the first two writing samples express a degree of impulsiveness, and historian Eliakim Littell concurs: "Marie Antoinette was cold at heart, though she had an easily excited surface sensibility, which made her hasty and impulsive." Also, her mother, Maria Theresa, wrote, "Marie-Antoinette's letters exhibit only the frigid phrases of glib conventionality. There is no true warmth in her expression. This constitutional coldness was probably a lucky accident under the circumstances which marked the early years of her wedded life."

"Flexible morality" is an interesting characteristic drawn from the dauphine's handwriting. Could this be a foreboding?

Letter from Marie Antoinette to M. de Clugny (1776)

The handwriting from Marie Antoinette's letter to M. de Clugny, the controller general of finance, is interesting because it contrasts with the previous analysis of the dauphine's "cold" character. This may be due to her feeling inferior or lacking self-confidence. The deep extension of the letters *f*, *j*, and *p* shows sublimation and fatality. The writing angle is vertical with only the slightest right slant, which shows neutrality and reserve. The slight right slant suggests that the reserve of the writer doesn't come off as being cold and rigid.

The disconnected nature of the script points to individualism, self-reliance, and egocentricity. The leveled direction of lines shows the writer to be methodical and of emotional control. This is reinforced by the regularity of the script.

Marie Antoinette's willpower and self-control are reminiscent of the inherited Hapsburg "fiber of obstinacy," and her mother was quite aware of this:

> I am more and more convinced that I have not been mistaken in the headstrong and pleasure-seeking character I have long attributed to my daughter. I have perfectly noticed that, notwithstanding professed deference to your remonstrances, she has never swerved from her course when it was a question of matters for which she had a fondness (Maria Theresa to Count Mercy, July 31, 1774).

Part IV

THE QUEEN'S REGRETS (1778–1792)

Louis XVI

10

CHARLOT AND TOINETTE'S LOVE AFFAIRS

A Play Stolen from V——★

Scilicet is superis labor est, ea cura quietas sollicitat.†

—Virgil, *The Aeneid*

During the reign of Louis XVI and Marie Antoinette, the French manifested a craze for satirical and pornographic writings. Unfortunately, the king and the queen were the targets of the scathing pamphlets that flooded France and abroad.

These types of publications, however, were not new to their reign. Henry III, with his mignons, was mocked for his homosexuality, Anne of Austria was accused of having an affair with Mazarin, Louis XIV was satirized for his exploits with the "old" Madame de Maintenon, and Louis XV was depicted as a debauched monster, indulging on young lasses to deflower in his Parc-aux-Cerfs. Louis XVI, however, was far from being depraved, and after seven years of alleged impotence, Marie Antoinette appeared to be the superior partner of the marriage and, therefore, the more popular target.

The first pamphlet about Marie Antoinette appeared in 1774, about the same time that Marie Antoinette's circle first included male admirers, such as the Baron de Besenval, the Duc de Coigny, and the Comte Valentin d'Esterházy. She had also befriended the Princesse de Lamballe among other ladies of the court by this time.

On June 26, 1774, Louis XVI sent the playwright and diplomat Pierre Beaumarchais to London to purchase the entire edition of a "frightful pamphlet" against Marie Antoinette, titled *Important Notice to the Spanish Branch on Its Rights to the Crown of France in Default of Heirs, and which may be very*

★ V——: Versailles

† That is indeed the task of the powers above; this trouble vexes their tranquil state.

121

useful to all the Bourbon Family, especially King Louis XVI and signed by G.A. (Guillaume Angelucci).* The pamphlet touted the king's impotence and the queen's taking lovers to give France an heir to the throne.

After buying up the entire edition or four thousand copies and having burned them, Beaumarchais reported, unfortunately, that Angelucci had escaped with a secret copy. After chasing Angelucci to Nuremberg, Beaumarchais concocted, according to his coachman, a story that he had caught Angelucci and retrieved the secret copy. After traveling to see Marie Antoinette's mother in Austria to republish the pamphlet without the scandalous parts about Marie Antoinette, the Austrians "smelled a rat" and had Beaumarchais imprisoned. He was released after the French government confirmed he was a diplomat, but his dealings have to this day been suspect in the affair.

It would not be long until it was necessary to search for copies of another pamphlet that damaged the queen's reputation. The anonymous *Les Amours de Charlot et Toinette* was printed in 1779 and was distributed so quickly outside France that Lieutenant General Lenoir of the Paris police sent Beaumarchais's rival, Goëzman, to England and the United Provinces to buy the seditious manuscripts, its lewd illustrations, and the print blocks. The pamphlet recounted in pornographic detail a torrid love affair between Marie Antoinette, or Toinette, and Louis XVI's youngest brother, the Comte d'Artois, or Charlot.

King Louis XVI's impotence and debility, Marie Antoinette's levity, and the Comte d'Artois's libertine lifestyle with free access to the queen's private chambers were known by the court of Versailles, giving rise to the subject matter for the pamphlet.

The question arises how these tales originated. Historians have theorized that the information and verses from courtiers were sold to merchants, who profited by having them published abroad and then distributing them. Real events and real people were the subject of the pamphlets and, therefore, the informant had to be current on the queen's frivolity at court and in Paris, her increasingly questionable entourage, her extravagance, and the ongoing problems with consummating her marriage.

> A young and frisky Queen,
> Whose very August Husband† was a bad f**k,
> From time to time, as a very prudent woman,

---

* Beaumarchais had been previously sent to London to find and destroy a pamphlet titled "Secrets of a Public Woman" against Madame du Barry.

† Louis-Auguste.

Diverted herself from her misery,
By taking care of the small business
Of a mind tired of waiting and a badly f★★ked C★★t.
In sweet reverie,
Her pretty little Body, naked, totally naked,
Sometimes on the cushion of a soft chair,
She rid herself at night of the day's constraint,
With the help of a certain finger, Love's Doorman,
And burned her Incense for the God of Cythera;★
Sometimes, dying of boredom in the middle of a beautiful day,
She trammeled all alone in her bed;
Her throbbing nipples, her beautiful eyes, and her mouth,
Half-open, softly panting,
Seemed to proudly invite the challenge of a good f★★k.
In these Obscene positions,
Antoinette would have rather not remained at foreplay,
And that Louis had f★★ked her better;
But what can one say about that?
It is well known that the poor Sire,
Condemned three or four times
By the healthy member,
For his complete impotence,
Cannot satisfy Antoinette.
Well convinced of this calamity,
Because his matchstick
Is about as thick as a blade of straw,
Always limp and curled up,
His C★★k is kept in his pouch;
Instead of f★★king, he is f★★ked
As was the bishop of Antioch.†

The purpose of the introductory section of the pamphlet is to express the queen's misery of being deprived of sexual satisfaction. She is young and attractive, but her husband is physically and emotionally unable to consummate their marriage. He is the "August" husband, which not only means "noble" but also refers to his middle name, which makes the story more personal.

Shown naked in a chair, the queen is portrayed as any other woman with natural desires—not as a queen in regal attire sitting upon a throne.

★ Cythera is where Aphrodite, the Hellene goddess of love and desire, first set foot on land.

† In 344, when orthodox representatives of Sardica visited Antioch, a harlot was found in their quarters during the night, and the scandal was traced back to Stephen, the Bishop of Antioch. As a result, he was deposed.

Self-satisfaction is her only recourse, until her brother-in-law arrives. The language is lyrical but interrupted by the almost shocking, crude vocabulary.

> D'A——,★ feeling the triumphant grace one day,
> Bracing the desire to f★★k,
> Falls at the Queen's feet, hoping and trembling;
> He loses his voice as he tries to speak to her,
> He embraces and caresses her beautiful hands,
> Letting his impatient flame flicker;
> He shows a little trouble, troubling her in turn;
> Pleasing Toinette finally only took a day:
> Princes and Kings are quick when it comes to love.
> In a beautiful alcove artfully gilded,
> That was not too dark and not too lighted up,
> On a soft sofa, covered in velvet,
> From the August beauty her charms are received;
> The Prince presents his c★★k to the Goddess:
> A delicious moment of f★★king and tenderness!

When the Comte d'Artois is introduced, he trembles and is a bit troubled at first. Is this because he is about to commit double adultery with his queen and thus committing an act of treason? But like all princes and kings, he is "quick" to act without attention to the consequences. Considering the number of mistresses and illegitimate children at the court of Versailles, such behavior had become the norm. Wives were merely political pawns.

But why is the Comte d'Artois the *prince charmant* in this pamphlet? He was the handsome, charming, youngest brother of Louis XVI and, unlike his fat, boring, awkward brothers, he was frivolous and adventurous like his sister-in-law Marie Antoinette. He was perhaps the most fashionable young man in France.

To justify the count's actions in the pamphlet, the queen is no longer a queen, nor his sister-in-law; she has become a goddess in a "not too dark and not too lighted up" alcove that resembles a cave where goddesses were worshipped in antiquity.

Or does this alcove represent the royal womb? In another pamphlet, *Vie de Marie Antoinette d'Autriche*, the royal womb is attacked: "Since the revolution, the monarchical club, of which Antoinette is the soul, has continued to make attempts. Each of the members who compose draw on the poison from the vagina of the Austrian. This pestiferous lair is the

---

★ D'A——: the Comte d'Artois, Louis XVI's brother.

receptacle of all vices, and there, each one comes to fill himself abundantly with his own dose."

> Her Heart is beating, love and the modesty
> Paint this beauty with a gorgeous blush;
> But the modesty passes, and the Love alone remains:
> The Queen weakly defends herself; she weeps.
> The eyes of the proud d'A——, dazzled, enchanted,
> Animated with a beautiful flame, ogle her beautiful features:
> Ah! Who could not help but to worship them!
> Below a finely turned neck, which puts alabaster to shame,
> Sit two pretty breasts, separated, rounded,
> Throbbing gently, curved with Love:
> On both of them a little Rose stands up,
> Breasts, charming Breasts, that never rest,
> You seem to invite one's hand to squeeze you,
> One's eyes to look at you, one's mouth to kiss you,
> Antoinette is divine, everything about her is charming:
> The sweet voluptuousness to which she succumbs,
> Seems to give her a new gracefulness:
> Pleasure embellishes her; Love is a great makeup.
> D'A—— knows her by heart and he kisses her all over,
> His member is a hot iron, his Heart a furnace.
> He kisses her lovely arms, her pretty little C★★t,
> Sometimes a buttock, sometimes a breast.
> He gently slaps her bouncing bottom,
> Thigh, belly, belly button, the center of everything good;
> The Prince kisses everywhere in his sweet madness;
> And without realizing he looks like a Rascal,
> He is carried away in his extreme ardor.
> He would like to shoot straight to the end of Friendship.
> Antoinette, feigning to avoid what she likes,
> With fear of the shock, she only gives halfway:
> D'A—— seizes the moment, and Toinette, conquered,
> At last feels how sweet it is to be so well f★★ked.

The pamphlet is presenting a scorching love scene, but it is not based on love. It is simply lust, where love is just "makeup," covering up the count's sexual drive. He more than likely knows the queen's body and "knows her by heart," having been included in her intimate circle and having accompanied her to the opera, to parties, and to the gardens of Versailles for their renowned nocturnal walks. He is also starkly contrasted with the king. The king is a "poor Sire" with a "matchstick" that cannot ignite, whereas the count is as hot as a "furnace" with a "hot iron." While the king keeps his emotions in his "pouch," the count is a real "Rascal."

> While love tenderly interweaves them,
> Charlot, holding her, makes her beg for mercy,
> Antoinette quivers, already in her eyes
> The pleasures of the Gods are portrayed:
> They are close to happiness, but destiny is a traitor:
> The Bell rings . . . a diligent page,
> Too busy to obey, disturbs them by entering . . .
> Opening and showing himself . . . sees all and disappears,
> It only took a second.
> Stupefied by his disgrace,
> D'A——left his place.
> The Beautiful Queen groaned,
> Lowered her eyes, blushed,
> Without speaking a word:
> The Prince consoles her with a new kiss:
> "Forget, dear Queen, forget this misfortune,
> If this too alert harasser
> Has delayed our happiness,
> Misfortune suffered often
> Gives pleasure more gusto.
> "So," said the handsome d'A——, "let's repair this loss."
> This way he tried
> A greater stroke
> Of which the Queen opposed
> With resistance,
> Which made their amorous transports pricklier,
> And only better spreading our all the little treasures.

Marie Antoinette is certainly the "Beautiful queen" in this pamphlet. Her sister-in-law Madame Clotilde once described the queen's radiance: "It was impossible to see anything but the Queen; Hebes and Floras, Helens and Graces are street-walkers to her.★ She is a statue of beauty when sitting or standing; grace itself when she moves."

When the queen and the count are interrupted by a bell, it is a court page who interrupts them. A bell commonly signifies an arrival or, morally, represents the voice of God. In any event, the count may feel as if he has

---

★ Written to the Countess of Ossory after Madame Clotilde's marriage (August 23, 1775).

sinned, because he is "stupefied by his disgrace." On the contrary, the queen feels no remorse. Lowering her eyes and blushing, she only appears embarrassed or disappointed.

The phrase "Misfortune suffered often Gives pleasure more gusto" highlights Marie Antoinette's lifestyle at Versailles. Her miserable marriage, the strict etiquette, and the prying eyes are all excuses for escape and entertainment, albeit unbefitting a queen. She only hopes for a better life, one far from the stifling court.

> Dear Reader, our lovers f★★ked each other so much
> That their asses gave them away.
> Up again rises "Sir Gervais"★ a second time:
> "What does Her Majesty want? . . ."
> "For god's sake! This is deliberate,"
> Said d'A—— angrily.
> "I know nothing about this mystery;
> Coming in here all the time
> What do these cruel guards want?"
> The Queen can hear no more . . . finally, when
> Their souls have barely recovered from their mistake,
> They search with great care,
> In every little corner,
> To discover the cause
> Of such a treacherous event;
> But they find nothing, Love mourns this pause,
> The Queen is in despair and starts to sob,
> Then drops, like a heavy lump,
> On a pile of tiles,
> Silent witnesses of her disgrace.
> The spell is broken then and her pretty body breaks
> The obstacle of their passion. . . . It's the damned cord
> Of the bell, whose tassel—
> Poisoned, rotten cause
> Of the day's accidents—
> Was caught between two cushions. . . .
> With each moment of their tenderness
> Of the sweets one tastes in Cyprus.

Religious connotations ring throughout the pamphlet. The Bishop of Antioch and the Archbishop of Rheims have fallen from grace, and not

---

★ Archbishop of Rheims who resigned after being declared unfit.

learning their lesson, the queen and the count's souls "barely recovered from their mistake" when they continued with their crime, even acknowledging the spiritual warning: "For god's sake! This is deliberate." However, humorously, they discover that the bell was rung because its tassel, under the couple's cushions, was tugged as they made love.

> A loud ring of the bell tolled their ecstasy.
> Oh! That the lechers would be captured
> If, in the middle of their incursions,
> They were thus to encounter the cords of bells!
> Our reassured lovers are still celebrating love
> Two or three good times before the end of the day:
> And, both plunged into the midst of delight,
> They seem to savor their precious positions.
> Each day happier, becoming more ardent,
> They offer Venus their everlasting flames;
> They f★★k each other often, and love and time,
> For these happy lovers, seem to have no more wings.
>
> As for me, if I am enslaved
> To enjoy great things, without laughter, to c★m, and to please,
> In order to save myself from such misery.
> I'd like better to cut my c★★k off.
> When we are told about virtue,
> It's often out of envy;
> After all, we wouldn't be alive
> If our fathers had not f★★ked.
> FIN.

Some historians have attributed *Les Amours de Charlot et Toinette* to Beaumarchais. The first edition was purchased by the publisher Boissière, who was paid 18,600 livres from Louis XVI's purse to suppress an obscenely illustrated edition of it in 1781. In March 1783, all editions found were confiscated and sent to the Bastille to be destroyed. The pamphlets, however, were difficult to track, and in the end, the shock of sexual, obscene language was successful in conveying messages that challenged the social and moral conventions of the last years of the Bourbon court.

11

THE AUSTRIAN WOMAN ON THE RAMPAGE, OR THE ROYAL ORGY

An Operatic Proverb

Veni, vidi.★

—composed by a royal bodyguard, published since by the
Freedom of the Press, and set to music by the queen

L'*Autrichienne en Goguettes ou l'Orgie Royale*, better known as *The Royal Orgy*, is an anti-royal pamphlet by Mayeur de Saint-Paul, author of plays, many licentious. In contrast to *Charlot et Toinette*, his work includes a lesbian scene between Queen Marie Antoinette and Madame de Polignac with the Comte d'Artois, and also a brief appearance by King Louis XVI.

Scene 1
The scene takes place in the queen's "petits appartements."

BODYGUARDS' CHORUS
(Drinking.)
Let's vary our pleasures,
Between Bacchus† and the God of the Cask.
The example they give us here
Intensifies our desires.

A GUARD
To arms! Here is Her Majesty.

★ I came, I saw..
† Roman god of wine and fertility.

ANOTHER GUARD
There will be an orgy tonight, the female Ganymede★ is with the Queen.

ANOTHER GUARD
And the beloved d'Artois is between vice and virtue. Guess who vice is.

A GUARD
There's nothing to guess. All I can see is this God proliferating.

Scene 2
The Comte d'Artois, the Queen, Madame de Polignac.

THE QUEEN
(To Madame de Polignac, who steps aside to let her pass.)
Come in, come in, my dear.

THE COMTE D'ARTOIS
(Gently pushing the Queen from behind, grabbing her bottom.)
In you go as well.
   (In the Queen's ear.)
Oh! What a bottom! It's so firm and flexible!

THE QUEEN
(In a low voice to the Comte d'Artois.)
If my heart were as firm, would we be so good together?

THE COMTE D'ARTOIS
Quiet, fool, or tonight I'll give my brother another son.

THE QUEEN
Oh no! Let's gather pleasure's flowers, but let's not bother with the fruit.

THE COMTE D'ARTOIS
So be it. I'll be prudent, if I can.

THE QUEEN
Let's be seated.

★ Madame de Polignac.

MADAME DE POLIGNAC

Where is the King?

THE QUEEN

What are you worried about? He'll come soon enough to bore us.

THE QUEEN

When I see Pleasure, Love, and the Graces around me
Put me in their footsteps,
It is happiness to follow the law.

THE COMTE D'ARTOIS

(To the Queen.)
Oh, supreme being, I am near the one I love;
My heart drowns in pleasure,
I have no other desires.

MADAME DE POLIGNAC

Adorable Princess, what happiness for me,
When I can at any moment
Plunge your senses
Into the sweetest intoxication!

TOGETHER

When I see around me
Pleasure, Love, and the Graces;
Put me in their footsteps,
It is happiness to follow the law.

MADAME DE POLIGNAC

Here is the King.

The first scene introduces Madame de Polignac as "Ganymede," who was the "most beautiful of mortals" in Greek mythology. The role would be fitting for Madame de Polignac, because she was beautiful. Even the queen's official portrait painter, Le Brun, agreed: "She had, besides her delightful beauty, an angelic sweetness and a most attractive, solid sense." However, the term "Ganymede" was also used then as "homosexual" or "faggot" is used today.

It is also interesting how the queen speaks of her husband when he is absent from her intimate circle: "He'll come soon enough to bore us." This rings true because the queen could not wait for him to retire in the evenings. Because he went to bed like clockwork every evening at ten o'clock, someone in the queen's group would set the clock forward, and when the king took his leave, the "intimate circle returned to its gaiety with his absence." When away from the court of Versailles and attending balls or parties with the king, the queen often ignored him, kept him out of her sight, or sometimes even left without him, accompanied by the Comte d'Artois or other men of her circle.

The Comte d'Artois had always been rumored to be the father of the queen's first son, the dauphin Louis Joseph. This is evident when the count says, "Tonight I'll give my brother another son." Similar to "Charlot et Toinette," the king's alleged impotence is highlighted from the very beginning of the pamphlet. But now the count has fathered the queen's first son, and he was the product of pleasurable sex: "Let's gather pleasure's flowers, but let's not bother with the fruit." In other words, the kingdom now has an heir and the king is not needed any longer.

It is now "happiness to follow the law" at court where conjugal relations are political and extramarital affairs are the norm.

Scene 3

(The same, Louis XVI.)

THE QUEEN

(Sneering.)
Why do you make us wait! What kept you?

LOUIS

I was busy finishing a lock, of which I'm very happy.

THE QUEEN

You must be very tired! Drink a big glass of bubbly champagne.

LOUIS

Gladly.
(He drinks.)

THE QUEEN

You won't have another?

LOUIS

No, I want to be sober tonight.
I must hold Council early in the morning; dulled senses
Don't give the mind the ability
Needed to judge properly.

THE QUEEN

As long as you are seated, it's all that is necessary.
Your council will do as it always does, following its own fancy.

LOUIS

It's true that I can't do anything right. Those gentlemen always
Manage to make me do something stupid.

THE QUEEN

That's still good enough for the frogs of the Seine.★

THE QUEEN

Let's laugh, let's revel,
Make use of our power;
Squander all the money
Of good Parisians.

TOGETHER

Let's laugh, let's revel,
Make use of our power
Squander all the money
Of our good Parisians.

(The King, who has emptied one bottle and three-fourths of the second, falls asleep with his head on the table.)

MADAME DE POLIGNAC

The Guards have retired, the King sleeps.

THE COMTE D'ARTOIS

That's what is called an obliging brother, a good and drunk scepter.

★ The queen is referring to the Parisians as frogs.

THE QUEEN
Let him have his fill and we'll make the most of it.

As soon as the king arrives, the queen asks, "What kept you?" This is ironic when we think of the seven years needed for the king to consummate his marriage. We also hear that he's been tinkering with locks in his workshop. He was, in fact, fascinated with locksmithing, more so than with governing his kingdom. The queen coaxing him to have a glass of champagne in this pamphlet is not unusual; the king is often inebriated in such pamphlets. However, it is well documented that he enjoyed drinking as much as he enjoyed eating. The journalist and politician Bertrand Barrère wrote in his memoirs about Louis "cultivating the bottle," noting that the king was on one occasion so "seriously intoxicated" that he had to be hoisted into his coach after the hunt, where he slept during the journey back to Versailles.

Louis XVI was also a glutton. He would have chicken, lamb chops, eggs, ham, and a bottle and a half of wine before going on the hunt in the mornings. Historian Louis Gottschalk reported that "he did not bother himself with cookery, nor with any refinements; to him, always afraid of not having enough to eat, sheer quantity was more important than anything else; he did not eat, he stuffed himself."

But in this case, the queen is trying to get Louis inebriated so he will retire early. When she asks the king to have a second glass, the king reveals that he needs to be clearheaded to work with his council the following day, but the queen rebuffs him: "Your council will do as it always does." This was pitifully true, and the king finally ends up drunk and passed out with his head on the table.

But behind these vulgar scenes are hidden political accusations: Marie Antoinette is France's enemy, she taints the legitimacy of the French monarchy with her infidelities, and she dominates her husband by emasculating him with drink. This is political pornography at its best.

THE COMTE D'ARTOIS
(Kissing the Queen on the mouth.)
Well said.
(All three get up from the table. The Queen goes to sit on a couch.)

THE QUEEN
(Stretching out.)
Oh, how nice it is here!

THE COMTE D'ARTOIS
(Slipping his hand under the Queen's skirt.)
Ah! It's even nicer there!
(Putting his middle finger on the royal private parts.)

THE QUEEN
(To the Comte d'Artois, who starts to move his finger faster.)
Ah, ah! . . . Stop it, d'Artois, you're making me c★★e.

MADAME DE POLIGNAC
What, Monsieur le Comte, you're usurping my rights?
That's horrible! I don't usurp yours!

THE COMTE D'ARTOIS
(The actions he has just performed put him in a vivid state.)
I believe so; you need a similar argument.
(He then exposes his maker of the human race★ to the two ladies' gazes.)

THE QUEEN
(Eyes animated and bosom throbbing.)
Ah! What a fine argument! What do you say, Polignac?

POLIGNAC
It would be unjust not to have the same opinion.

THE COMTE D'ARTOIS
(Placing a leg between the Queen's knees.)
Allow me to press my argument home.
Forgive my intoxication
I don't want to only half
Prove my affection.

THE QUEEN
No, leave me be, my friend;
Gently, you're hurting me.
Get a grip on your desire,
When happiness brings us together,

★ His "maker of the human race" (*régénérateur de l'espèce humaine*) refers to his penis.

"What, Monsieur le Comte, you are usurping my rights?" Marie Antoinette, Madame de Polignac, and the Comte d'Artois

Let's drown together
In waves of pleasures.
That's good.

D'ARTOIS

Oh wait . . .

(A moment of silence and Madame de Polignac faces the couple.)

MADAME DE POLIGNAC

(To the Queen.)

Faster. . . . What a delicious moment!

D'ARTOIS

Ah! The way you move!

What a wonderful movement!

THE QUEEN

Ah! Ah! That's so good. . . . I'm c★★ing!

D'ARTOIS

You are going to receive my soul.

(Together.)

In this moment full of sweetness, let's drain the cup of happiness.

(Madame de Polignac contemplates the happy couple.)

POLIGNAC

Happily, while you were busy.

I had the "Porter of the Charter House"★ in one hand, and my other was not idle.

THE QUEEN

(To the Comte d'Artois.)

Ah, my dear count, your climax is so delicious!

You've left me beside myself. . . .

I am still savoring the pleasure you've just given me to taste.

D'ARTOIS

I hope my Priapus† won't stop there. Here's my instrument still full and strong.

And you will see it ready for another go.

MADAME DE POLIGNAC

The good Monarch is giving you plenty of time; he's snoring like a Templar.

★ *Histoire de Dom Bougre, Portier des Chartreux* (1741), a French erotic novel.

† Priapus was a god of fertility and known for his oversized penis.

THE QUEEN

By Jove! His sound asleep gives me a wildest idea!

D'ARTOIS

What is it?

THE QUEEN

He must assist in our frolics. His position fits in with my scheme.
I'm laughing already.

D'ARTOIS

Let's do it now.

THE QUEEN

Yes, yes, I can't hold my laugher any longer. . . . Let's sit like this.
*(The Queen pulls up two stools on either side of the King's back. Madame de
Polignac sits on Louis XVI's back and, parting her legs, places each of her feet
on a stool. Antoinette leans forward into Polignac's arms, embracing her tight,
while her tongue seeks and plays with that of the Confidante. She thereby offers
Comte d'Artois the most beautiful ass in the world.)*

THE QUEEN

Well, Count, you can see what route remains for you to take.
*(D'Artois lifts up a light linen petticoat, uncovering her bottom, white as
snow; and, furtively opening up with his hand the route to voluptuousness, he
launches the arrow of love into the temple of bliss. While the women's tongues
are flicking, while supple loins are moving, seeking new pleasures, the Confidante introduces her little finger into the portal of the Temple into which the
Count has introduced himself by a detour.)*

THE QUEEN

The poor old Monarch! I'm sure that if he woke up now,
I could make him believe he's seeing things.
It's so easy for me to get him to believe anything I want.

THE QUEEN

(To the Comte d'Artois, who's still going strong.)
Stop for a moment.

THE QUEEN

(To the Duchess.)

You too, Polignac; let me laugh for a moment about our scene.
This new ensemble should be added to Aretino's postures.* . . . Ah!

(Lascivious Antoinette's voice fails her, and a voluptuous silence follows the joke. But a bodyguard who saw everything through the doorway promises himself to stage this proverbial-opera scene, whose motto will be: Dimmi con chi tu vai, e sapero qual che fai.† And he wrote the following quatrain, inspired by the sight of this scene.)

QUATRAIN

On a human Monarch's back
I see the Mother of Vices
Immerse herself in frightful pleasures,
A rogue Prince and a prostitute Queen.

From Catherine de Médicis to Anne of Austria, a queen has never exercised power in France without causing disturbances or clashes. And the libels never stopped drawing parallels between Marie Antoinette and Catherine de Médicis or other hated queens in French history. Moreover, the image of an uncertain and hesitant king fading behind the authoritarian and daring personality of his queen was pure fodder for pamphleteers.

Marie Antoinette had been thrown in the political intrigues as an inexperienced princess, and deprived of the advice and firm convictions from her wavering husband, she had a natural tendency to ask her family and the Austrian ambassador in Paris, the Comte de Mercy-Argenteau, to enlighten and guide her, only further isolating the queen from her adopted people. It was a vicious circle: the more the pamphlets denounced the stranglehold of "the Austrian" on political life, the more Marie Antoinette felt rejected by the French and the more she sought support from her family.

The police were unable to stop the ever-increasing distribution of these pamphlets because enemies either had them printed or protected their printing, and these enemies were often courtiers or princes of the blood. The Parisians gave credence to these libels, taking the most shameless lies

---

* Pietro Aretino was best known for his sixteenth-century illustrations of different positions for sexual activity.

† Tell me whom you go with and I'll know what you do.

seriously. Although the libels were not directly responsible for the revolution on the horizon, they did damage the queen's reputation to the point that no revival of the love she experienced as a dauphine could save them.

Mentioning the work *Portier des Chartreux* was a curious tactic, as if the work from 1741 foretold what was to come. When its main character Dom Bougre was dragged off to the Bicêtre prison, he lamented, "Sorrow petrified me, fever seized me, and I got well only to fall sick with a much crueler illness: venereal disease." His cure included emasculation, while his mistress, whom he rediscovered in a brothel, dies.

In *The Royal Orgy*, the king is emasculated with his queen committing adultery behind the "human monarch's back." Venereal disease will strike the court of Versailles in due time.

12

DESCRIPTION OF THE ROYAL MENAGERIE OF LIVING ANIMALS

Established in the Tuileries, near the National Terrace, with their names, features, colors, and characteristics.

—F. Dantalle, 1789

In the *Royal Zoo*, a pamphlet written by F. Dantalle and provided below, each member of the royal family is given an insulting name, such as the venomous asp for the Comte d'Artois. All are monstrous beasts, except for the timid king, and Marie Antoinette, the daughter of a monkey, who will usurp the king's power and rule as regent for her son, Dauphin Louis Charles.

Some time ago, there was a truly curious zoo in Henri IV's castle—as curious for the rarity of the animals there as for the excessive expenditure that its upkeep cost the nation.

The public has inspected the ferocious beasts in their respective cages in the park at Versailles where they can watch more comfortably, and without too much trouble, a number of quadrupeds gathered at the Louvre. We will list the most remarkable of these ferocious beasts, noting their habits and their inclinations, their manner of feeding, and their characteristics.

The Royal Veto

This animal is around five feet and five inches tall. He walks on his hind legs like men do. The color of his fur is tawny, He has beast eyes, a fairly wide face, a red muzzle, and big ears; not much of a mane; his cry resembles the grunt of a pig; HE DOESN'T HAVE A TAIL.

He is voracious by nature; he eats, or rather, crassly devours, anything one throws at him. He is a drunk and never stops drinking, from rising in the morning until going to bed at night.

The Royale Veto is as timid as a rabbit, and as stupid as an ostrich; in all, he is a fat animal, which, it seems, nature regretted creating it.

His food costs about twenty-five to thirty million a year. And he is also not grateful; on the contrary, he seeks only to do harm, and his cunning and rude spirit often leads him against the walls of the national terrace, where he sometimes breaks his nose.

He is thirty-four to thirty-six years old. He was born at Versailles and given the nickname "Louis XVI."

The Female Royal Veto

The female of the Royal Veto is a monster found in Vienna, Austria, in the wardrobe of Empress Maria Theresa, the crowned female monkey who probably had an unnatural urge; she undoubtedly had herself bedded by a tiger or a bear and she brought MARIE ANTOINETTE into the world.

This thirty-three-year-old monster was brought to France in the days of the incestuous Louis XV, whose memory is odious. To the falseness of her country she added the deceit of beasts, by first presenting herself to the people as angelically sweet as a priest. The people cried: LONG LIVE THE QUEEN! Now, once she was assured that she could acknowledge the onlookers' allegiance with a few grimaces, she lifted her mask and was known for what she really was.

Married for political reasons to an oaf who spends his time making locks and bolts. Like Dion of Syracuse,★ she soon created ways to amuse herself at the expense of the kingdom. Everyone heard talk of the Parc-aux-Cerfs, Bagatelle, Trianon, Décampativos, and famous festivities of people from the four corners of the earth, in which the Royal Veto was always the chamber pot. There was talk of the Artois couple and Polignac women, Vaudreuil and bodyguards, the king and his Swiss guards, the Cardinal and Cagliostro, the necklace and unfortunate Oliva, and death by poison. The Heavens spurned the abominations and crimes of the Austrian woman, who mocked the Heavens and the nation. The people rise up, and then the Austrian Siren takes a child in her arms (the dauphin); she escapes from the same hands she would like to have seen in irons.

And so is the Versailles zoo transferred to Paris! Now you have the female of the Royal Veto conspiring with an animal called Lafayette, a

★ Dion usurped the power of Dionysius at the end of the fifth century BC.

little trip to the border; now she is the chameleon passing herself off as the Baroness de Korff, and Louis XVI, King of France, her manservant, who was made to sit behind the carriage too, as if another male was in heat. Then the group is stopped and driven back to Paris, where the cabal starts again, and Marie-Antoinette of Austria entertains herself by disturbing the peace of free France.

A prostitute has just been condemned to six months' imprisonment for having insulted a citizen. If Marie-Antoinette were judged as she merits, she would be in good company in Salpêtrière.★

The female of the Royal Veto is tall, ugly, wrinkled, worn-out, faded, hideous, and frightening, but like the nation she is dumb enough to feed its tyrants, she eats France's money in the hope of one day devouring the French, one at a time.

The Delphinus (Louis Charles)

We won't say anything about the Delphinus. We have noticed that on a rotten tree there is sometimes a good shoot . . . whose son is the Delphinus? Hopefully he will not be poisoned like his unfortunate brother.

The Royal Madame

This little female, undoubtedly destined like the spiders of the French Cape to suck the blood of slaves, already has all her mother's pride and perhaps her vices, too. It would not hurt to train her in some kind of trade; instead of being queen, she could one day mend socks.

The Elisabeth Veto

The sister of the Royal Veto is as evil as she was pretty. This evil carcass would like to see the nation go to the devil; but she has a pittance from the tyrant, and she earns her meals well. Who does keep her?

"What a swarm of parasites on that one branch of the royal tree," wrote historian Henry Williams. Madame Elisabeth was said to consume 30,000 livres worth of fish; meat and game, to the amount of 70,000 livres; and candles, to the amount of 60,000 livres in a year.

★ It served as a prison for prostitutes, and a holding place for women who were learning disabled, mentally ill, or epileptic, as well as poor; it was also notable for its population of rats.

The Royal Veto Provence

All that is most cunning in the fox is found thousands and thousands of times more in the folds and creases of the heart of the Royal Veto Provence.

This hypocritical monster, on learning that Favras* had compromised him, waits for the ill-fated man to expire before going in pomp to the Hôtel de Ville, with his tail between his legs, to assure his fellow citizens of his attachment to the Constitution; then, he suddenly departs for Koblenz, without paying his debts, and tries to stir up that country's wolf cubs against us.

There is more to say about this animal.

The Royal Veto Provence is a fat dolt like his elder brother; he looks vile and treacherous. . . . The Bourbon race undoubtedly resembles the descendants of Cain, bearing on their muzzle the mark of their reprobation in infamy. We will say nothing about his habits. He used to amuse himself by biting his fingernails; he might one day bite his fingers for having ingratiated himself with our traitors, among whom he couldn't fail to shine for his evil deeds. But if, having escaped from the royal menagerie, this animal is ever caught . . . put LOUISE in place.†

The Royal Veto d'Artois

Resembling the venomous asp, but lively and lightly built, the Royal Veto d'Artois is perhaps the prettiest beast of all the royal menagerie, but not at all the least vicious.

An animal without morals, having the lasciviousness of a wild boar,‡ the lewdness of Louis XV, the debauched dissoluteness characteristic of the louts of the court, d'Artois, before the revolution, only showed vice and a heart made for crime; all he lacked for glory was a counter revolution; but what horrors would come before!

The clammy ANTOINETTE, that same female of the ROYAL VETO, was not different from him. He found her worth the trouble . . . Bagatelles, Trianon, Meudon, the thickets and caverns resounded to the sound of their erotic spasms. . . . D'Artois flew into the arms of girls with tiaras and naughty skirts. It was all the same to him. A depraved libertine without faith, without honor, and without God—here you have another

---

* Favras, in 1789, was involved in the Comte de Provence's plans to save the king and end the French Revolution. He negotiated a loan of 2,000,000 francs but was betrayed by officers he took into his confidence.

† Louise, the little machine that cuts heads off so well.

‡ Male pig.

of these animals who imagine that all they have to do is act, blowing away all principles, and they'll succeed in people, not for liberty, crawl under their iron rod! We will shortly return to the subject of this ferocious beast; we will not forget the bragging and boasting of that other fugitive animal, called Condé.★ Let us examine our enemies' conduct a little. Let's no longer amuse ourselves by making futile reproaches. It is their manifest in hand against which we must wage an outrageous war. It is important for us; it is important for the children of liberty to show supporters of slavery that nothing can shake us.

But, less outraged by the boastfulness of Prussia or Hungary than filled with the deepest contempt for instigators in our war, we indignantly reject the treacherous advice that the courts of France, Berlin, and Vienna give us.

Indeed, so is the man, the least crazy who would prefer the old order to the new . . . and who had admitted that the current order of things cannot last longer. You see that this treacherous Louis XVI is unworthy to rule over you.

I'll prove what I am arguing: either Louis XVI is an aristocrat, or he is a patriot.

If he is an aristocrat, I ask the first anti-revolutionary if he does not find, in Louis XVI, a sickly party chief. Has not the apparent evil done to the aristocrats by the King stayed in their souls? Can they see a protector in Louis XVI? Does he arm himself with daggers? Aren't they kicked in the ass in front of him. . . . Did they want to drag him to Montmédy, they are confounded, and Louis XVI does as he pleases? Thus is this well-reasoned love for an untruthful king! Poor Louis XVI, can you not see that if the aristocrats only represent the Ancien Régime and if they want to reestablish the nobility and the monasteries, it would only be to dethrone you and lock you away in a cloister? There, with your head shaved and dressed in a long monk's frock, reduced to a modest existence, you would be perfectly certain of the eternal scorn of those whom your wife calls her dear gentlemen and her holy priests.

Now I would like to know of what Louis XVI's patriotism consists.

Tell us, Marie-Antoinette: what have you done to your husband's heart? You have set your spouse on edge; you have cleverly stupefied him. One could not speak to his majesty because his MAJESTY WAS DRUNK. One could not speak to his majesty; HE WAS MAKING LOCKS. One could not speak to his majesty; HE WAS HUNTING.

And you, flitting from pleasure to pleasure, from intrigues to intrigues, you were reigning in his name, you did everything in his name.

★ Marie Antoinette once offended the royalist Prince Louis Joseph of Condé when she snubbed his illicit mistress.

What baseness and arrogance, what audacity and duplicity, what protests of civism and sinister plots!

Distorted mother, you abandon your son on his death bed! Ah, you know well who pushed him to his grave! His last words denounce you. "Take," he said to his governor, "take this lock of my hair to my mother, so she will remember me. . . ." Answer, foul mother! . . . He is dead! . . .

Wife without decency, you prostitute yourself to frightful pleasures. . . . Born to be the most contemptible of courtesans, all that you have of royalty is impudence; of maternity, the name; of modesty, nothing, not even the appearance; of frankness, no knowledge; of virtue, no practice.

Monster in all aspects, one cannot look at you without trembling or imagine you without thinking of Jezebel. . . . There is no Jehovah to sacrifice you to, we despise you too much . . . but there are dogs to revel in your corpse. . . . They are waiting for you . . .

Soon enough, imperious one, you will want to mimic Semiramis.* . . . It is true you have not yet killed your husband, but isn't it just this action that you wanted to commit on your journey from Versailles, during your departure for Montmédy, Baronne de Korff?† Your king was your manservant!

You come with your son in your arms and tell us that you will bring him up according to the constitution!

No doubt, the constitution of Koblenz . . .‡

You graciously welcome the National Guard—you would like to bathe in its blood.

You have lost your husband. . . . You have torn from him the heart of the French people; you have sacrificed him to your pride, to your d'Artois!

Thousands and thousands of plots are traced before your eyes. . . . You draw them all together! . . .

Antoinette! . . . There is a prison where they lock up bad women. . . .

And king, king without a crown, since you don't want to wear it any longer. . . . Stupid man without character; let's see, what should be done with you?

Louis . . . there is still time, you can win back the esteem of the nation, even the love of the French . . . you have only one means of succeeding, it is to give a list of all those who have cheated you! . . . it is to abandon

---

* The legendary, beautiful queen of Assyria, who was associated with promiscuity and lustfulness. She ruled for her son until he reached maturity. (Was Dantalle insinuating this could occur with Marie Antoinette and the dauphin?)

† The pamphleteer is referring to Marie Antoinette as taking on the identity of Baronne de Korff on the flight to Varennes; however, it was Madame de Tourzel who played this role. Marie Antoinette played the role of her governess.

‡ This refers to the Brunswick Manifesto, promising that, if the royal family is not harmed, the Allies would not harm the French or loot when they invaded France.

your Louvre to the evil ones, until they are expulsed from it! . . . then you could be happy . . . everything would be all right . . . but there is no going back . . . or you will be deposed.

F. DANTALLE

The essence of this pamphlet is less sexual and more political than *The Love Affairs of Charlot and Toinette* and *The Royal Orgy*. The queen has now over-powered, weakened, emasculated, and reduced the king to the role of valet, and turned him into a heartless soul. Like a monstrous beast, she "tore from him the heart of the French people."

Confining the members of the royal family to a zoo is a fascinating tactic, allowing the French to discover the peculiar and practically foreign nature of royalty in an entertaining manner. The purpose of this zoo is to keep danger-ous animals like the royal family in captivity, as well as educate people about the creatures. The zoo reeks of foul odors and the stench of animal droppings, and the yowling, grunting, and sounds of "erotic spasms" of the zoo only add to the foul, indecent environment of Versailles, Trianon, and the Bagatelle.

The Rare Animals

In sum, the pamphlets were propaganda in the war against the queen, and their success was undeniable against her. The war was even waged within the royal family with a degree of protection. For example, the police did not have the right to enter the Royal Palace or the Duc d'Orléans's palace, where many pamphleteers took refuge.

The war also gained momentum when the queen's eccentric taste for luxury and her frivolity was made public during the Affair of the Queen's Necklace. This scandal only gave credibility to all pamphlets previously written and obscenely illustrated.

The use of pornography was especially effective in separating the king from the queen, especially if the king was to rule over a new constitutional monarchy. He needed to be free of the Autrichienne who dominated him, who exploited the kingdom's coffers, and whose decadence demeaned the halls of Versailles.

Unlike the Comte d'Artois, who would one day become king, Marie Antoinette never mended her stained reputation so blatantly damaged in the pamphlets. Her slandered character became incorrigible.

The question remains today: what is fiction and what is truth? Prosecutor Fouquier-Tinville drew upon the pamphlets to accuse the fallen queen at the Revolutionary Tribunal in 1793. Almost every slander and crime was available in the pamphlets for evidence at the trial— except for one: Marie Antoinette's incestuous relations with her son while incarcerated at the Temple Prison.

13

FILTH, SEX, AND EROTICA
IN MAGNIFICENCE

*The unpleasant odours in the park, gardens, even the château, make
one's gorge rise.*

—Denis-Laurian Turmeau de La Morandière

Since the reign of Louis XIV, life at Versailles had been a public affair
rather than a private one. To be absent from court was a self-imposed
penance, an involuntary hardship, or due to ostracism. Almost purely theatrical, life revolved around ceremony, being seen at court, and if fortunate,
being acknowledged by the king.

Unfortunately, a sense of family life was superseded by these social re-
sponsibilities. Children, being raised by governesses or governors, were not
allowed to attend court. The king and his male courtiers kept mistresses and
fathered illegitimate children. Women were occupied with the intrigue and
gossipmongering at court. All the while, the king's elite, who were required
to reside at Versailles, gave up the most elementary provisions they enjoyed
on their own estates.

In fact, everything was sacrificed for the royals. The king and his family were afforded spacious chambers, gold-gilded furniture, and the finest
decorations, while the nobles had to content themselves living in cramped
and unsanitary conditions in the wings. The lodgings in the dark, narrow
mezzanines were cramped and hardly hygienic, but at least the nobles were
near their sovereign and overlooked the inconveniences just for a smile or
a word from him.

It was no wonder, however, that the nobles often craved a retreat from
the ceaseless babble of tongues and crowdedness. Marie Antoinette knew
this craving well and spent much time in her *petits cabinets* or her boudoir

at the Petit Trianon far from the spying eyes of the courtiers. At Trianon, whether she was hiding an illicit rendezvous or not, no visitor, not even her husband, was permitted on the grounds without her consent.

However, Marie Antoinette may also have sought refuge from the foul-smelling and trash-ridden premises of Versailles. Although an army of valets was constantly collecting and disposing the contents of chamber pots in ditches, the cries "gare à l'eau!" (watch for the water!) warned passersby below when pots were emptied from windows. In fact, according to a journalist of the time, Marie Antoinette had been the victim of just such an unfortunate mishap:

> *Special Police of Versailles.* The shortcoming of the Versailles Police affects every good citizen; garbage of all species in the streets and at each marker: kitchen refuse, dishwater, and fecal material are thrown out of windows. Madame la Dauphine was not immune to these indignities when, a few years ago, a chamber pot was emptied out the window from the second floor of the Grand Commun,★ landing on her sedan chair. It also splashed on her Chaplain and his following, obliging them to abandon her and go change their clothes. The perpetrators of this crime have been known and not punished.

Such a mishap happened more than once too. When Dauphine Marie Antoinette and her sister-in-law the Comtesse de Provence were headed for Madame Victoire's apartment one morning, their *chaise à porteurs* (sedan chair) stopped at an inner courtyard for a moment when, just at that instant, a servant emptied a chamber pot out the window, hitting the princesses' sedan chair. The window belonged to the dauphine's archnemesis, Madame du Barry, and the question arises: could it have been done on purpose?

Consequently, the palace of Versailles during the reign of the Bourbons, as depicted in this work, has nothing in common with the luxurious palace that today receives thousands of visitors daily. The sparkling clean museum today was then a "vast cesspool, reeking of filth and befouled with ordure." There were public latrines about the palace, but the palace was large, and to avoid any accidents, *chaises percées*† (pierced chairs) were placed behind screens in some corridors. However, servants, courtiers, aristocrats, and an occasional beggar often relieved themselves under the staircases or wherever possible, leaving the passages, courtyards, corridors, and buildings in the wings "full of urine and feces." The existence of private latrines also did not

---

★ Louis XIV erected this building close to the palace to accommodate the pantry, servants, and secondary officers.

† The *chaise percée* was a chair with a seat that raised to show an opening for the chamber pot.

prevent the king's subjects from relieving themselves in the gardens, where beds of hyacinths, narcissus, and jasmine were planted to mask the odors.

The perfumed plants may not have helped much because the stench of livestock defecating outside could reach the king's chamber. Moreover, the avenue leading to the palace was covered with "stagnant water and dead cats."

Sanitation, as a science, was not even in its infancy then. Historian Godfrey Bradby wrote that the French of the eighteenth century had none of the Dutch passion for cleanliness: "Pet dogs were often permitted to turn the private apartments into something little better than a kennel; rubbish was allowed to accumulate; and courtyards and streets were regarded as the natural dumping-ground for offal."

During the reign of Louis XIV, the Bishop of Noyon was once so overcome by an urgent need that, as he passed the chapel of Versailles, he entered a section reserved for the royal family and peed over the balustrade, "his urine bouncing off the consecrated floor of the church below."

The king's sister-in-law Elisabeth Charlotte did not hold back and bluntly discussed the problem of courtiers relieving themselves in the palace: "The people stationed in the galleries in front of our room piss in all the corners. It is impossible to leave one's apartments without seeing someone pissing."

Versailles had always been seen as the gold standard of refinement, but some habits died hard. The "cheerfully accepted" Princess d'Harcourt sometimes relieved herself in her skirts, leaving a "foul trail behind her for the servants to clean up." But then again, even members of the royal family often gave audiences to subjects or chatted with intimates while sitting upon their chaises percées.

Odors were not the only problems that plagued the Château of Versailles. Bright and colorful walls and wall hangings were, during the reign of the Bourbons, faded and darkened by the soot from the chimneys and thousands of candles, as well as the condensation caused by the breath of hundreds of courtiers. Because the chimneys did not draw well, rooms were often full of smoke in the winter, and the sooty odor permeated the upholstery, the wall tapestries, and the carpets, as well as courtiers' expensive clothing and wigs.

Moreover, personal hygiene was not always a priority at Versailles. Ladies applied rouge and makeup in the morning, reapplied it in the evening, and left it on overnight. When they woke up, they reapplied a fresh layer to ensure any "spots, pimples, or open sores" were well covered. Most courtiers only bathed once a month. Believing that "evil humors" could more easily infiltrate the pores of wet skin, they wore their undergarments in the bath and hardly ever washed their hair.

Marie Antoinette, however, was ahead of her time. She cleansed her face every morning with a mixture of fruits, herbs, camphor, white wine, and stewed pigeons, and she bathed frequently. She had her own English toilet,* but to keep the stench of Versailles at bay, she was "constantly dousing herself with orange blossom water," and she kept fresh flowers, pouches of perfume, and vases of potpourri throughout her chambers.

Most of the courtiers and members of the royal family at Versailles, however, appeared to be indifferent to the unforgettable stench. When an elderly noble lady returned to Versailles during the reign of Louis XVIII, she remarked that the "stench of excrement awoke nostalgia" for her lost youth during the ancien régime in the Versailles of Louis XVI.

These are not isolated instances of problems with sanitation. Louis XIV's chronicler Voltaire complained about the stink from nearby latrines when he was lodged in the north wing of Versailles. Louis XV's daughter, Madame Adélaïde, requested new rooms for her lady-in-waiting lodged "far too near the privy." And Louis XVI's dressers and one of the queen's chaplains petitioned for the closure of the fourth-floor latrine, because the smell penetrated the lodgings, infecting "furnishing, clothes, and linen." They also complained that the area had been used by "riff-raff," who used it as a meeting place for sexual trysts.

Latrines were not the only hideaways at Versailles for illicit encounters. The gardens were poorly policed and perfect for secret rendezvous, prostitution, and even "philosophical vice," or homosexual activities. Put simply, the entire palace was known for open debauchery. Even Louis XIV created a special corridor, the passage du roi, which allowed him to move discreetly from his chambers to those of the queen without passing through a "series of public rooms where he might encounter groups of nudging and winking courtiers." His valets also created a spy network, using the Swiss Guards to frequent the corridors, passages, and gardens day and night, to report on any indecencies.

Marie Antoinette, however, had the Petit Trianon, but she also had arranged for a secret chamber in the attic above her private chambers for her rendezvous with Axel von Fersen. And to conceal his lodging here, Fersen told his father that he had moved into another apartment in the palace, thus giving him an "official" address at Versailles. Moreover, the queen had furnished the secret chamber with a *poele suédois* (Swedish stove) to keep it warm for Count Fersen.

---

* English water closets installed at Versailles were reserved for the king and Marie Antoinette.

Marie Antoinette also had another special hideaway, a boudoir with a secret library, where she and members of her entourage could find refuge from the prying eyes of Versailles. In fact, she had two libraries, not including her library later at the Tuileries. The first, the *bibliothèque*, was located in the palace, and the second, the *boudoir de la reine*, in the Petit Trianon. Whereas the books in the bibliothèque were considered more honorable and prestigious readings, the books in the boudoir were of a more frivolous and libertine nature. In fact, naming a chamber as one's boudoir invoked a "space of sexual intrigue and moral laxity" used by courtesans.

Erotic literature was not reserved just for the lower classes. Aristocrats and upper classes collected examples of it for their private libraries—as did Marie Antoinette. The nineteenth-century bibliophile Ernest Quentin-Bauchart wrote that her library was no more morally disreputable than those of many other great ladies of the time: "In fact, there was nothing at all scandalous about it. The books from the boudoir were exactly the type of reading that the moral police might expect from a discredited queen."

When Louis Lacour published the list of Marie Antoinette's books in his *Livres du boudoir de la reine Marie-Antoinette* in 1862, he created quite a stir but claimed he never intended any harm to the queen's memory. He reasoned that the most honest and virtuous ladies at that time had these fashionable books and novels, which "seem scandalous to us today but did not produce such an effect then."

Historians disagree today whether Marie Antoinette was an avid reader or not. She had a very busy schedule and often did not have time to write her mother when she arrived at Versailles. As for reading, the Comte de Mercy wrote that "she devotes too little time to that employment," which was a great source of anxiety for her mother:

> Try to furnish out your mind with a little good reading. . . . Do not neglect this resource, which is more necessary to you than to another, since you have learned neither music, nor drawing, nor dancing, nor painting, nor any pleasing accomplishment. Return, then, to your reading; and you must charge the abbe to send me every month an account of what you have finished and of what you intend to begin.

Marie Antoinette became angry after she read her mother's letter, telling the Comte de Mercy, "Truly, she would make me pass for an animal!"

Then calming herself, she continued, "Ah, well! I shall answer that it will be impossible for me to undertake any reading during the Carnaval, but that I shall do so in Lent. Will that do?"

"Yes, Madame," replied the count, "provided that you are in earnest."

Soon afterward, Marie Antoinette prepared a schedule and presented it to the count. She would, on rising, spend the first moments of her day in prayer; then she would busy herself with her music, dancing, and one hour of "sensible reading." Her toilette, a visit to the king, mass, and dinner would occupy the rest of the morning.

Surprisingly, in the afternoon she scheduled another hour and a half for the "continuation of the sensible reading," a walk or the hunt, and conversation with Monsieur the Dauphin and other members of the royal family.

The count respectfully encouraged the dauphine not to depart from a "so wise and well-arranged a plan." And she replied with her usual good faith, "I do not know if I shall fulfil all this very exactly, but I shall hold myself to it as far as possible."

When winter arrived and social activities at Versailles calmed down, the dauphine was devoting not one but two hours to reading, and two hours more for music and dancing.

The Comte de Mercy wrote the empress about the improvement: "The days are suitably well filled, and I think that Your Majesty has every reason to be satisfied with her."

Whether Marie Antoinette devoted two hours a day for "sensible reading" is not known. However, most women at that time read little more than novels, plays, and poetry—all of which could be found in the queen's boudoir. And according to bibliophile Émile Desjardins, Marie Antoinette's library included more than two thousand works, of which 536 volumes were novels and 408 were plays. When asked about the scandal of attributing a number of libertine books to the queen, Desjardins answered,

> What is scandalous about a worldly, little devoted, thirty-year-old woman leafing through fashionable books to entertain herself and taking the precaution to lock them up? In the eighteenth century, the allure of society, the tone of conversation, and, consequently, current literature were much looser and freer than modern prudery would have it. Was one worth less for it then? Are we better today? I leave it to the moralists to decide. One would have found, at that time, the books of her boudoir in other people's libraries as well.

If Marie Antoinette did not like to read, as some historians report, why did she need a library? And why did she periodically request new books from her mentor, Abbé de Vermond? Perhaps when she first arrived at Versailles, she had other motives for wanting a library. For example, the apartments for the newlywed couple were being restored when she arrived at Versailles in 1770, but they were far from being ready. The ceilings were still in ruin, and the paintings, sculptures, and plasterwork were worn and rotting. Palace workers were also threatening to quit if they were not paid for prior work completed.

Patience was not one of the dauphine's virtues. As work progressed on her royal chambers, she would temporarily accept an undecorated white ceiling without artwork and sculpture but only under the condition that it would be completed immediately.

After taking over her apartment, Marie Antoinette must have become bored because she was dissatisfied with the bookshelves left in place in an adjoining room since the death of Queen Marie Leszczinska. The dauphine made imperial demands to have them transformed according to her fantasies, and all the work had to be completed before returning from a short trip. The architect, Ange-Jacques Gabriel, was called upon to demolish the shelving and replace it with armoires in glass and decorated encasements without delay.

This new interest was not due to the princess's taste for books. She simply wanted a library because one was being built for her sister-in-law, the Comtesse de Provence, and there were also plans in the making for a new library for her other sister-in-law, the Comtesse d'Artois. Her taste for reading, and a *certain genre* of books, would come later.

Empress Maria Theresa supported building a new library for her "lazy" daughter, where she could retire and read historical and moral works as assigned by Vermond. The cost of the restoration was 15,000 livres, but building funds in the royal treasury were limited, if not nonexistent. Gabriel wrote the following memo to Louis XV:

> Monsieur, Madame la Dauphine told Mr. Lecuyer to build a library in a room near her chambers. . . . Because Madame la Dauphine told me she wanted to enjoy this library upon her return from Fontainebleau, I begged her to request that the General Controller, the first time she would see him, supply the funds that we needed. Mr. Lécuyer and I will continue to follow the wishes of Madame la Dauphine, but we will stop if the funding should stop.

Of course, the old king could not refuse his delightful little granddaughter's request. Despite the drain on the treasury, the final touches on her library were completed a month later (at the same time as that of the Comtesse de Provence's library).

When the library in the boudoir was complete, it was soon overstocked with volumes adorned with the *fleurs-de-lys* and an annex had to be constructed. Marie Antoinette had no idea that the publication of her library's inventory would one day create such a scandal.

How many readers were horrified when they perused the inventory of her library in the boudoir to find titles such as *La Comtesse d'Alibre*? In this story, the Count d'Alibre was away when his wife gave birth to her lover's son. She tried to keep the event secret, but her husband had spies, and when he heard about the infidelity, his vengeance was uncontrollable. He had the countess and her son locked in an underground cave without food, hoping she would succumb to eating her own offspring. The boy died, but the countess's lover saved her, although not until he had knifed her husband. Curiously, this is reminiscent of Marie Antoinette's incarceration in the Temple with her own son after the king was executed in 1793.

Another risqué book in the queen's library was *Mémoires de Fanny Spingler*, a novel in the form of letters in which Madame Beccary writes of the misfortunes of a poor orphan girl, Fanny, who was brought up by Monsieur Dorblac, a friend of her father's. Dorblac also had a daughter, who was Fanny's friend, and a son, who was Fanny's lover. Because the young couple was poor, Dorblac could not give them permission to marry until his son could secure employment.

Sir George Malgarde, a relative of Fanny's mother, visited Dorblac and took an interest in Fanny and brought her to London to live with his family. He was rich with a beautiful soul, but his wife was haughty, cold, and an unloving woman, who, along with her daughter Miss Malgarde, intimidated Fanny.

When young Dorblac arrived to work for Sir George and live with his family, he had hopes of making it in the world and marrying Fanny. However, he was corrupted by the new world he entered when he befriended Sir Harris. Also, Sir George's wife tells Dorblac that her husband and Fanny are having a relationship. Subsequently, Dorblac became perversely reckless, living precariously, and took Miss Malgarde for his wife. However, they both die young, along with Sir Harris.

The moral of the story is the consequence of pursuing a libertine lifestyle. Harris reflects on his agonizing "destroyed health" that resulted from his follies. Syphilis was serious, it was painful, and it was contagious. A cure for venereal disease in the eighteenth century was not assured. The primary stage could be treated with bed rest to the extent that symptoms disappeared; however, the disease was not cured and remained in the body as an affliction that could "injure the brain, spinal cord, major blood vessels, bones, or other tissues."

Other treatments were tried, but with little success. Casanova used rigorous fasting in his search for a cure, but he was forced to resort to mercury, the favorite, but often deadly, treatment of Rétif de la Bretonne, another author to be found in Marie Antoinette's library.

More licentious than *Mémoires de Fanny Springler* is Bretonne's decadent work *Le Paysan perverti* (The perverted peasant).★ It became a success and ensured his reputation as a libertine author throughout Europe. It was also perhaps the most decadent novel found in Marie Antoinette's library.

Le Paysan perverti narrated the corruption of a young peasant boy, Edmund, who married a girl who had been impregnated by his boss. However, Edmund was only interested in the conquest of the ladies, including his boss's wife and his cousin, which culminated in their pregnancies and subsequent suicides. He then moved to the dangerous and lustful world of Paris where he went on a sex spree, only to become infected with syphilis.

The topic of syphilis was not limited to the works of Madame Beccary and Rétif in Marie Antoinette's library—and understandably so, because the sexually transmitted disease was spreading across Europe at the time, extending as far as Siberia. Historian Marcel Benabou wrote,

> I've seen more than fifty people die of it, including especially a great army general and a very wise minister of state. Few lungs resist the illness and the remedy. . . . Little distinction in made between venereal diseases. A "galanterie," which usually indicated gonorrhea, not infrequently is used indiscriminately to refer to syphilis. Of course, literature also represented the hinder side: syphilitics were also termed rotten, gangrenous, pox ridden, and rotten to the marrow.

Rétif's novel not only addressed the scourge of venereal disease but also vividly described a shocking scene of attempted rape:

> Fatal f★★k! It destroyed the calm and the most violent storm resulted. It was not love; no, my friend; it was not the most delightful sentiment which seized my heart. It was an odious frenzy, a sort of rage. . . . In my anger, I crumpled, I wounded with abominable brutality these enchanting charms, these delicate beings, who must receive only adoration and caresses. . . . Use violence. . . . Oh, God! . . . And I used it. . . . And with whom? Who was the victim of this horrible offense? . . . She who I respect the most in the world.

It is astonishing to find the title of another novel, *The Danger of Loving a Stranger* (or *History of Milady Chester and a French Duke*), in the queen's possession. After all, the courtiers who fell in love with Marie Antoinette, were they not "loving a stranger," a foreign princess on French soil? Did not the Austrian Marie Antoinette, in turn, love a Swedish count?

★ After the success of this novel, Rétif followed it with a series of letters written by the peasant's sister in *La Paysanne pervertie*, which described the slow but certain perversion of an innocent peasant girl who went to Paris to help her brother.

This story charts the adventure of the young French Duc de Durcé, who took refuge in England following a duel in which he had killed his rival. When Milady Chester meets the duke, the relationship becomes passionate despite the objections of a current lover and her family. Milady Chester is also a very independent young widow who fears losing her autonomy should she every marry again.

The drama surrounding the affair threatens her health and she becomes bedridden at her uncle's house, where the duke is not permitted to visit her. However, he wins over one of the servants who doubles the dose of Milady Chester's sedative and takes advantage of her, being guilty of "the most cowardly action."

The duke returns to France and is about to marry another when Milady Chester arrives in desperation. She tells him she is pregnant and cannot face the shame. She finds her lover, causes a duel with the duke, and is killed at his side. But by the time the independent Milady Chester dies at the end of the novel, she has already been emotionally destroyed and socially abandoned by her love for the duke.

If Marie Antoinette read this tragic story, did she relate to Milady Chester's abandonment and the social disorientation when pursuing a relationship with a foreign prince? A woman can find herself isolated and without family in a foreign country when someone has cheated on her, has abandoned her, or has neglected her after marriage.

In 1784, Marie Antoinette acquired the work *Les confessions d'une courtesan* (The confessions of a courtesan), which recounts the adventures of a prostitute who gives up her life of depravity for one of virtue.

The preface of this book is reminiscent of Marie Antoinette's longing for the simple life: "It is by traversing the circle of false pleasures that she has known about the void and its satiety; it was after her soul was overwhelmed by the weight of depravity, that she savored with more delight, the inexpressible sweetness of a quiet life, free from reproach, and which, employed in the practice of her duties, alone, can lead to true happiness."

About this time, Queen Marie Antoinette was designing the *hameau*, a model hamlet in the garden of the Petit Trianon. The queen's popularity had long been on the wane, and although it was somewhat revived with the birth of the princess and dauphin, pamphlets and jingles about her were becoming increasingly malicious.

The hamlet, constructed in 1783, was a fairy-tale village with lakes, a stream with a mill for grinding grain, a farmhouse with cottages, and dozens of gardens. Giving up the majestic palace of Versailles, the monarchy of France was stripped of its respect and dignity—the queen was now but a simple milkmaid.

À SAVOIR

Marie Antoinette's Handwriting (1778–1792)

On February 13, 1779, Marie Antoinette signed an invoice to approve its payment and the signature has been analyzed by the graphologist:

- Although the lower zone still leans to the right, the middle zone is vertical as opposed to the slight forward lean this writer has. This suggests neutrality and self-control. This can come off as a lack of pity in some cases.
- The heavy *i* dots suggest calmness. The disconnected nature of the signature shows the writer to be a consequential thinker. It also suggests over-adaptability.
- The signature is slow; this indicates caution and steadiness.
- The straightforward nature of the signature combined with its irregularity suggests the writer is impressionable.
- The letter *t* stays close to the middle zone. This characteristic, coupled with the firmly placed bars, suggests prudence.
- This signature shows yieldingness as suggested by the first stroke of *M* looking like a small letter, and the letter *a* in Antoinette being a small letter.
- The high pressure combined with the irregularity reinforces the over-adaptability of the writer.

Adaptability is the personality trait that helps determine how you respond to change. People with high adaptability are often described as "flexible" or "malleable." Marie Antoinette was certainly flexible in the sense that she was easily swayed by her favorites, from the Princesse de Lamballe to the Princesse de Guéménée and then to Madame de Polignac.

Letter to Mother (1780)

On October 11, 1780, Marie Antoinette sent a letter to her mother: "Madame, my very dear mother. My daughter's health has occupied me and worried me a little for three weeks. Several teeth all came in at once, causing her great pain and giving her a fever. . . . I am touched by the sweetness and patience of this poor little girl in the midst of her sufferings, which in certain moments have been very intense."

- This lettering is small, but the pressure is higher. This shows the writer feels more natural. The high pressure combined with the regularity of the script shows great willpower.
- The high regularity of the script symbolizes self-conquest, harmony, and moderation.
- Here, the placement of the *i* dots is not consistent, showing resolution in the writer.

- The left movement of the upper zone shows intellectual and moral freedom.
- The lower zone is deep and moves strongly to the left. This suggests the writer intensely enjoys material pleasures, sexual pleasures, eating, and drinking.
- The script remains disconnected and is a bit arcade. This shows there is a bit of skepticism and distance in the writer.

Characteristics such as "moral freedom" and "sexual pleasures" are interesting, because it is about this time that Marie Antoinette gives her new favorite, Madame de Polignac, 400,000 livres for her debts, the promise of an estate worth 35,000 livres a year, and 800,000 livres in cash as a dowry for her daughter. In addition, the queen was gambling heavily and keeping company with "undesirables":

> Here play went on madly to ruin; here every kind of intrigue was set on foot by calculating individuals, and here the young and thoughtless queen was thrown together with spendthrifts and with rakes, a crew of headlong votaries of dissipation. Amongst the names of those who were the familiar habitats of the Polignac circle, it will be hard to find one entitled to consideration; more than one was notorious for grave blemishes. The list comprises Vaudreuil and Coigny, Esterhazy and Besenval, the Chevalier de Luxembourg, "ambitious and evil-minded," and the Duc de Lauzun, "that most dangerous man from his audacious mind and the combination of every kind of evil quality."

On August 30, 1786, Marie Antoinette wrote a letter to Maréchal de Castries: "I am angry, Mr. Marshal, that you did not ask to see me yesterday. Despite the short time I have, I would always have found some to see you."

- This script leans more strongly to the right, which suggests the writer's personality is extroverted here.
- Also, the signature here is genuine, as opposed to the pseudo-personality shown in the previous payment approval.
- The letters in this script are not elaborate, which suggests honesty.
- This script is also small, which suggests greater devotion, humility, and tolerance.
- This script is pasty, which suggests warmth.
- The placing of the *i* dots is all over the place; this rarely happened with the 1788 letter to Polignac. For the most part, the *i* dots show

perception and imagination, but it also shows a level of irresolution in the writer.

- The disconnected nature of the script symbolizes intuitive thinking and individualism.
- The straight direction of lines shows perseverance and emotional control.
- The leanness in the upper zone suggests the writer is an ethical thinker and has an analytical mind.

Only Marie Antoinette's signature is in her handwriting in a letter to her brother-in-law, Ferdinand IV, the king of Naples, on September 24, 1788. The simple nature of the signature shows maturity and orderliness. The high pressure in combination with the regularity of the script symbolizes

Letter to Castries (1786)

willpower, tenacity and self-control. This may be due to the formality of the letter.

- This script is narrow, which suggests a movement toward the ego. There are inhibitions in the writer's personal relationships.
- The *t* bars are placed higher up than in previous letters. This shows progressiveness and curiosity.
- The good distribution of space and high pressure suggests courage.
- The placement of the *i* dots is not irregular as seen in the 1786 to Castries and the 1780 letter to mother. This suggests the writer has more stability here.
- The upper and lower zones are consistent with the other letters analyzed and remain lean. This shows the writer to be a rational thinker.
- Although pastiness is interpreted as having warmth, this level of pastiness shows an increased sensuousness in the writer.
- The direction of lines is leveled; this suggests emotional control and perseverance.
- There is a sense of superiority in the writer as suggested by the larger script size.
- The script is disconnected and regular, which is consistent with the other letters. This suggests individualism, self-reliance, and egocentricity.

Individualism and egocentricity could best be seen in the queen's appearance, including the fashions with which the milliner Rose Bertin dazzled her and the yard-high hairstyles that the eccentric hairdresser Léonard concocted for her.

In a letter to Madame de Polignac on December 2, 1788, Marie Antoinette refers to the nomination of a cardinal: "I don't need to tell you, my heart, what a pleasure the king felt in finishing the affair of Mr. de Luxembourg."

- The forward lean shows the writer to be an extrovert.
- The small script size shows respect; the writer is a tolerant person.
- The right slant shows extroversion and progression. The writer is an expressive person.
- The disconnected script suggests the writer is intuitive and self-reliant. Also, this person can be a bit egocentric.
- The script has good space distribution between words; however, it is narrow. This suggests the writer relies on his/her instincts a lot.

- The direction of lines is leveled, and the script is regular. This shows the writer is consistent and shows indifference.
- The pen pressure, combined with the regularity of the script, suggests the writer has great self-control and is adaptable.
- The writer's public persona is different from their private persona as suggested by the differences between the signature and the body of the letter. A larger signature with a smaller script suggests an overrating of the writer's ego in relation to society.
- The lower zone is deep and moves strongly to the left. This suggests the writer enjoys material pleasures such as sexual pleasures, eating, and drinking, intensely.

An interesting characteristic from the analysis is the reference to "drinking." Marie Antoinette only drank water and, like her mother, did not drink wine. However, records from the queen's pharmacist Robert reveal that the queen did consume a special potion consisting of one ounce of *Syrop de capilaire* (maidenhair fern), one ounce of *Eau de fleurs d'oranger* (orange blossom water), three ounces of *Eau de fleurs de tilleul* (linden tree flower water), and fifty grams of *Gouttes d'Hoffmann* (spirit of ether).

Marie Antoinette may not have drunk alcohol, but her elixir, Gouttes d'Hoffmann, was more potent, being a mixture of alcohol and ether.

On March 4, 1790, Marie Antoinette wrote to Madame de Polignac's husband, Jules de Polignac, regarding the marriage of his son in Venice: "I showed your letter to the king, and you must not doubt sir, of the pleasure we have in consenting to the marriage of your son."

- The upper zone, especially the *t* bars, is hasty and high, which shows enthusiasm and curiosity. The right-tending *t* bars suggest authority.
- The disconnected script is seen positively as self-reliance and negatively as loneliness.
- This script maintains a good space distribution; this speaks more about the writer's organizational abilities (good) than anything else.
- The *i* dots are heavy, high, and mostly placed to the right, which shows perception and a bit of impatience.
- The script is regular, which suggests self-conquest. The regularity combined with the high pressure suggests the writer is adaptable and receptive.
- The direction of lines is not as leveled as found in previous letters. This indicates the writer is more ambitious here than in previous letters.

- The upper zone is lean, which shows mental clarity. The lower zone extends deeply but remains lean. This shows business-mindedness and realism.
- This script is quite large compared to the previous ones. This suggests more sense of superiority and generosity in the writer.
- The forward lean in the middle zone is more intense than in the previous letters. This suggests the writer is becoming more expressive.

A sense of realism, clarity, and superiority are notable factors in the analysis of Marie Antoinette's letter in 1790. The storming of the Bastille and the adoption of the *La Déclaration des Droits de l'Homme et du Citoyen* (*The Declaration of the Rights of Man and the Citizen*) had been sobering events, and the queen was increasingly more active in politics.

Letter to Hans Axel von Fersen (1791)

Of a letter believed written to Count Axel von Fersen in 1790, the graphologist has analyzed the queen's handwriting:

- There is a bit more of a fullness in the lower zone than in previous scripts. However, it isn't significant enough to be considered a full lower zone. This suggests an increase in the writer's sensuousness.
- This script has more space distribution than previous ones. This indicates the writer has more orderliness in thinking than he/she previously portrayed.
- The upper zone of the letter *d* doesn't extend to the left as much as in previous scripts. This indicates less reflective and meditative qualities.
- The lower zone isn't as deep as in previous scripts, which suggests sublimation.
- The upper zone has more loop than in previous scripts, which indicates more imagination.
- The script is disconnected, which shows individualism and self-reliance.
- The script starts out irregular and gradually becomes regular as it goes on (though still not as regular as in other script samples). This indicates the writer was impulsive and impressionable at the start of the letter but gradually became less impulsive and showed more moderation.
- The right slant symbolizes extroversion and progression. The slight right slant suggests a balance between expressiveness and self-control or reserve.
- This script is wider than previous samples, which suggests the writer has less inhibition or self-control in personal relationships than they did as of when writing the other letters.
- The direction of lines is leveled, which shows perseverance. There is a balance in the pen pressure that suggests a balance between willpower and impressionability
- This script is more ornamental, which suggests a greater sense of pride.

On February 27, 1791, Marie Antoinette wrote her brother Leopold when she and her family were under house arrest in the Tuileries.

- This handwriting sample maintains a good standard of form level.
- The slightly larger script size suggests more superiority and pride in the writer.

- The slight right slant shows expressiveness and sociability, but not overly so.
- This script is disconnected, indicating self-reliance; the writer is an intuitive thinker. The wider script shows more vivacity and extroversion.
- The script has good spacing and is regular. This shows moderation and a bit of indifference.
- The leveled direction of lines on this script shows the writer to be social but methodical and to have emotional control.
- High pressure combined with a regular script symbolizes willpower, tenacity, and self-control.
- The *t* bars are hasty and sharp and sit closer to the top. This indicates loftiness, trust, and optimism.
- The fullness in the upper zone suggests the writer is imaginative and has vision.

With the revolution on the horizon, the analysis of Marie Antoinette's handwriting reveals a sense of superiority, willpower, and tenacity. Her husband, Louis XVI, has by this time become weak, both personally and politically, forcing the queen to play a more prominent role in his reign.

Part V

A QUEEN DETHRONED
AND DISEASED (1792–1793)

Marie Antoinette on the Way to the Guillotine *by
Jacques-Louis David*

14

MALADIES VÉNÉRIENNES AT THE COURT OF VERSAILLES

The best treatment is mercury; it is used once or twice a day on the patient's arms and legs until the first signs of intolerance appear, or until the teeth become bothersome.

—Vigo, 1898

M aladies *vénériennes* (venereal diseases) were rampant in eighteenth-century France, and no social classes were spared—not even those of upper nobility and royalty. If prostitutes, actresses, and opera dancers were infected, so too were their admirers, especially the counts and dukes who lavished fortunes upon them—and subsequently their unsuspecting princesses and wives.

Children, too, could be infected at birth from mothers with venereal disease; unfortunately, their symptoms were often not detected until years later, when the illness was usually diagnosed as "consumption" (now recognized as tuberculosis). Also, physicians were reluctant to associate venereal disease with the children of "people of rank and fortune" and would attribute their deaths to other causes.

The French often called syphilis the *grosse vérole* to distinguish it from smallpox, the *petite vérole.* The grosse vérole, however, was an umbrella term for a range of venereal diseases, such as gonorrhea, chlamydia, and other genital and urinary disorders that had not yet been defined. Gonorrhea, for example, was thought to be a secretion of a syphilitic infection. Due to the wide range of symptoms caused by venereal disease, physicians routinely confused it with other illnesses, and it would not be until the nineteenth century that physicians could differentiate between syphilis and gonorrhea.*

---

* In 1837, the French physician Philippe Ricord showed that gonorrhea and syphilis were two distinct diseases.

Women were not usually aware of their infection until later stages of the disease; if they were aware, however, they were not comfortable revealing it to anyone. Men, too, refrained from revealing their condition to anyone; nevertheless, although infected, they were known to continue their promiscuous escapades. In the second half of the eighteenth century, however, there was a "surprisingly cavalier attitude toward the disease." Men described the unpleasant inconvenience simply as a *galanterie*, or a minor indiscretion.

Venereal disease in men was particularly easy to identify if there were visible symptoms. Most symptoms, however, normally disappeared after a short period of time, with serious manifestations surfacing later in life. In extreme cases, patients' noses caved into their faces, giving rise to artificial noses that could be enameled or painted to resemble the original.

The grosse vérole was considered not only a disease of debauchery but also one that "followed armies like flies after a dung pile." Voltaire wrote that two-thirds of the French army contracted the disease: "On their flippant way through Italy, the French carelessly picked up Genoa, Naples and syphilis. Then they were thrown out and deprived of Naples and Genoa. But they did not lose everything—syphilis went with them."

In fact, the problem was so prevalent that Louis XV's royal physician, Jean Astruc, wrote a major treatise on the disease, *De Morbus Veneris*, in 1736. Unaware that there was more than one type of venereal disease, physicians attributed the symptoms of syphilis, gonorrhea, and chlamydia to the same disease. Furthermore, Astruc mentioned only five ways in which the infection could be transmitted: male-female intercourse, nursing, kissing, sharing bedding, and manual transmission when midwives or physicians touched an infected person's genitals. Not included in Astruc's list was same-sex transmission and mother-to-child transmission, an understandable oversight due to lack of research.

Syphilis was largely unknown in Europe until almost the end of the fifteenth century, when it was first noticed after Columbus's return from the New World. It spread rapidly but was not recognized as being "venereal" until confirmed by Giovanni da Vigo in 1514 as well as Ulrich von Hutten in 1519. King Charles VIII of France was said to have died of venereal disease in 1498, and one of his successors, King Francis I, suffered the same fate in 1547.

Francis, the ninth king of the House of Valois, had suffered a devastating defeat in battle and was captured and imprisoned in Spain. This defeat and confinement aggravated his migraines, which were a consequence of old wounds and of "newly contacted syphilis." He blamed his impending death on "the weight of a crown that he had first perceived as a gift from God"; it was another type of gift, however, that led to his demise. Francis I had also infected his queen, Claude, with the "pox" before she died in 1524.

Other monarchs were likely infected by the grande vérole, a Pandora's box of diseases, but may have not been diagnosed with it. Most physicians were taken aback by the speed with which the new disease spread; because they had no knowledge whatsoever about the disease, they preferred to "reject the sick because they were so horrified by them."

In 1589, the House of Valois became extinct in the male line and was succeeded by the House of Bourbon, a dynasty that was not left unscathed by venereal disease. On a sad note, Louis XIII's sister Élisabeth was "exchanged" in 1615 for the Spanish Infanta Anne of Austria, who left her native Spain to marry Élisabeth's brother, Louis XIII. In turn, Élisabeth married the future King Philip IV of Spain and quickly became pregnant; however, the child was premature and did not survive. Weakened by multiple pregnancies and miscarriages, Élisabeth died while giving birth to her ninth child. It is very likely that Élisabeth's miscarriages were the result of a venereal disease Philip IV had received from one of his mistresses and transmitted to the queen.

Other members of the Bourbon dynasty inflicted with sexually transmitted diseases included Francois Louis de Bourbon; Prince de Conti, a libertine who engaged in scandalous debaucheries with members of both sexes; Henriette de Bourbon-Conti, the Duchesse de Chartres, who had numerous extramarital affairs; and Louis Joseph, Duc de Vendome, a successful French army commander in Louis XIV's army.

Patients infected with venereal disease could live long lives without any outward show of symptoms and could have children; eventually, however, as the disease intensified, subsequent babies either were stillborn or lived briefly—for hours, months, or a few years—although some survived to experience a "sickly" adulthood.

Historians have speculated that Louis XIV's brother Philippe, the Duc d'Orléans, and Philippe's lover, the Chevalier de Lorraine, both had syphilis, as did many other men at that time. In fact, they were the founding members of a secret brotherhood of homosexuals that "met at various Parisian higher-class taverns, brothels and country-houses" to engage in sex with each other and with prostitutes.

It is documented that King Louis XIV had syphilis, as well as "youthful gonorrhea," and that either he or his brother could have transmitted an infection to Philippe's first wife, Henrietta. Consequently, seven of Philippe's eleven children did not survive childhood.

As the intensity of the disease waned over the years, couples could eventually have healthy children. This could also have been the case with Philippe and Henrietta. Although their first child, Marie Louise d'Orléans, survived, she was unable to give her husband, King Charles II of Spain, an heir. Henrietta's subsequent six pregnancies resulted in stillbirths or miscarriages, but her last child survived upon the waning of Philippe's disease.

Philippe's last three children with his second wife, Elizabeth of the Palatinate, also survived. After the birth of their last child, Philippe and Elizabeth no longer shared a bed but "maintained a mutual and tender esteem." Being generous, Philippe also gave his second wife a souvenir, the gift of the "intimate illness."

Elizabeth, and any other royals who were infected with venereal disease in the seventeenth and eighteenth centuries, might not have sought treatment for many reasons. They may not have known they were infected, or they might not have wanted their condition made public. However, some treatments, the use of mercury being the most common, did exist at the time. Astruc wrote the following: "Thanks to mercury's speed in the circulation, it will destroy the venereal virus whatever it is and wherever it is . . . it will be destroyed, uprooted and driven out by all the excretory ducts."

In *De Morbo Gallicus*, Giovanni da Vigo, an Italian surgeon appointed to Pope Julius II, agreed that the best treatment for venereal disease was mercury. It could be used as an ointment "once or twice a day on the patient's arms and legs" and covered with plasters until the "first signs of intolerance appeared, or until the teeth became bothersome." Despite confidence in his therapy, however, Vigo admitted that recurrence was frequent, and it was necessary to repeat the treatment several times a year.

The main objective of mercury treatments was hypersalivation, which was considered beneficial in treatment. The excretion caused by the treatment was indeed excessive: "some few liters per diem." It was reasoned that pituita, the body humor presumably causing the symptoms and signs of syphilis, could be expelled via the saliva. Over a long period of time, however, the absorption of too much mercury could lead to ulcerations of the lips, tongue, palate, and jaw, resulting in fetid breath and the loss of teeth.

Fumigation was also a form of treatment in which patients were seated or made to stand in a cabin. A stove in which tablets of mercury were burned was placed at their feet to create vapors. Patients had to breathe the mercury fumes for thirty days, a process that often led to death from heart failure, dehydration, or suffocation.

It is uncertain whether Louis XV had treatment for his venereal disease, which was a touchy subject with the king. His valet physically exam-

"For One Pleasure a Thousand Pains" (circa 1659)

ined all the young ladies in Louis's private bordello, Parc-aux-Cerfs, for any symptoms. The king's minister, Maurepas, was also exiled for disrespecting Louis's first official mistress, Madame de Pompadour. Maurepas had written an epigram that was read by Louis XV's courtiers:

> Your noble and honest manners,
> Pompadour, enchain hearts;
> All your steps are paved with flowers,
> But they are only white flowers.

Such an epigram may have appeared harmless at first sight, but "white flowers" was an allusion to venereal disease, more specifically to leucorrhea, a vaginal swelling with a white, foul-smelling discharge often attributed to sexually transmitted disease. Historians have reported that the king's favorite, in addition to several miscarriages, also suffered from leucorrhea.

Louis XV did not live long enough to shudder at the debaucheries of his and his queen's godson, Louis-Alexandre-Joseph-Stanislas de Bourbon, the Prince de Lamballe, who died of syphilis in 1768 at the age of twenty. The prince had been drawn into a licentious lifestyle by his cousin, the Duc de Chartres, whose residence, the Palais Royal, was known as a "sumptuous temple of prostitution." When orgiastic soirees were held here, prostitutes and guests supped "stark naked." And at the end of each banquet, the Duc de Chartres gave a signal resulting in "everyone taking his own pleasure, in his own way."

The cost of sexual freedom was high. The Duc de Chartres's grandmother wrote that her grandson and noble friends had suffered from several bouts of venereal disease: "Out of nine . . . seven had the French sickness [grande vérole]."

The Prince de Lamballe's father, to help change his only son's debauched ways and hopefully secure an heir for the family fortune, married him to the gentle, pious Marie Louise de Savoie in 1767. However, the new Princesse de Lamballe was unable to lead her husband from his dissolute lifestyle of recurrent infidelities and gambling. Before dying a year later with the grande vérole and suffering the devastating effects of mercury treatments, the prince had to sell his wife's jewelry to pay off his debts. She was perhaps not too concerned, however; upon her husband's death, she became one of the wealthiest heiresses in France.

After a period of mourning, the Princesse de Lamballe withdrew to the Palace of Rambouillet until she was presented to the new dauphine, Marie Antoinette, in 1770. When her cousins married Marie Antoinette's brothers-in-law, the Comtes de Provence and d'Artois, the Princesse de Lamballe joined the dauphine's circle of friends, which included the counts and their new wives.

The Princesse de Lamballe did not remarry. Was this because she had been infected with the grande vérole by her wayward prince? Although she put on a pious and chaste front, there was reason to believe that she had indeed been infected:

> A young, lively and amiable Princess, married last winter to a very young husband too, could not stand the repeated infidelities of her husband, some fatal to their love, even for this modern Theseus; she could not see, without a marked jealousy, her estrangement, her deviations: she conceived envy at the center of the most despicable objects which the Prince honored with his glances; she had contracted a profound melancholy and convulsive vapors. The fashionable physicians have not been able to calm this evil more moral than physical.

According to the Princess of Lamballe's physician, Doctor Saiffert, it appears that her self-indulgent husband gave her more than just a broken heart. She left court for a series of treatments in July 1787 for symptoms of venereal disease. "The symptoms announced by Saiffert appeared just as he had expected; she had a fever, along with a red rash all over the skin of the body."

Moreover, the princess's father, Prince Louis Victor of Savoy-Carignan, had gone so far as to write to Louis XV, asking him to "take action against the contaminating agent." This would suggest that the princess had confided in her parents about her infliction. In any event, she would have wanted to keep the condition a secret to avoid as much gossipmongering as possible at court. Considering her wealth and status at court, it would have also been doubtful that any doctors called to her bedside in the coming years would dare mention the "bonne galanterie."

Marie Antoinette's brother-in-law, the Comte d'Artois, was a member of the new circle of friends and was well acquainted with the gossipmongers' viciousness. A close friend and confidant of the future queen, he was accused of having seduced her. Whether true or not, the count did transmit the grande vérole to his wife, who transmitted it to their daughter, Mademoiselle d'Angoulême, at birth; the child died seven years later.

The Comte d'Artois, future king Charles X, was no saint. He had an affair with the famous dancer and opera singer Anne Victoire Dervieux, and later carried on a lifelong love affair with Louise de Polastron, the sister-in-law of Marie Antoinette's favorite, the Duchess of Polignac.

It is interesting to note that it was common in Paris at this time to advertise treatments for the grande vérole. One poster read, "Popular treatment of venereal disease for adults, for children, administered free in Paris by order of the government." Physicians, too, posted advertisements for new cures, such as anti-venereal baths and anti-venereal chocolate. This chocolate remedy was actually sold on the Rue Croix-des-Petits-Champs by an apothecary named Martin, who was also known as the "apothecary of Monseigneur the Comte d'Artois." Ironically, venereal disease came from the Americas as did the chocolate used to treat it.

15

MALADIES VÉNÉRIENNES AND THE UNTHINKABLE

Chlamydia in females was seldom detected in the 18th century; if it was, it was thought to be cured with plenty of rest.

—Lemuel B. Bangs and William A. Hardaway, 1898

The dethroned Queen Marie Antoinette suffered from uterine hemor-rhaging while imprisoned in the Conciergerie in 1793. It was un-known then that untreated venereal disease could spread to the uterus and fallopian tubes, causing pelvic inflammatory disease and bleeding. It was also not known that mothers who contracted the disease were more prone to miscarriage or premature delivery; children who acquired the infections suffered from osteitis, pneumonia, and lung infections. Marie Antoinette had two miscarriages; her four surviving children suffered from one or more of these infections, and three of them died. Although royal doctors diagnosed the children as having scrofula (tuberculosis of the lymph nodes), this was impossible: scrofula was hereditary, and the queen and king had no family history of the disease in their Bourbon and Hapsburg ancestries.

Due to the provocative nature of this chapter, it has been written with the greatest care. Pamphlets abundantly touted the queen's promiscuity at a time when the court was plagued with intrigue and whisperings of venereal disease. That a sexually transmitted disease could have been possible is based not only on the facts regarding the royal family's health history but also on a study of those close to the queen who had been exposed to such infections.

This chapter has drawn on many historical sources, such as physicians' reports, autopsies, and memoirs describing the illnesses of the queen, her children, and those in her closest circles, giving rise to an unsettling pos-sibility: Marie Antoinette, the queen of France, could have contracted a sexually transmitted disease. If this was the case, several questions arise: Was the disease passed on to any of her children at birth? Was it the cause of her miscarriages? Was it the cause of her illness in the Conciergerie?

By the time Marie Antoinette was thirty years old, she had given birth to four children and suffered two miscarriages. Only her first daughter lived to adulthood. In 1778, at the age of twenty-two, Marie Antoinette gave birth to Marie-Thérèse Charlotte, who lived to the age of seventy-two. The birth of the princess nearly cost the life of the queen. The noise of the throngs that surrounded her bed combined with the heat, and possibly disappointment that the child was not a son, brought on a sudden fainting fit.

"Air! Warm water!" the midwife cried. "The queen must be bled."

The room was filled with chaos and confusion. The window could not be opened, and there was little air in the room until the king rushed forward and broke a pane of window glass. The crowd, which had forced its way in, was ejected by the soldiers and servants. The queen did not open her eyes for nearly an hour afterward, but her life was saved, and the princess was healthy.

However, Princess Marie-Thérèse was unable to bear children during her marriage to her cousin, Louis Antoine of Artois, the son of the Comte d'Artois. She was also known to have poor eyesight, bad teeth, and a red-blotched complexion; these characteristics, however, were not necessarily symptomatic of congenital venereal disease.

Marie Antoinette's second pregnancy ended in a miscarriage early in July 1779, as confirmed in her letters to her mother, Empress Maria Theresa. In June 1783, Marie Antoinette announced a new pregnancy but suffered another miscarriage on the morning of November 2, her twenty-eighth birthday. These miscarriages could have been the result of a venereal disease such as chlamydia, but they alone could not be considered proof of any such infection.

In 1781, at the age of twenty-five, the queen gave birth to her second child, the Dauphin Louis Joseph, the long-awaited heir to the throne. All was well until the beginning of 1784, when his first high fevers appeared; these passed after the dauphin convalesced at the Château de la Muette; the fevers returned in 1786, accompanied by curvature of the spine. When the prince was taken from his governess and placed in the hands of male mentors, he had difficulty walking, and there were traces of blisters and tumors on his body, often signs of congenital venereal disease.

To help correct his curved spine, the prince wore an iron corset for two years but experienced no improvement. At the end of 1788, his health declined further, with higher fevers, one shoulder that was higher than the other, and gangrene occurring in several of his vertebrae. A year later, the prince lost flexibility in his hands and legs. Bedridden, his health declined rapidly, and he died at the age of seven in 1789.

Congenital or sexually acquired forms of infection have been known to increase the risk of developing spondyloarthritis and syphilitic disease of the spine. Spondyloarthritis, a type of inflammatory arthritis, could have been responsible for the inflammation in the child's joints and surrounding areas, causing pain and stiffness in his back. Syphilitic disease of the spine could have caused spinal degeneration with necrosis and gangrene of the vertebrae, as well as Charcot spine, a disability caused by congenital syphilis.

Marie Antoinette, at the age of twenty-nine, gave birth to a second son, Louis Charles, in 1785, exactly nine months after Fersen's return, leading to doubt as to the paternity of the child. Moreover, the queen called him her *chou d'amour*, or cabbage of love. The king, however, seemed to imply that the child was not his. In his journal, on the morning of Louis Charles's birth, he wrote, "The queen gave birth to the Duc de Normandie at seven-thirty. Everything happened just like that of my son."

Louis XVI was referring to his older son Louis Joseph, the dauphin, when he wrote "my son," and the question arises why he does not consider the Duc de Normandie "his son." But he was not the only one in doubt. A scandalous anecdote was recorded that the queen one day asked the Countess Diane, "Is it true that there is a rumor that I have lovers?"

"There are more words than that said about Your Majesty," replied the countess.

"What are they?"

"It is said that the handsome Fersen is father of the dauphin, M. de Coigny of Madame Royale, and the Comte d'Artois of Monsieur de Normandy."

"And the miscarriage?" asked the queen.

Even the Comte de Provence had his doubts. When the Duc de Normandie was christened, the comte said, "But Monsieur l'Abbé, is it not necessary to know who the father of the child you are about to baptize is?"

Louis Charles, the Duc de Normandie, was stooped at an early age and was frail and often ill. His sister, Marie-Thérèse, recollected in her memoirs that he had been known to suffer from fevers and convulsions. When the child was imprisoned in solitary confinement at the Temple before his death, he was badly mistreated by his caretakers and guards until the government intervened to provide greater care. However, the fevers continued, he experienced swelling of his knees, and his illness grew worse every day until his death at the age of ten in 1795.

Dauphin Louis Charles and Count Axel von Fersen

Although the child spent a period of time in unsanitary conditions during his incarceration, physicians recorded his death as a result of consumption (tuberculosis). However, tubercular osteitis was strongly linked to congenital syphilis, and children from the age of two to fifteen years who suffered from late congenital syphilis presented certain signs not usually regarded as diagnostic of the disease. A history of miscarriages, premature births, a family history of high infant mortality, convulsions, retarded physical development, rickets, and hydrocele (testicular inflammation) are extremely suggestive of congenital syphilis.

Furthermore, the child had been treated for what was called "an injury to his testicle." A physician attributed the testicular inflammation to an accidental trauma to the area, excess masturbation (which was noted by his aunt), or an infection due to uncleanliness. However, he noted a more delicate matter: the child may have contracted a venereal disease from his mother: "Could a mother, or a woman of a certain age, sleeping with her child, and disposed of leucorrhea, contaminate her child? Yes, contact, even involuntary, could be responsible for the contagion to occur."

In 1786, at the age of thirty, the queen gave birth to Sophie Hélène Béatrix, a daughter who was born prematurely and died a month before her first birthday. At birth, the child appeared to be larger than normal, and her development was also abnormal. She died while suffering convulsions, and doctors attributed her death to pulmonary tuberculosis or pneumonia. However, chlamydia could have been the cause of preterm delivery as well as pneumonitis or trachomatis in newborns. Syphilis of the lung might not have been as uncommon as was formerly believed, and many cases diagnosed as tuberculosis or peribranchial phthisis were actually cases of syphilis.

In her midthirties, Marie Antoinette was becoming weaker and weaker; suffering from uterine hemorrhaging, her blood stained the seat of the coach that took her from the Temple to the Conciergerie Prison on the night of August 1, 1793. She was treated with medicinal soups in the prison until the prosecutor Fouquier-Tinville discontinued the treatment, an act to ensure she would be too weak to think straight at her trial.

Rosalie, the prison maid, noticed that the queen was growing weaker due to the hemorrhaging. In her memoir, Rosalie described an instance in which the queen asked her for some clean linen: "I immediately cut up one of my chemises and put those strips of cloth under her bolster."

On the morning of Marie Antoinette's execution, Rosalie wrote that the queen had "lost all her blood." In fact, before being sent to the guillotine, the queen removed her bloody linen and stuffed it into the cracks of her dungeon wall.

Historians have attributed Marie Antoinette's bleeding to cervical cancer, but another cause could have been pelvic inflammatory disease, caused by untreated chlamydia in up to 40 percent of those infected. Another condition caused by chlamydia was cervicitis, an inflammation of the cervix with symptoms of unusual bleeding. Venereal disease was never reported in Marie Antoinette's case, but it should be noted that chlamydia in females was seldom detected in the eighteenth century; if it was, the supposed cure was plenty of rest.

Marie Antoinette was frail, white-haired, and looked twice her age on the day of her execution. She had poor vision and was nearly blind in one eye before being guillotined at the age of thirty-seven.

If rumors are true that Marie Antoinette had illicit affairs with her brother-in-law, the Comte d'Artois; her favorite, the Princesse de Lamballe; or any of her suitors at Versailles, she might have been infected with venereal disease. As for her husband, considering his timidity and the lack of solid evidence of any mistress or illicit affairs, it is unlikely that he could have infected his queen.

The symptoms present in the family case studies could certainly have been the result of an untreated sexually transmitted disease. Cases of untreated chlamydia and the resulting miscarriages and congenital infection would have been of great concern to physicians if the disease had been known at the time.

Moreover, an inquiry about the sexual partners of the queen would have been initiated, especially one in particular, Count Axel von Fersen. If

Thursday, August 30: He feels he is slowly getting better and not suffering from hemorrhoids.

Friday, August 31, 1792: He has not suffered from his hemorrhoids but has applied a Vigo mercury plaster. This is important because such a plaster was a common treatment for venereal disease.

Sunday, September 16: Sixth *friction*, or application of mercury ointment on the right leg.

Monday, September 17: Doing better for two days, but has been concerned about the redness, his thighs, and some yellow creases near the penis. He was told it was caused by the lymph gland. He drank a beverage with *eau de vie* and put powder on the affected area.

Pages from Fersen's journal

the queen was having a carnal relationship with Fersen, it would have been presumed that the count was also infected with the grande vérole.

And he was.

Fersen kept a very detailed journal, which is preserved in the Swedish Archives. On November 18 and 19, 1793, he wrote,

Saturday 18: Rain and wind. Hardly suffered (hemorrhoids). Stomach swollen in front. Dined at Craufurd's. News from Paris as well as news from Luxembourg of the arrivals.

Sunday 19: Rain and wind all day long in the cold, at 7 a.m. I was awakened by a strong erection, heat in my lower abdomen and pain in my right testicle which was sore. The Abbe Muires and Mr. Deveux said it was a swelling of the spermatic vessels caused by an abundance of materials. They combined a poultice of Goular's water with milk and made a barley-water drink for therapeutic uses with quack grass and licorice water.

I stayed in bed all day long and my greatest sorrow was because of her (?) and not seeing her, she came to see me for a moment at 8 o'clock in the evening, she comes in the morning. Her new courier from Luxembourg sent the new project of the Regency and Monsieur.★

Untreated venereal disease could have resulted in epididymis, swelling of the testicles, infection in the tube that carries sperm to the testicles, and inflammation and tenderness in the scrotum. In addition to the detailed descriptions of his symptoms, Fersen also left a daily account of the pain he endured as well as the mercury treatments with ointments and plasters for his venereal disease.

Friction was a cure that consisted first of preparing patients by bathing, purging, and following a strict diet to ensure that the mercury would be well absorbed. On the first day, in the morning, patients rubbed a prescribed quantity of mercury on their legs; on the third day, on their thighs; on the sixth day, on their arms from the wrists to the shoulders; on the eighth or ninth day, on their backs from the hips to the neck; and from the seventh to the fifteenth day, according to circumstances, on any of these areas as advised by their physicians.

Between the fourteenth and sixteenth day, patients often became restless, grew short of breath, and had swollen stomachs. On the sixteenth day, rubbings continued in the evenings with purges the following morning until the twenty-fifth day. On the twenty-sixth day patients were put into a warm bath and, after half an hour, washed clean with soap and then dried.

Axel von Fersen's venereal disease did not lead to his death. Marie Antoinette's lover died at the hands of a Stockholm lynch mob in 1810 during a period of popular unrest.

★ Comte de Provence, Louis XVI's brother, and future Louis XVIII.

16

CANCER RISING
AND SUN IN SCORPIO

It is said that the astrologer who showed Marie Antoinette her natal chart, also laid before her one for the year and the day she was guillotined, begging her to take warning. For astrology teaches that "man is his own star" and that though destiny is marked out, one may overcome it by the force of will to a great extent.

—Henry C. Hodges

In the year 1755, at half past seven o'clock in the evening on the second of November, Marie Antoinette came into this world. She was born in Scorpio, with the sun in the fifth house of Leo, and with Venus, the moon, and Jupiter also in the fifth, Mercury in the sixth, Saturn in the eighth, and Uranus in the tenth house. An astrological chart has been created based on the mathematically precise positions of the planets, the sun, and the moon at the time, date, and place of Marie Antoinette's birth.

Such a chart is designed to provide insight into one's character and personal life potentials by indicating the strengths and challenges experienced in life. The accompanying report based on the time, date, and place of birth covers the subject's primary motivation in life, emotions, mentality, love and sexuality, and spirituality.

In some parts of the report based on Marie Antoinette's chart, there will be apparent contradictions in the descriptions of her character. This is to be expected. People are complex, have many contradictory facets to their personality, and can be influenced by many other factors.

THE FIRST HOUSE

The first house cusp is, in most cases, the ascendant or rising sign of the natal chart. The house placement of the first house ruler shows those areas of life that are of primary importance, including your self-expression and vitality, physical appearance, and interaction with others. Also, planets in the first house influence how you present yourself to the world.

Ascendant in Cancer. The primary motivation in life is to feel emotionally secure. You are sensitive and emotional but can also be over-sensitive and easily hurt by people. You are receptive to the needs of others and have a natural desire to care for or protect others. Family and domestic matters are always important, and the home is your retreat and sanctuary. You are also susceptible to changeable moods, irritability, and petulance.

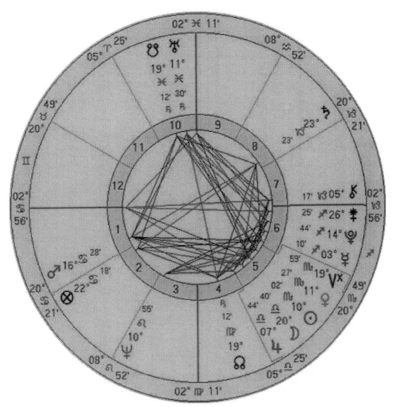

Natal chart for Marie Antoinette, November 2, 1755, 19:30:00 LMT—01:05:20, Vienna, Austria, 16e20'00, 48n13'00. Geocentric Tropical Zodiac—Placidus House System

Marie Antoinette was obstinately proud, but surrounded by enemies in the viper's nest at the court of Versailles, she would have been motivated to pursue a sense of security. Questionable, however, was her attention to the needs of others. Granted, she was charitable on several well-publicized occasions, one of which she wrote about to her mother: "I asked the king for 12,000 francs, which I thought proper to send to Paris for the poor who are held in prison . . . and 4,000 francs here at Versailles, also for the poor. . . . I know my dear mother's good heart too well not to hope that she will approve."

Marie Antoinette's predecessors were well known for their good works. Louis XIII's Queen Anne of Austria, whose "piety was at all times remarkable," once pretended to lose her jewels in order to give them to the poor. She was also a fervent supporter of convents and hospitals. Louis XIV's Queen Maria Theresa of Spain was famous for her piety and gave generously to charity, establishing a home for unwed mothers and patronizing the *Maison Philanthropique de Paris*, a society for the elderly, blind, and widowed. Louis XV's Queen Maria Leszczinska dedicated her life to charity and was popular for her generosity.

Marie Antoinette, however, could not have been as charitable as her predecessors. She had an immoderate taste for gambling, giving rise to great losses despite the king's disapproval of the games. In fact, after the complacent king found the means to pay his queen's debts, she unabashedly and without embarrassment continued to play her favorite game of pharaoh.

Queen Marie Antoinette also had a taste for fantasy, going so far as to have a small village, her hamlet, created for her own amusement—while her subjects in real villages were suffering. Her frivolous village included eight cottages surrounded by a garden planted with vegetables and fruit trees. The roofs were thatched, and the windows were fitted with leaded panes of glass. There were even barns with wooden staircases to access the granaries. In other words, the hamlet was complete, and nothing constituting a real hamlet—the farm, the grange, the poultry yard, the gardener's and guard's houses, or the mill with its turning wheel—was lacking. The queen and her architect, Hubert Robert, thought of everything, "even to painting the fissures in the rocks, the cracks in the plaster, the bulging of the beams, and bricks in the walls."

Family and domestic matters would only have been important to Marie Antoinette, upon her arrival at Versailles, insofar as producing an heir to the crown. Unlike Schönbrunn in Vienna, where court etiquette was characteristically relaxed, the Château of Versailles was far from comfortable for Marie Antoinette. After giving birth, her children were raised by governesses, and she spent very little time with them or her husband until the family's first imprisonment at the Temple.

Finally, Marie Antoinette may have been susceptible to irritable and petulant moods, especially when confronted with Madame du Barry's control over Louis XV or with Madame Etiquette's constant vexing. Her lightheartedness was well known. According to Stefan Zweig, "How could she fail to be a victim of levity when everything came so lightly, so easily; when as much money as she wanted was as obtainable by merely scribbling her name upon a piece of paper; when precious stones, gardens, and palaces could be secured at will by writing the word '*payez*' or 'pay' on the invoices?"

> *1st House Cusp Ruler, Moon, in the 5th House.* You realize your primary motivation in life through expressing your creativity. You may be involved with the entertainment sectors, theatre, or sports. Love affairs and sex are important to you.

Marie Antoinette's love of the theater as both a spectator and a participant has been well documented. At just ten years old, the archduchess was already entertaining in a ballet at her brother Joseph II's wedding celebration at Schönbrunn. As dauphine, she acted in plays at Versailles, but only with her sisters-in-law and in private because playacting was not appropriate for a princess.

At her Petit Trianon, which was already compared to Louis XV's Parc-aux-Cerfs, Marie Antoinette organized a theatrical performance in the summer of 1780 with favorites from her intimate circle and the Comte d'Artois. The only spectators were the king, the Comte de Provence, and her sisters-in-law. Creating an outcry, the court, including the Princesse de Lamballe, was not permitted to attend the performances; however, the queen did invite her ladies-in-waiting and their children to fill the audience for the sake of appearance.

In later productions, the Comte de Mercy was invited: "I saw," he wrote, "the two little comic operas, *Rose et Colas* and *Le Devin de Village*." The Comte d'Artois, the Duc de Guiche, the Comte d'Adhemar, the Duchesse de Polignac, the Duchesse de Guiche, and the Comte de Vaudreuil appeared in various roles. Mercy reported that the queen's voice was "agreeable and in perfect tune," and her manner of acting was "noble and full of grace." However, the count was worried—and with good reason, considering the rumors of illicit affairs—about the appearance of certain members of the queen's court.

There is no question that "love affairs and sex" were important in Marie Antoinette's life. There were love affairs and there was sex, at least with Axel von Fersen. The queen wrote the following letter to the Swedish count in 1792:

> I can tell you I love you and I only have time for that. Do not be anxious upon my account, as I am quite well, and I wish I could learn that you were the same. Write to me in cipher by the post; address the letter to M. de Browne, and a second envelope to M. Gougens. Have the addresses written by your valet. Tell me where to address such letters as I shall be able to write to you, for I cannot live without writing. Goodbye, most beloved and loving of men; I kiss you with all my heart.

Is this proof of an intimate liaison? The letter was unquestionably passionate, and historian Lucien Maury concurred: "Nowhere, as far as I know, is a clearer confession of the royal passion to be found." The French aristocrat and writer Madame de Boigne was brought up at Versailles and spoke to the relationship between the queen and Fersen: "There was little doubt among her friends that she yielded to her passion for M. de Fersen."

Moreover, love affairs and sex with the queen's other admirers, especially during the seven years of her unconsummated marriage, although more questionable, are not beyond the realm of possibility.

> *Mars in the 1st House.* You are bold, combative and impatient by nature. You can tend to act first and think later or jump to conclusions too quickly. Not content with just watching life from the side-lines, you need to have direct experiences. Equally, you can be headstrong and inconsiderate; wanting things your own way or not at all. Physically, you should enjoy good stamina and body strength. However, with your tendency to impulsiveness, there may be accidents and injuries.

Marie Antoinette definitely had Mars in the first house; it is dominant in her horoscope, and history agrees that the queen was possessed of much force of character and reckless courage with the subtlety of the scorpion. On one occasion, while Queen Marie Antoinette was riding a donkey, the animal threw her to the ground, provoking her into such a fit of laughter that she could not be persuaded to get up until the bewildered Duchess of Noailles attended to her where she sat. Then, putting on a grave, inquiring face, the queen asked mischievously, "Pray, Madame Etiquette, when the queen and her donkey tumble down together, who ought to be the first to get up?"

As seen by her conduct as a child at Schönbrunn, Zweig wrote, "She had no idea of putting up with anything irksome, or of not freely indulging in fancies. Not that she was a person of really warm affection. Marie-Antoinette was cold at heart, though she had an easily excited surface sensibility, which made her hasty and impulsive."

Maria Theresa confirmed this coldness from her daughter's letters from Versailles: "There is no true warmth in her expression. This constitutional coldness was probably a lucky accident under the circumstances which marked the early years of her wedded life." Though Marie Antoinette did not feel deeply, she was given to near-instant likes and dislikes, which she indulged with petulant vehemence.

> *Mars Trine Sun (6d 26m A).* With Mars in Cancer, you have an abundance of energy, which you express positively and confidently. You have strong willpower and the drive to achieve whatever is important to you in life. Naturally assertive, you like taking charge of situations and making your intentions known. Self-motivated and ambitious, you enjoy an active lifestyle. Advancements you make in life are based on your personal efforts and determination.

That Marie Antoinette had a highly charged and active lifestyle is an understatement. Her schedule was hectic, and she attended balls and fêtes until the wee hours of the morning. It was not uncommon for her to arrive at Versailles at seven in the morning just in time for mass, immediately after which she would retreat to bed.

Marie Antoinette was also strong-willed. Maria Theresa admitted this when her daughter was a child at Schönbrunn: "I am more and more convinced that I have not been mistaken in the headstrong and pleasure-seeking character I have long attributed to my daughter. I have perfectly noticed that, notwithstanding professed deference to your remonstrances, she has never swerved from her course when it was a question of matters for which she had a fondness."

> *Mars Square Moon (4d 12m S).* You are naturally bold and forthright and generally up-front in your dealings with others. You have the capacity for leadership and are often motivated to take charge of situations. Competitive or aggressive situations bring out the fighter in you. You have a strong resistance to restriction and being ordered around by others. You are not afraid to take risks; however, you can expect setbacks caused by impulsiveness or impatience. At home, you tend to rule the roost. Marital quarrels are likely.

Perhaps the most interesting characteristic revealed here was the queen's "strong resistance to restriction." She did take risks when breaking the palace rules of etiquette. When dauphine, she kept her chambers messy and played with the servants' children. She also refused to wear a corset.

When queen, it could be said that, at home, Marie Antoinette did "rule the roost," and marital quarrels were unlikely because the king loved his queen. Mercy wrote that Louis "prides himself on the charms and qualities of the queen, that he loves her as much as it is possible to love." But Louis may also have feared his wife's boldness. Mercy added that Louis "feared her as much as he loved her."

The Abbé de Véri took this opinion a step further, saying, "The king feared her rather than loved her, because you could find the king just as happy and even more at ease at parties which she didn't attend."

> *Mars Trine Venus (5d 00m A).* You are a warm-hearted person who is passionate and friendly towards other people. You tend to be favored in love, as you express affection easily and are naturally attractive to others. You enjoy social activity, demonstrate a lively and outgoing personality and are generally relaxed in company. Artistic talent is highly likely, particularly creative expressions requiring physical or technical ability, such as dance, drama, ceramics, or sculpture.

The position of Venus signifies artistic talents and accomplishments, and this rings true when considering the queen's passion for the theater. She had also studied and played the harp and the harpsichord.

> *Mars Opposition Saturn (6d 55m A).* This particular combination of planets is challenging to say the least. The enthusiastic and adventure-seeking nature of Mars is in conflict with the obstructive and restraining tendencies of Saturn. Negatively, at times, progress in life can seem frustratingly slow; you may find it difficult to manage anger and irritability. At approximately seven-year intervals, you may be forced to contend with restrictions and periods of low physical energy.

Marie Antoinette's life was encumbered with restrictions, especially during the seven-year interval (1770–1777) in which she waited for her marriage to be consummated. Why did it take seven years? Because her husband suffered, supposedly, from a small defect called phimosis, a penile deformity in which the foreskin was so narrow that it interfered with sexual intercourse. In addition to preventing an heir to the throne, the malady caused the couple's bed sheets to be humiliatingly checked every morning for blood or emissions. The intimate life of the couple became public information, spurring rumors and ridicule.

A few days after the queen's recovery from giving birth to her first child, Madame Royale, the curé of La Madeleine of Paris wrote to the queen's lady-in-waiting, Madame de Campan, and requested a private interview with her. He wanted to personally deliver a little box containing the queen's wedding ring. He wrote to the queen, "I have received under the seal of confession a ring to send to your Majesty, with an avowal that it was stolen from you in 1771, in order to be used in sorceries and prevent you from having any children."

On seeing her ring again, Marie Antoinette said that she had in fact lost it about seven years before, while washing her hands. Furthermore, she decided not to identify the superstitious woman who had wronged her.

Curiously, the Seven Years' War, which involved Austria and France, ended when Marie Antoinette was seven years old.

THE SECOND HOUSE

The second house is associated with personal assets and financial affairs. It governs all movable possessions and wealth.

> *2nd House Cusp in Cancer.* You have a natural talent for dealing in real estate or property development. A cautious investor, you tend to make financial decisions and purchases based on gut instincts. You are naturally security conscious and appreciate the need to keep something in reserve for a rainy day.

Marie Antoinette had a natural talent for "dealing" in real estate, especially property development, such as her work at the Petit Trianon, the costly hamlet, and Saint-Cloud, which Louis purchased for her in 1785. Convinced that the air of Saint-Cloud would be healthier for her and her children, the king bought the château from the Duc d'Orléans for six million livres.

Marie Antoinette proposed to the king that Saint-Cloud should be bought in her name, to keep the acquisition from being too costly. She argued that, if the château was not in the king's name, the appointment of a governor, deputy governors, and corresponding staff would not be required. She would only require a porter at the outer gate. The king acquiesced, but his subjects were outraged at the purchase at a time when promises had been made to cut back on royal expenditures. Moreover, there was "something not only impolitic but immoral" about the idea of a palace belonging to the Autrichienne.

Saint-Cloud, to which the queen had always been partial, was finally hers, and for the next five years, she divided her attention to it with the Trianon, proving that she had no propensity to save or "keep something in reserve for a rainy day." In fact, the monarchy was facing financial difficulties and was forced to cut back on expenses at Versailles. The king cut back by disbanding some of his Swiss Guards and reducing his hunting expenses. The queen's efforts, however, backfired on her.

Thinking that the nobles would take part in her budgeting plans, Marie Antoinette began cutting back expenditures by depriving her favorite, the Duc de Coigny, of his hundred-thousand-livre yearly pension for supervising one of the palace stables, La Petite Écurie, or the Small Stable. Consequently, the entire court was in an uproar. The queen's favorite, Besenval, commented, "It is frightful to live in a country where one can be sure of nothing."

When the Duc de Coigny approached the queen, she said, "My lord, do you bring reproaches against me too? Are you also discontented?"

"And why should I be contented, your majesty?" he said. "I am deprived of a post which hitherto has been held for life, and does your majesty desire that I should be contented? No, I am not contented. No, I do as the others do. I am full of anger and pain to see that nothing is secure more, that nothing is stable more, that one can rely upon nothing more—not even upon the word of kings."

"My lord duke," said Marie Antoinette, "you go too far, you forget that you are speaking to your queen."

"Madame," he said, even louder, "here in Trianon there is no queen, there are no subjects! You yourself have said it, and I at least will hold to your words, even if you yourself do not."

2nd House Cusp Ruler, Moon, in 5th House. Your livelihood may be associated with the arts and entertainment industries. You may make money as an artist or through dealing in artwork. Whatever you do to earn a living must also give pleasure and enjoyment. You may work with children as a coach or teacher. Money may also be gained (or lost) through sports, gambling or the stock market.

Marie Antoinette's livelihood was not associated with the arts and entertainment industries, and she did not earn money as an artist, but her role as queen, unlike past queens of France, was to give pleasure and enjoyment. She did play a role in bringing up her children, but it was very limited until she gave birth to her fourth child, Sophie. After months of abstinence from the gambling and balls, due to her pregnancies, she soon found it more agreeable to spend time with her children.

THE THIRD HOUSE

The third house is associated with your immediate environment. It rules your neighbors and your relationships with your relatives, especially your siblings and cousins. It also rules all forms of communication. It describes your early education and ability to learn.

> *3rd House Cusp in Leo.* You naturally adopt a leading position in conversations and in your interaction with people that you are familiar with. Taking charge and offering ideas and suggestions is second nature to you. You tend to dominate or organize your siblings or extended family members and, possibly, the neighbors.

Marie Antoinette, thanks to her position at court, would have had no problem leading in conversations and interacting with the courtiers of Versailles. Once queen, she would have taken charge. She did not, however, "dominate or organize" her siblings or extended family members.

As for courtiers at Versailles, she dominated them in the sense that she excluded them from her personal retreat at Trianon.

> *Neptune in 3rd House.* You can be given to daydreaming but also to idealistic and inspired thinking. At times, you can have difficulty explaining your thoughts and ideas clearly to others. Relations with relatives or neighbors can be difficult due to misunderstandings or miscommunications.

It is doubtful that Marie Antoinette had any difficulty explaining her thoughts clearly to others. She spoke French "with much grace," according to Madame Campan. As for misunderstandings, the queen's relationships with her mother, Maria Theresa, and her brother, Joseph, were riddled with contradictions. Maria Theresa expected her children's marriages to advance the interests of Austria, and for that, a sense of court and marital harmony was needed. At court, dauphine Marie Antoinette failed to follow etiquette by not acknowledging the king's mistress, Madame du Barry. This concerned her mother, especially with respect to dishonoring the king's wishes, who chastised her daughter:

I cannot keep silent longer; after your conversation with Mercy, and all that he told you the king desired,★ and which it was your duty to fulfil, that you should have dared to fail him! What good reason have you to give? None. You should not regard the Du Barry in any other light than as a lady admitted to the court and to the society of the king. You are his first subject. . . . And yet you fail him on the first occasion that offers for you to oblige him and show him your affection, —an occasion which may not return again so soon. . . . You are afraid to speak to the king, and you are not afraid to disobey and disoblige him!

As for Marie Antoinette's marriage and the problem consummating it, her mother stressed that a wife should be "submissive in everything to her husband and should have no thought but to please him and to do his will." Although her mother's marriage had been a happy one in appearances only, Maria Theresa wrote that the "only true happiness in this world lies in a happy marriage; I know whereof I speak. Everything depends on the wife if she be yielding, sweet, and amusing."

> *Neptune in Leo.* You have a flair for the dramatic. You have idealistic notions about your leadership abilities. You are part of a generation that tends to have romantic ideas about leaders and celebrities.

Marie Antoinette's flair for the dramatic was accentuated by her over-the-top hairstyles. Noble ladies of the court of Versailles felt obliged to imitate the queen's new and daring hairstyles, including the yard-high pouf, despite the danger of becoming burning infernos should they brush against the candles of the palace chandeliers.

The young ladies of Paris were also enthralled with the trends, drastically increasing their coiffure expenses and incurring large debts. Mothers and husbands grumbled, family fights ensued, and many relationships were irreparably damaged. In all, the general consensus of the French people was well publicized—the queen was bankrupting all the women of France, financially and morally.

> *Neptune Square Sun (0d 53m A).* You are highly sensitive and impressionable. You have a tendency to be easily swayed by others and are prone to seducing influences and stimulants. Equally, you may be prone to recycling periods of low vitality and physical weakness. There is a susceptibility to self-deception and seducing influences that can lead to undermining activity. You have compassion and an ability to understand the needs of others with sympathy and empathy.

★ Louis XV had asked the Comte de Mercy to persuade the dauphine to greet Madame du Barry at court.

Neptune is the planet of illusions and deceptions, and Marie Antoinette was exceptionally impressionable. Whether succumbing to the Comte d'Artois's whims, Madame de Guéménée's gambling dens, or the sly maneuvers of Madame de Polignac's greedy clan, Marie Antoinette was easily swayed by others. She also understood the needs of others with sympathy and empathy, but only if they were members of her intimate circle.

> *Neptune Square Venus (0d 32m S).* You possess good taste, refinement and artistic appreciation, or talent. You have a keen sense of beauty, coupled with creative imagination and inspiration. Emotionally, you are highly romantic and inclined to dream and wish for perfect love.

Marie Antoinette had good taste, as can be seen in her attention to fashion, music, furnishings, and the appreciation of art. However, the most interesting part of this horoscope pertains to the romantic ideals of "perfect love." Marie Antoinette, on more than one occasion, asked her male favorites to attend her court in their military uniforms. Her favorites had chivalrous dispositions and were romantically brave at fighting in the American Revolution or abroad. She had her own set of bodyguards outfitted in red and silver uniforms at her Petit Trianon.

THE FOURTH HOUSE

The fourth house is associated with home and family matters. It describes your parents—especially the father—and your relationship with them. It gives information on your family history or ancestry and on the nature of your later life.

> *4th House Cusp in Virgo.* You prefer your domestic circumstances to be modest and easy to manage. You can be fussy and particular about certain things within the home. You may work from home, or at least have a study or workshop on the property. There can be a tendency to worry about family members.

Madame Campan fulfilled her role as lady-in-waiting in proximity to the queen for a long time, and she had firsthand knowledge of the queen's battle against useless etiquette at court. She even complained about it in her memoirs: "It was the disdain of the grave uselessness of etiquette which became the pretext of the first reproaches addressed to the queen." She added that

Marie Antoinette's extreme simplicity was "the first and perhaps the only wrong for which we reproach her."

That was not quite true. Madame Campan and the court were not too happy with all the queen's changes, such as abandoning the paniers, or side hoops, which extended the width of skirts at the side while leaving the front and back flat. Madame Campan called the abandonment "absurd."

Moon's North Node Sextile Venus (7d 45m A). You have well-developed social skills. Possessing charm and good taste, you prefer the company of cultured and refined people. You tend to cultivate friendships with creative people and move in artistic circles. Popular and well-liked, you enjoy an active social life and have many opportunities for love.

Marie Antoinette was unlike the queens of Versailles before her; they kept themselves busy in the background with good works and with giving their husbands heirs to the throne. On the other hand, she was an extrovert. She enjoyed the social life at court, where she was the most coquettish, the most fashionably dressed, and "the most amused woman" at Versailles.

Moon's North Node Trine Saturn (4d 11m S). You have a sense of responsibility towards the important people in your life and can be relied upon to be loyal and dependable. Your associations with others of a wide-age difference—either older or younger—are generally harmonious and free from stress or pressure. You enjoy the company of older people for their knowledge and experience and, likewise, you appreciate young people for their fresh outlooks and vitality. You enjoy change and variety with regard to your associations and can be inclined to make and break contacts suddenly and unexpectedly. When meeting new people, you tend to assess their character intuitively and quickly. You may associate with people who expose you to unsettling or disruptive experiences.

Marie Antoinette was loyal to those in her intimate circle, but only to a certain extent. When Madame de Polignac was presented at court for the first time, the queen was attracted to her charms and beauty. Unfortunately, this attraction took precedence over the tender affection that the queen had for the Princesse de Lamballe. Was this because Madame de Polignac, being an outsider, had so little attachment to the court?

Curiously, Marie Antoinette had a close relationship with her children's governess, Madame de Guéménée, with whom she enjoyed partying and gambling in her salon. However, when Monsieur de Guéménée suffered financial ruin and bankruptcy, the queen coldly ended the relationship with her former partner in crime, giving the position of governess to her new favorite, Madame de Polignac. Was this separation with Madame de Guéménée cruel? Had Marie Antoinette not participated in the ruin of this couple? Did she not take part in their numerous fêtes and gambling soirées?

THE FIFTH HOUSE

The fifth house is associated with pleasure, sex, love affairs, and children. It also governs artistic creativity, music, the fine arts, fashion, social entertainment, games, and speculations.

> *Venus Trine Uranus (0d 03m A)*. You tend to be choosy in love because you need someone who can accommodate your need for freedom and independence. You are attracted to exotic and unusual partners who are independent and up to date in their outlooks. Romantically, you are spontaneous with your affections, adventurous, and quickly aroused. Flirtatious behavior can result in romantic whirlwinds, which quickly flare up and swiftly fizzle out.

Yes, yes, and yes. Marie Antoinette was independent, spontaneous, and flirtatious. Most of her alleged flings with male favorites quickly "fizzled" out, except for that with Axel von Fersen.

> *Jupiter Sextile Pluto (7d 00m A)*. You can handle power responsibly. Others will generally respond favorably to being organized and led by you. The secret to your success with others is that you lead by example. You are motivated by the desire to improve yourself and the conditions of those around you.

No, no, and no. Marie Antoinette was not a leader, and by the time she *did* try to take the reins of the monarchy when her husband was weakened, it was too late. Louis XVI had generally been considered morally upright and honest; he loathed bloodshed, but his weakness led to his downfall. He had willingly accepted numerous concessions to give his people more power, but many of his advisers, including the queen, were just as incompetent as he in reforming the government. At a time when France needed a strong leader, Louis was a shy and awkward monarch.

Marie Antoinette, on the other hand, was in many ways stronger and more intelligent than her husband. Moreover, she was in a good position to exert power over him. And that she did, especially after the royal family was removed from Versailles and put under house arrest at the Tuileries Palace. Until the family was sent to the Temple three years later, Louis remained apathetic and depressed, unable to face the problems of his time, even as these problems inched ever closer to the walls of his palace.

> *Jupiter Square Ascendant (4d 49m A).* Broad-minded and enthusiastic, you have an eagerness for knowledge and travel.

Marie Antoinette was gracious, materialistic, and coquettishly assertive. However, whether she had an eagerness for knowledge and travel is questionable. For example, after arriving in France, Marie Antoinette never ventured more than a few miles from Paris, except on one occasion when she, her husband, and her immediate family attempted to escape. The purpose of the escape was to initiate a counterrevolution with the help of loyal troops and royalist officers near Montmédy on the border; however, the escape succeeded only to the small town of Varennes, where they were arrested.

> *Sun Trine Uranus (1d 28m A).* You are open to anything contemporary and progressive, including the possibilities offered by modern technology or science.

It is interesting that Marie Antoinette was open to new ideas and scientific marvels. She had heard about vaccination for smallpox before coming to France. Because she had caught a mild case of smallpox when she was two years old, she was immune to it. However, on June 8, 1774, she insisted that her husband be inoculated against the disease. When his brothers and sisters-in-law were also vaccinated, the court was in a frenzy. The entire royal family was at risk, and the queen would be blamed for any resultant disaster.

Marie Antoinette and the king invited the Montgolfier brothers to Versailles for a demonstration, on September 19, 1783, of the *Aérostat Réveillon*, a balloon flown with the first living beings in a basket: a sheep called Montauciel (Climb-to-the-sky), a duck, and a rooster. The flight lasted approximately eight minutes, covered two miles, and obtained an altitude of about 1,500 feet. The craft landed safely after flying, and no animals were injured in the process.

> *Sun Trine Mid-Heaven (7d 51m A).* You have an awareness of your purpose in life from an early age. You have the ability to attain a measure of distinction and recognition in your career. Your parents may assist you in deciding your vocational direction and your family will probably support your career moves.

A measure of distinction and recognition was certainly attained when the archiduchesse of Austria, Marie Antoinette, became queen of France and mother of the future king. Like her sisters, she was well aware of her imperial mother's direction in planning her royal career. She and her siblings were no more than political pawns.

But Maria Theresa was just as affectionate a mother as she was an empress. Every three weeks, couriers were regularly sent to Paris, Naples, and Parma to her daughters, Marie Antoinette, Caroline, and Amalia, respectively, with long letters full of motherly advice and anxious inquiries about their health, their doings, and especially their children. If one of the princesses was with child, a courier was sent every nine days.

THE SIXTH HOUSE

The sixth house is associated with work and employment or service. It describes your dependents, such as pets, employees, servants, and tenants, if you have any. It is the house of health and sickness.

> *Pluto Square Uranus (3d 14m S).* Sometimes you can be confronted with situations that are so intense that the only thing you can do is take sudden or drastic measures. Exposure to volatility and forces beyond personal control is not uncommon.

Two occasions immediately come to mind about exposure to dangerous and volatile situations over which Marie Antoinette had no control. The first took place on October 5, 1789, when an angry mob of fishwives marched in the rain from Paris to Versailles—armed with pikes and pitchforks and demanding bread.

By the time the women reached the palace, they were no longer calling for bread. They were calling for Marie Antoinette's head, but she was spared. Two of her bodyguards, however, were less fortunate; their severed heads were impaled on pikes.

> More revealing, however, was Madame Campan's version of the event that evening, as revealed to Napoleon, when the mob stormed the palace. Axel von Fersen was in the queen's chambers where, according to the queen's lady-in-waiting, he often spent the night. When the mob arrived, "Marie Antoinette had fled undressed from her own chamber to that of the kin for shelter, and 'the lover' descended from the window. On going to seek the queen in her bedroom, Madame Campan found she

was absent, but discovered a pair of breeches, which the favorite had left behind in his haste, and which were immediately recognized."

The breeches were easily recognized as those belonging to Axel von Fersen, and historian Lord Holland attests to Madame Campan's close relationship with Marie Antoinette: "Madame Campan was in fact the confidante of Marie-Antoinette's amours. These amours were not numerous, scandalous, or degrading, *but they were amours.*"

If Fersen was indeed at Versailles on October 5, then he would have no doubt remained at the château all day and night like any loyal royalist to protect the royal family. In fact, he wrote in his journal that he witnessed *tout* (everything):

> Paris, October 9, 1789–All the public papers will inform you, my dear father, of what happened in Versailles on Monday 5 and Tuesday 6 [of October], and of the king's arrival in Paris with the whole family Royal. I witnessed everything, and returned to Paris, following in one of the King's coaches; we were half past six on the way. God preserve me from ever seeing a spectacle as distressing as that of these two days.

Charles-Maurice de Talleyrand, a historian who was generally averse to providing any anecdotes derogatory to the royal family, twice assured Lord Holland that Axel von Fersen "escaped observation with considerable difficulty that night in a disguise that she, Madame Campan, herself procured for him." Although it is still unclear if Madame Campan was actually on duty in the palace that evening, her sister Adélaïde was there with their father, and Marie Antoinette rewarded Adélaïde with the name "my lioness" for her bravery that terrible night.

It should also be noted that when Marie Antoinette was questioned during her trial about the twenty-five louis found on her person, she answered that Adélaïde had lent it to her. She begged the court to repay her faithful "lioness," as she had called her "ever since the terrible events of October 6, 1789, when Madame Campan's sister had saved her mistress's life by her courage and promptitude."

On October 6, when the Parisian women cried out for the queen to appear from her balcony, she emerged with her children (as human shields?), but the crowd was not satisfied. They demanded her to appear in front of them alone. When she did so, even those who a moment before wanted to disembowel her, joined in the cry of "Long live the queen!"

Marie Antoinette was not the dupe of this outcry, because she also heard the crowd shouting another alarming cry: "To Paris with the king!"

When she left the balcony, she said sadly, "They are going to make the king and me go to Paris, with our guards' heads carried waved in front of us on the ends of their pikes."

Louis XVI, always good-natured, decided to obey this impertinent demand from his subjects. He only asked that he should not be separated from his wife and children.

THE SEVENTH HOUSE

The seventh house is associated with partnerships, both personal and professional. It rules your relationship with other people generally, including those who oppose you. It also describes the sort of person you will attract as a mate.

> *7th House Cusp in Capricorn.* You are an emotional and sensitive person who requires someone to lean or depend upon.

Marie Antoinette had her favorites and her alleged lovers for emotional support during the first years of her reign. However, her relationships with her husband's siblings were complicated, especially her relationship with her sister-in-law, Élisabeth. Marie Antoinette reportedly found Élisabeth delightful when she first received her at court. A courtier wrote, "The Queen is enchanted with her. She tells everyone that there is no one more amiable, that she did not know her well before, but that now she has made her her friend and that it will be for life."

Élisabeth, however, was very close to her aunts, the Mesdames Tantes, who were members of the anti-Austrian party at court and were known for their animosity toward their nephew's new wife. The aunts were also deeply opposed to Marie Antoinette's informal reforms in court life, and Élisabeth therefore regarded the queen's disregard of etiquette as a threat to the monarchy. She remarked, "If sovereigns descended among the people, the people would approach near enough to see that the Queen was only a pretty woman, and that they would soon conclude that the King was merely the first among officials."

The sisters-in-law grew closer, however, as the clouds of revolution gathered on the horizon. In fact, Élisabeth refused to emigrate with other members of the royal family when the gravity of the situation became apparent. After the execution of Louis XVI on January 21, 1793, and the separation of her nephew, the young Louis Charles, from the rest of the family on

July 3, Élisabeth was left with Marie Antoinette and Princess Marie-Thérèse in their chambers in the Tower Prison. The former queen was taken to the Conciergerie on August 2, 1793. When Marie Antoinette was transferred to the Conciergerie, both Élisabeth and her niece mournfully asked for permission to join Marie Antoinette—their requests were denied.

THE EIGHTH HOUSE

The eighth house is the house of shared resources and other people's money, including your partner's. It is associated with wills, inheritances, death, and loss.

> *8th House Cusp Ruler, Saturn, in 8th House.* You may encounter situations that test your survival instincts. Your will is strong and unyielding.

THE NINTH HOUSE

The ninth house is associated with philosophy, wisdom, spirituality, religion, higher education, and travel. It also rules those you seek for advice, such as lawyers, priests, and astrologers.

> *9th House Cusp Ruler, Saturn, in 8th House.* Your faith may be tested from time to time. It is possible that you may journey to dangerous places.

THE TENTH HOUSE

The tenth house is associated with your status in the world. It describes your reputation and level of public success. It is the house of career and, traditionally, the house of the mother.

> *Uranus in 10th House.* Your path in life may be unique and prone to sudden changes of direction. You may be suited to unusual or progressive careers. You may be inclined to rebel against authority figures.

When the young Louis-Auguste married the Austrian archduchess, Marie Antoinette, many of the grandes dames of the court of Versailles were shocked by the newcomer's light and frivolous manners, especially her disregard of tradition. The dauphine's dame d'honneur, Comtesse de Noailles, did her best to persuade the dauphine to acknowledge the court's customs, but the dauphine laughed in her face, going so far as to call her "Madame Etiquette."

THE ELEVENTH HOUSE

The eleventh house is traditionally known as the "house of good fortune." Your friends and benefactors are described here, as well as your hopes and wishes.

> *11th House Cusp in Aries.* Your friends tend to be energetic and direct in manner. They are usually busy people, who enjoy physical pursuits, sports, and outdoor activities. They may also be naturally competitive and inclined to compete with you, or among themselves.

THE TWELFTH HOUSE

The twelfth house is the house of ill luck. It is associated with sorrow and sadness, your self-undoing and downfall, and your secrets, worries, and anxieties.

> *12th House Cusp in Taurus.* It rules hospitals, retreats, hideaways, and prisons.

Secrets, worries, sorrows, and anxieties all resulted from Marie Antoinette's imprisonment and two-day trial at the Revolutionary Tribunal. One particular sorrow was the vile accusation by her son against her, which the witness Jacques Hébert offered to the court.

Simon, the caretaker of the young Louis Charles, had requested weeks before that Hébert come to the Temple Prison, where the child remained with his aunt and sister, although kept separate from them. Simon told Hébert that he had surprised the boy alone—in the "commission of very unnatural acts." Also, he was astonished to see a child committing such "crimes" at such an early age.

When Simon asked him who had been his instructors, Louis Charles Capet* answered "with all the naiveté and candor of his age" that he had been taught by his mother and his aunt as he slept between them. Moreover, he reported that his mother had molested him.

---

* Stripped of his royal and noble titles, Louis XVI became known as "Citizen Louis Capet," a name derived from his ancestors. His son, Louis Charles, became known as Louis Charles Capet instead of Dauphin Louis Charles.

Hébert referred to the child's behavior as "criminal enjoyment," a piece of political strategy intent on degrading the child's physical and mental health.* This would allow the mother to rule as regent for the incompetent child if he would one day occupy the throne.

When Herman, the president of the tribunal, asked the queen how she would answer the charges, she replied with a "scornful but dignified" look: "I have no knowledge of these facts to which Hébert refers."

Then, before Herman proceeded to call another witness, a jury member asked him to order the queen to respond to the crimes, "the proof of which rested on the declarations of the young Capet."

Marie Antoinette faced the jury and said, "I remained silent on that subject because nature holds all such crimes in abhorrence."

Then, she turned to face the people in the courtroom: "I appeal to the hearts of all the mothers here [*J'en appelle au cœur de toutes les mères ici présentes*]. I ask whether they hold such a crime to be possible?"

Marie Antoinette referred to this dreadful charge in the letter she wrote to her sister-in-law Élisabeth in the early morning before her execution, a letter that was, at the same time, her testament and farewell to life.

Another particular "secret, worry, sorry, or anxiety" on that cold October morning before her execution might have been the hemorrhaging she experienced. This last humiliation had been kept secret for many days, and

"J'en appelle au cœur de toutes les mères ici présentes."

---

* The word *jouissance* is here translated as "enjoyment." However, Hébert's use of the term could have been deemed outrageous in this context because the word also denoted orgasm.

her undergarments were soiled with it. Historian Stefan Zweig describes the humiliation in great detail:

> Having a natural desire to go to her death clean, she wanted to put on fresh undergarments, and she begged the gendarme to withdraw for a few minutes. But he had been given strict orders not to let her out of his sight for a moment. The Queen, therefore, crouched in the narrow space between the bed and the wall, and, while she was changing her shift, the kitchen-maid [Rosalie] stood between her and the gendarme, to hide her nakedness.

But what was to be done with the bloodstained undergarment? Marie Antoinette quickly rolled it up into a small bundle and stuffed it into a crevice behind the stove. Was she ashamed at the thought of leaving her soiled linen for the prying eyes of those who, within a few hours, would enter her cell to pore over all that she had left there?

Or was Marie Antoinette worried that the source of the blood might be reported? Could her secret vaginal bleeding be related to untreated venereal disease? After all, it was from here, according to the pamphleteers, that monarchical poison was extracted against the people and their revolution: "Since the revolution, the monarchical club, of which Antoinette is the soul, has continued to make attempts. Each of the members who compose draw on the poison from the vagina of the Austrian. This pestiferous lair is the receptacle of all vices, and there, each one comes to fill himself abundantly with his own dose."

À SAVOIR

Marie Antoinette's Handwriting (1792–1793)

The following letter that Marie Antoinette wrote to Antoine Barnave had to have been written after June 1791, because she had not met Barnave until the time of the family's arrest during the flight to Varennes on June 21. Barnave was appointed to bring the family back to Paris. During this journey, Barnave became sympathetic to Queen Marie Antoinette and her family's plight.

- The small script size points to humility and tolerance.
- The script maintains the slight right slant the writer is known to have. This shows the writer is sociable and expressive.
- The disconnected script shows self-reliance and intuitive thinking.
- The script width is balanced, and the space distribution is normal. This shows orderliness of thinking.
- The leveled direction of lines shows the writer is methodical and of emotional control.
- This script is a bit irregular. This suggests there is a bit of impulsivity and impressionability in the writer.
- The pen pressure is higher than usual. This has to be interpreted in conjunction with the irregularity of the script, suggesting high emotions (could be excitement or moodiness).
- The pastiness of the script suggests warmth and sensuality.
- The left-tending movements in the upper zone suggest intellectual and moral freedom.
- The left-tending movements in the lower zone points to mystical impressionability and an instinctual perception of the past/bias.
- The *t* bars are placed high. This shows excitement and curiosity. The firm placement of the *t* bars shows optimism.

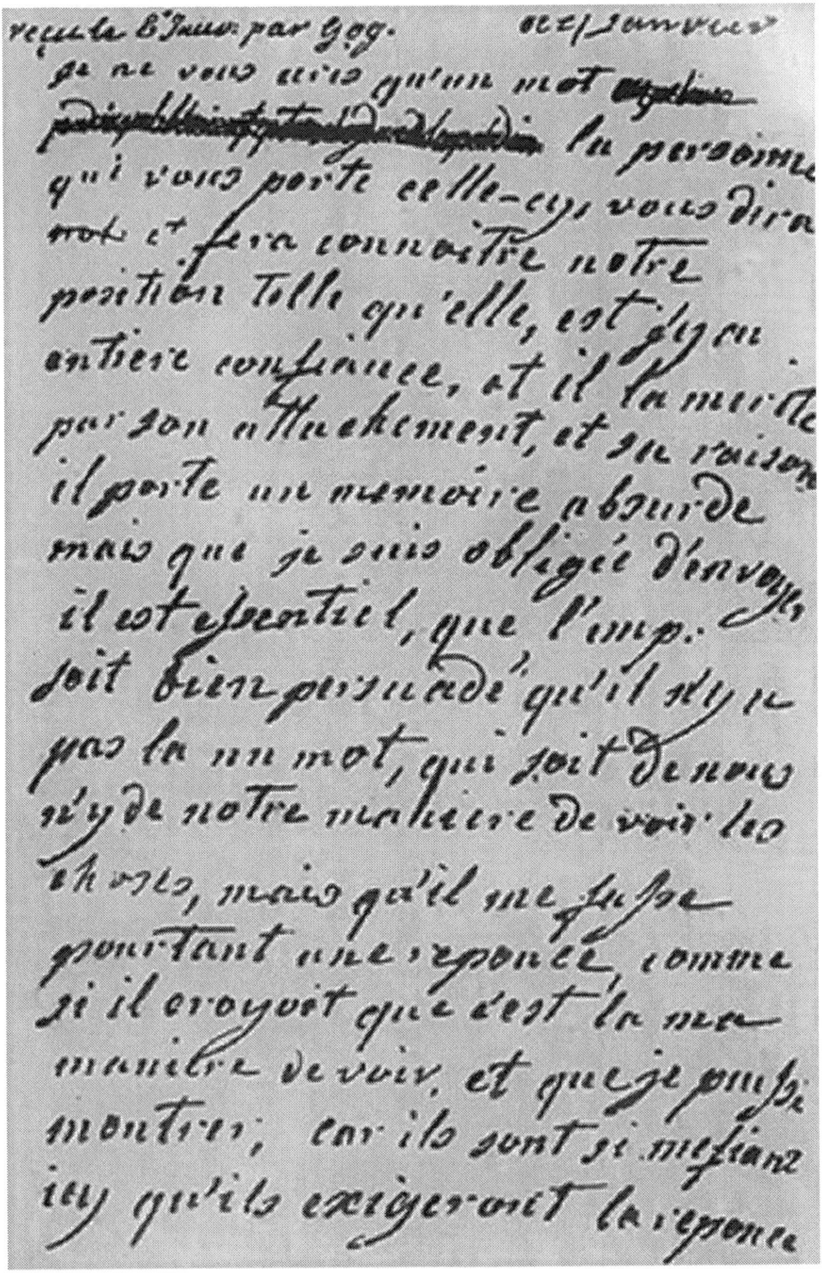

Letter to Barnave (1791)

It is said that Marie Antoinette was able to charm Barnave during the return to Paris and earn his favor politically. This could account for the sensuality and impressionability found in the handwriting. It was also rumored that the queen and Barnave had a sexual relationship: According to Barnave's biographer, Jules Janin, Barnave was "a ridiculous lover of the queen" and he "was in love with Marie Antoinette, in all probability, long before he had ever seen her."

General François Jarjayes, along with the guard Toulan, had organized an escape of the royal family in the Temple after the execution of Louis XVI, but the plan had to be abandoned at the last minute due to the impossibility of rescuing all the prisoners: the queen, her sister-in-law, and her two children. However, preparations were made to save the queen only, whose life was in greatest danger.

When Toulan arrived the next day to rescue her, the queen could not leave her children behind: "You will be angry with me, but I have been thinking it over. We are, indeed, encompassed with dangers here, but it is better to die than to act against one's conscience." The queen then wrote Jarjayes:

> We have dreamed a lovely dream—that is all! But we have gained much, in that we have a fresh proof of your affection for us. My confidence in you is unbounded. You will always find me strong and courageous. But the interests of my son are my only guide, and great as would have been my happiness to leave these walls, I cannot consent to a separation from

Letter to General Jarjayes written from the Temple Prison

him. I recognize your devotion in all that you expressed yesterday, and you must feel assured that I grasp the truth of every argument you can put forward. But nothing could give me pleasure in the absence of my children, and it is this which prevents my feeling any regret.

- The left-tending movements in the lower zone suggest a motherly instinct and mystical impressionability.
- The placement of the *i* dots is inconsistent. This level of inconsistency suggests unusually high excitement, moodiness, or irritability.
- The short, straight lower-zone extension suggests a lack of interest in primary pleasures such as sexual activities, eating, and drinking.
- The script is mostly disconnected, which suggests self-reliance.
- This script is irregular. Some parts stay disconnected, and some have an arcade connection. The arcade connections show diplomacy and distance.
- The space distribution between words is average. This suggests spontaneity and creative thinking.
- The irregularity points to impressionability. This combined with the high pressure of the script can be seen as impulsiveness.
- The left-tending movements in the upper zone show intellectual and moral freedom.
- The extended terminal strokes in the middle zone show sociality.
- There are discrepancies in the writer's social and private behavior as suggested by the signature being larger than the script. The writer acts more prominent than they actually are.

Motherly instinct would undoubtedly be pronounced at this time. She could not leave her children, Louis Charles, the uncrowned Louis XVII, and Marie-Thérèse, who would remain imprisoned in the Temple with her and their aunt Élisabeth. That said, any interest in primary pleasures such as sexual activities, eating, and drinking would be unthinkable.

Part VI

THE VERDICT

The Verdict

17

THE LAST TESTAMENT

It is to you, sister, that I write for the last time.

—Marie Antoinette, Conciergerie Prison,
October 16, 1793, at 4:00 a.m.

Marie Antoinette penned her last letter in the early morning hours of October 16, 1793, to Madame Élisabeth, completing it just a few hours before her execution at midday. It was past four o'clock in the morning, and the ex-queen was overwhelmed with fatigue, cold, and uterine hemorrhaging as she returned to her cell for the last time, where she asked Warden Bault for a pen and paper. He complied and then left her alone.

In this famous letter, sometimes referred to as the Last Testament of Marie Antoinette, the queen commends her soul to God and her children to Madame Élisabeth's care. To better understand these last moments of the queen's life, the handwriting of the letter has been analyzed by a graphologist:

- This handwriting has a good standard of form level.
- The small handwriting shows devotion, humility, and tolerance.
- The scripts right slant indicates sociability.
- The normal script width suggests a balance in vivacity and timidity.
- The arcade nature of the script shows the writer is more reserved here than previously.
- The disconnected letters suggests the writer is a self-reliant person.
- The words have great space distribution. However, descending direction of lines points to fatigue.

- The regularity of the script suggests moderation and self-conquest. This characteristic, coupled with the high pressure, shows willpower and self-control.
- The upper zone is a bit fuller; this shows the writer has more imagination here.
- Although the lower zone remains mainly lean, the slight fullness in letters shows the writer has a bit more sensuousness, fantasies, and sublimation.

In all fairness to Marie Antoinette, the letter is a painful reminder of the queen's sadness and humility. If we look at the first five lines, we notice that the first word of each line begins in an ascending direction, as if declaring innocence to the heavens. However, the futility of the situation takes hold, and the lines quickly begin to diagonally descend across the page, with the last words of each line practically falling off the paper. All the while, the

Excerpt from Marie Antoinette's last letter

words are neatly written in a sharp manner and with simplicity, making the testament even more remarkable than her earlier writings. Notable, too, is that all the commas are placed where needed.

We see the same pattern, even more pronounced, after she cries out to her *Adieu*. The words "puisse" and "pensez" at the beginning of the two phrases "that you receive this letter" and "always think of me" rise strongly, but the following words then fall heartbreakingly.

As we approach the end of the letter, the lines are all descending after "Adieu, adieu." The soul is tortured, and resistance is impossible. The very last words, "absolument étranger," are emphasized by crossing the two *t*'s with one bold line. Her nature is unshakable, almost heroic. Then, Marie Antoinette signs majestically as the queen she once was, using capital *A* and *M*—the only capitals used in the entire document. However, the last three letters, *tte*, of her last name fall off the page, as if all hope is lost.

If we examine the testament more closely, the first line of Marie Antoinette's letter immediately exonerates herself from any wrongdoing after being condemned to death in the Revolutionary Tribunal:

> I write to you, my sister, for the last time. I have been condemned, not to a disgraceful death—that only awaits criminals—but to go and rejoin your brother. Innocent as he, I hope to show the same firmness as he did in his last moments. I grieve bitterly at leaving my poor children; you know that I existed but for them and you—you who have by your friendship sacrificed all to be with us. In what a position do I leave you! I have learned, by the pleadings on my trial, that my daughter is separated from you. Alas, poor child—I dare not write to her for she would not receive my letter; I know not even if this may reach you.

Marie Antoinette was not being punished as a criminal; rather, she was being reunited with her husband, who she felt was also innocent and falsely condemned to death. When she was escorted to her own death, the queen did indeed show courage and firmness in countenance.★ In fact, contemporary tabloids reported that the queen faced death with the utmost bravery. The *Glaive vengeur de la République française* reported, "She stepped on the scaffold with courage." And the *Moniteur* reported, "She mounted the scaffold with enough courage." The following verse published in the *Révolution en vaudeville* also spoke to the queen's strength:

★ Marie Antoinette's last words were "Pardon me, Sir, I did not do it on purpose" after she accidentally stepped on her executioner's foot.

> Against the widow Antoinette,
> France gave only one cry;
> She underwent the same test
> As the sire her husband! (repeat)
> To quell this former queen,
> The iron blade did not succeed.
> Her majesty sovereign
> Showed herself just as firm!

Louis XVI, too, showed strength, if not an eerie sense of serenity, at the time of his death. Before his execution, he had asked his jailer, Antoine Santerre, if he could "speak of mercy" to his subjects, but Santerre refused his request. When the king arrived at the scaffold on January 23, 1793, at ten o'clock in the morning, he mounted the scaffold alone and advanced toward the guillotine with a "steady" countenance, addressing the crowd in a "firm" voice: "Frenchmen, I die innocent; I forgive my enemies. I wish that my death may be useful to the people."

He then placed himself on the plank, praying aloud in Latin: "I commend my soul to God." His head was instantly severed from his body, and during the next few minutes, the most profound silence prevailed. "Not a murmur, not a motion, not a breath was heard" until his head was shown to the spectators and their roar of "Vive la République!" was heard.

Marie Antoinette left responsibility for her children, Louis Charles and Marie-Thérèse, in Élisabeth's hands. Having spent the past few years with them under house arrest at the Tuileries and while incarcerated at the Temple Prison, she would have certainly grieved "bitterly." It was not clear in the trial's proceedings why the queen believed her daughter had been separated from her aunt, but this presumption explains why the letter was addressed only to Élisabeth. And if the queen had thought that this letter would not reach Élisabeth, a possible reason for writing it anyway may have been to convince herself that her children would grow up together.

But this was a fantasy; she knew all too well that her son had already been separated from his family—both physically and mentally. She also knew that the young uncrowned king would never sit on the throne of France, let alone be in a position to take revenge on his family's captors.

Or better yet, if the queen truly thought the letter would not reach Élisabeth, she may have written it as her last testament for posterity and to rehabilitate her legacy. After all, the document (756 words) could be scored extremely high in self-referencing words (70)—more than 10 percent of the total. Marie Antoinette used the word *I* thirty-nine times, *my* twenty-six times, and *me* five times.

Do receive my blessing for both. I hope one day, when they are older, they may rejoin you and rejoice in liberty at your tender care. May they both think on a lesson that I have never ceased to inspire them with, that sound principles and the exact performance of their duties are the chief foundation of life; and then mutual affection and confidence in one another will constitute its happiness. May their friendship and mutual confidence form their happiness! May my daughter feel that at her age she ought always to aid her brother with that advice with which the greater experience she possesses, and her friendship, should inspire her! May my son, on his part, render to his sister every care and service which affection can dictate! May they, in short, both feel, in whatever position they may find themselves, that they can never be truly happy but by their union!

Let them take example by us. How much consolation has our friendship given us in our misfortunes, and in happiness to share it with a friend is doubly sweet? Where can one find any more tender or dearer than in one's own family? Let my son never forget his father's last words. I repeat them to him purposely—*Let him never seek to revenge our death.*

Despite the picture painted by the Revolutionary Tribunal of Marie Antoinette as an incestuous and wanton mother, the queen begs Madame Élisabeth to care for her two children and instill in them that "sound principles and the exact performance of their duties are the chief foundation of life."

Another possible reason for writing this letter may have been to allow Marie Antoinette to reiterate the absurdity of the charges leveled against her by her young son. She could only "hope" that the child, obviously coerced, would one day be in a condition to know better.

I must now speak to you of a matter most painful to my heart. I know how much trouble this child must have given you. Pardon him, my dear sister; think of his age and how easy it is to make a child say what one wishes and what he even does not comprehend. A day will arrive, I hope, when he will the better feel all the value of your kindness and affection for them both.

The queen next addressed her spirituality. She told Élisabeth that she did not know if she would receive her last rites because she would not accept the services of a sworn priest. During the Terror, the clergy were required to take an oath to the constitution, literally cutting them off from communion with the Church. Those priests who did not take the oath either emigrated or went into hiding.

It still remains to me to confide to you my last thoughts. I had desired to write them from the commencement of the trial; but, exclusively of their not permitting me to write, the proceedings have been so rapid that I should really not have had the time. I die in the Catholic, Apostolic, and Roman religion; in that of my fathers; in that in which I have been bred and which I have always professed, having no spiritual consolation to expect, not knowing if priests of this religion [unsworn] still exist here—and even the place in which I am would expose them too much, were they once to enter it.

There was debate about whether the queen's last letter was authentic, particularly when she wrote that she would die in the "Catholic, Apostolic, and Roman religion," because she had not received any spiritual consolation, according to her statement "not knowing if priests of this religion still exist." However, evidence suggests that the queen did receive last rites from the Abbé Magnin, so the question arises as to why she said she did not know whether any true Catholic priests existed. Some historians believe she did not mention her rites to keep Magnin out of danger.

I sincerely ask pardon of God for all the errors I may have committed during my life. I hope that in his kindness he will accept my last vows, as well as those I have long since made, that he may vouchsafe to receive my soul in his mercy and goodness. I ask pardon of all those with whom I am acquainted, and of you, my sister, in particular, for all the trouble which, without desiring it, I may have caused you. I forgive all my enemies the evil they have done me.

Marie Antoinette asked pardon for "all the errors" she may have committed. Curiously, she mentioned none. She would not have asked forgiveness for any crimes against the nation, nor for any misuse of the treasury's funds, nor for treason. This would only have given credence to her guilt at the tribunal. She would not have asked forgiveness for any of the seven deadly sins—pride, greed, lust, envy, gluttony, wrath, and sloth—even if she had committed them; for that, she was too proud.

Excerpts from Marie Antoinette's last letter

The queen concluded her letter with touching farewells to her friends and family, but she ended it on a peculiar note. She was still uncertain of her spiritual salvation, not willing to see a priest who was not unsworn.

> I say here adieu to my aunts and to all my brothers and sisters. I had friends, and the idea of being separated forever from them and their sorrows causes me the greatest regret I experience in dying. Let them, at least, know that in my last moments I have thought of them. Adieu, my good and kind sister! May this letter reach you! Think of me always! I embrace you with all my heart, as well as those poor dear children. My God, how heartrending it is to quit them forever! Adieu! Adieu! I ought no longer to occupy myself but with my spiritual duties. As I am not mistress of my actions, they may bring me perhaps a priest. But I here protest that I will not tell him one word and that I will treat him absolutely as a stranger.

Adieu, my good and kind sister! May this letter reach you! Having asked Élisabeth to care for her children, Marie Antoinette surely had no idea that the revolutionaries would ever harm her children or Madame Élisabeth. Of the three, only the queen's daughter, the Duchesse d'Angoulême, would survive. Louis Charles died a horrible death in the Temple Prison, and Élisabeth was guillotined. Élisabeth never received her sister-in-law's last testament.*

When Marie Antoinette finished the letter, she kissed each page, folded it, and gave it unsealed to Warden Bault.† The gendarme standing guard outside her cell must have observed this because, when Bault left the queen, the guard confiscated the letter and took it to Fouquier-Tinville, who passed it on to Robespierre.

Robespierre, not known for any compassion for the royals, placed the letter beneath his mattress, where it remained until his death by guillotine on July 28, 1794. Fortunately, the Committee of Public Safety later found the letter beneath the mattress, and it was turned over to a member of the convention, Courtois, for safekeeping.‡ He protected it for twenty years before presenting it to Élisabeth's brother, the Comte de Provence, who was now sitting on the throne as Louis XVIII in the Bourbon Restoration.

The queen's daughter, Marie-Thérèse, is said to have fainted when she recognized her mother's writing, and she promised she "would live her life

---

* The authorities may not have wanted the queen's testament published; royalist sentiment was revived when Louis XVI's testament was circulated just days after his execution.

† Marie Antoinette did not write this letter entirely in her own hand; the last page bears the following five signatures: A. Q. Fouquier, Lecointre, Legot, Guffroy, and Massieu.

‡ Edme Bonaventure Courtois was a member of the commission in charge of the inventory of Robespierre's papers, including Marie Antoinette's last testament.

devoted to the memory of her parents and to serving and promoting the Bourbon cause."

Curiously, Marie-Thérèse had visits from her mother's lover, Axel von Fersen, but the princess appeared cold and standoffish, not allowing him a private audience. Was the princess too emotionally vulnerable to meet someone who would remind her of a horrific past, including the ill-fated flight to Varennes, which the Swedish count had organized? Or, loving her father more than her mother, was she ashamed of the count's relationship with the queen? Worse yet, did she possibly believe that her brother was actually fathered by the count?

Just six years after Marie Antoinette's death, the Swedish government sent Fersen to the Congress of Rastatt,★ but Napoleon told Baron Edelsheim that he would not negotiate with Fersen due to his royalist affiliations, and also because he "had slept with the queen." The remark, "avait couché avec la reine," was obscene at a time when one would have normally only said "had relations with the queen."

When Edelsheim reported this to Fersen, according to historian Stefan Zweig, Fersen simply lowered his head. He did not say Napoleon was lying, nor did he defend the queen's reputation. His silence spoke louder than words.

★ The Second Congress of Rastatt, November 1797, was held to negotiate a general peace between the French Republic and the Holy Roman Empire.

18

GUILTY?

If there is a man who commits adultery with another man's wife, or
who commits adultery with his friend's wife, the adulterer and the
adulteress shall surely be put to death.

—Leviticus 20:10 (NASB)

In France, there was no death penalty in the eighteenth century for adultery; it was a century of "false eloquence" during which writers and poets endeavored to ridicule fidelity. Gentlemen, courtiers, nobles, and royals alike extolled adultery, prostitution, and the corruption of innocence. King Louis XVI, unlike his predecessors who ruled at Versailles, could not be included in this depraved group.

That is not to say there were no projects to induce the timid Louis XVI to debauchery. When the king showed extraordinary interest in Louise Contat's performance as Suzanne in the *Marriage of Figaro*, his advisers had hopes that he might take her as his mistress, forcing Marie Antoinette into the background, similar to Louis XIV's queen Maria Theresa or Louis XV's Marie Leszczinska. However, their hopes were futile.

If Louis XVI was without a doubt innocent of any infidelity, what about Marie Antoinette? What is the verdict with respect to her alleged adultery at Versailles? Was she guilty of sexual infidelity with men, or at least with Axel von Fersen? Was she guilty of sexual infidelity with women? Or was she at least guilty of emotional infidelity?

The queen's fidelity had become a political issue by the onset of the revolution. General Lafayette had a project to force Louis XVI to divorce Queen Marie Antoinette. In order to intimidate the queen and force her to agree to divorce, Lafayette planned to blackmail her with threats of exposing her adultery. The Comte de la Marck confirmed this in a letter to Comte de Mercy on November 9, 1790: "[Lafayette] had, a few days ago, a long conference with the queen. He employed the most odious means to cause trouble in her soul, and she was even told that, in order to obtain a divorce, he would report on her adultery."

One might ask why the queen of France would ever consider committing adultery. Unable to consummate her marriage for seven years, Marie Antoinette may have struggled with low self-esteem. She was certainly humiliated by having to sleep next to a snoring, overweight, and often inebriated spouse with digestive problems who could not fulfill his royal duty. When Louis asked her one morning if she had slept well, she answered, "Yes, very well, because no one was there to keep me from it."

In a sense, Marie Antoinette was emotionally abused. Her husband was obsessed with hunting, tinkering in his workshop, and satisfying himself with food and drink at the royal buffet. He left his wife feeling bored, neglected, lonely, and longing for the excitement of being young and sexually attractive—which only left her open for emotional attachment in another's arms, whether male or female. When suffering from boredom, especially in the first years of their marriage, Marie Antoinette found the perfect accomplice for thrill-seeking in her charismatic brother-in-law, the Comte d'Artois. They amused themselves at the opera, at masquerade balls incognito, at the gambling tables, and with horse racing, nocturnal promenades, and the scandalous déscampativos. They amused others, too, with their characterizations in the obscene pamphlets that flourished throughout Europe.

Many of Marie Antoinette's contemporaries believed that her private conduct went far beyond the limits of mere naivete. Even those who acknowledged her moral innocence conceded that she displayed a lightness of behavior, or *légèreté*, which could be easily misconstrued. After all, Marie Antoinette spent most of her time at the center of a small intimate circle, to which higher nobility were seldom admitted, including her husband; moreover, the character of the members of this circle was debauched and corrupt in the eyes of the aristocracy as well as her majesty's subjects. Historian Thomas Wright wrote, "Her personal attachments were violent and unduly demonstrative, and, as is generally the result, of short duration."

Thus, the question remains: could Marie Antoinette have been guilty of committing adultery? In eighteenth-century France, adultery had to be proved by either "witnesses" to the sexual act or some strong tangible evidence of guilt, such as pregnancy or catching a venereal disease. Witnessing such illicit acts normally followed a set of "pre-determined and time-worn" forms that were enshrined in legal texts: "Depositions hinged on legally sanctioned acts of clandestine surveillance: peering through cracks in walls, chinks in curtains or hangings, or the keyholes of locked doors."

A confession on the part of the guilty party provided the strongest grounds for proof, but "such material was often not forthcoming." However, evidence that the accused had the chance to have sexual relations coupled with a desire, or opportunity and inclination, might have been sufficient to prove guilt. A legal source reported,

> Letters in which the accused parties have written about their amorous feelings or clandestine encounters may be introduced in court to support the assertion that the parties had the inclination to engage in sexual relations. Character evidence indicating the good or bad reputation of each party may be brought before the jury. Evidence of a woman's sexual relationships with men other than the party to the adultery generally cannot be used; however, if her reputation as a prostitute can be demonstrated, it may be offered as evidence.

Marie Antoinette was certainly not a prostitute, but she did leave a record of amorous letters written to her favorites, especially the Princesse de Lamballe, Madame de Polignac, and Count Axel von Fersen.

To the princess she wrote, "Farewell, my dear Lamballe, I embrace you with the best of my heart as I will love you all my life." And to Madame de Polignac she wrote, "I cannot resist the pleasure of kissing you again." Fortunately, same-sex relationships between women lacked recognition in the eyes of the law; however, sexual contact with other women was on rare occasions cited as "additional evidence of a woman's licentious character."

Finally, Marie Antoinette wrote Fersen, "I will finish, but not without telling you, my dear and tender friend, that I love you madly and there will never ever be a moment without adoring you." Her clandestine encounters and rendezvous were too numerous to cite, but Fersen's nocturnal visits at Versailles, the Château de Saint-Cloud, and the Tuileries Palace have all been well documented.

Fersen confirms staying overnight with the queen in his diary, and historian Imbert de Saint-Amand narrated the rendezvous:

> He left Stockholm under an assumed name and with the passport of a Swedish courier and reached Paris without incident on February 13, 1792. He was so adroit and prudent that no one suspected his presence. On the very evening of his arrival he wrote in his journal: "Went to the Queen by my usual road; very few National Guards; did not see the King."

Fersen had entered the palace under darkness by a private entrance to which he had a key. Fortunately on this evening the entrance was unguarded. Stefan Zweig reported, "He effected his entry unobserved. After eight months of cruel severance, eight months during which the world had changed, Fersen and Marie Antoinette were together for the last time."

Would Marie Antoinette have felt guilty for committing adultery, or even be judged as guilty by those in her intimate circle? Perhaps not, considering that sexual relations with Louis were unfulfilling, if not lacking. He was often absent or simply not interested, leaving his sexually deprived queen feeling justified in seeking a relationship elsewhere. The relationships may have been sporadic and casual at first, since there were no children involved; however, once an heir to the throne was provided to the House of Bourbon, a romantic affair could be more plausible—the queen was no longer pressured into sexual relations with the king.

From the viewpoint of the queen's subjects, adultery was a crime of larceny in that it passed off illegitimate children as heirs, an occurrence also feared by the princes of the blood. It was homicide in that an adulterous woman was murdering two souls, hers and her lover's. And finally, it was considered idolatry for a woman to worship her lover instead of her husband.

The church would have thought differently: adultery was a sin of lust, it was fornication, and it was wrong. But we have to remember that it was not anything unusual at the vile Château of Versailles ever since the days of Louis XIII. By the eighteenth century, the regent's mother, Elizabeth Charlotte, wrote of the moral situation at court:

> All the youth of both sexes lead a most reprehensible life in France; the more it is out of order, the better. They do not follow my example of having regular hours, and I am very determined not to take as a model their conduct, which seems to me that of pigs and sows. Now, more than ever, one needs the grace of God, because ours is a terrible time; we hear of nothing but quarrels, disputes, robberies, murders, and vices of all kinds. The old serpent, the devil, has been delivered from his chains and his reign in the air. All good Christians must therefore give themselves up to prayer.

Interestingly enough, Louis XIII did give himself up to prayer when his physician told him he had but two hours to live: "Well, my God, I consent with all my heart." His son, Louis XIV, who was known for years of adultery and infidelity, went a step further by marrying the pious Madame de Maintenon, who exercised an extraordinary ascendancy and powerful religious influence over him for the last thirty years of his life.

Even more depraved, Louis XV, despite his transgressions of the Seventh Commandment,★ was religious and scrupulously observed the final rites. When he became deathly ill while in battle in Metz in 1744, he confessed his sins, but the priest could not give him absolution until he "asked pardon for the scandal which he had caused and sent away" his mistress Marie-Anne de Mailly, the Duchesse de Châteauroux, who had been his "war-baggage." The weeping king complied.

Before dying in 1774, Louis XV was instructed to prepare for the final rites, and that same evening, he informed Madame du Barry, "We cannot recommence the scandal of Metz. If I had known what I know now, you would not have been admitted. I owe it to God and to my people. Therefore, you have to leave tomorrow." She left, and he received his final rites.

In each of these three reigns at Versailles, the kings were sinners and the queens were saints. Not so, however, in the reign of Louis XVI, who was more or less the saint, and his queen, Marie Antoinette, who was essentially the sinner. However, she too gave herself up to prayer, asking for forgiveness in the *dernière lettre* to Madame Élisabeth: "I sincerely ask pardon of God for all the errors I may have committed during my life."

Although repentant, was Marie Antoinette still guilty of intrigue, infidelity, and adultery to the point of exposure to sexually transmitted disease? Perhaps revisiting a text on the subject at the time of her death could shed light on this dilemma: "Not only is there no known instance of God forgiving an unrepentant sinner; God cannot forgive an unrepentant sinner. God is merciful to the repentant. How merciful and indulgent God is to repentant sinners."

Final Verdict. The empress Maria Theresa, for political purposes, condemned her daughter, the radiant Marie Antoinette, to a life in the vile environment of the Château of Versailles. The Austrian princess, a central figure at court, stood before the public gaze and her gaieties were the topic of daily gossip. She ruled her weak and lethargic husband, for whom she had little love in the earlier years of their marriage and for whom perhaps no passion ever existed at all. The king could not provide his queen those conditions that are essential to the life of a young wife. Was Marie Antoinette still guilty for seeking consolation elsewhere?

Yes, but she was also forgiven.

★ "Thou shalt not commit adultery."

ACKNOWLEDGMENTS

There are a number of people I must thank for their help with guiding this project. First, I must express my gratitude to the staff at Rowman & Littlefield and especially my editors, Susan McEachern and Katelyn Turner, whose patience and invaluable advice were exemplary. Also, Janice Braunstein, the book's project editor, and Chloe Batch, the cover designer, have contributed so skillfully to make this book possible.

Second, I can never forget the supportive staffs at the libraries and archives I visited while researching and writing this book, including the National Archives and the National Library of France, the Ohio State University Library, and the National Archives of Sweden. It is also with the deepest gratitude that I acknowledge the handwriting analysis by Marie Antoinette's graphologist, Bella Choji; the expert assistance for her natal chart from the Astrology House New Zealand; and the invaluable assistance in French from Stéphane Gagnon and Jean-François Robichon.

Finally, recognition must go to my family, who has always supported and encouraged me, even though the miles between us were many at times. It saddens me that my mother and grandmother cannot see this book—they would have been so proud. My brother, however, remains a constant source of inspiration, and this book is lovingly dedicated to him.

NOTES

AUTHOR'S NOTE

ix   *If it can happen that we feel thirsty*: Plato, *The Republic*, trans. John Llewelyn Davies and David James Vaughan, 2nd ed. (1860; repr., London: University Press for Macmillan, 1866), 143.

ix   **"the so little-known intimate life of the royal family"**: Pierre de Nolhac, *Études sur la cour de France: Marie-Antoinette dauphine, d'après de nouveaux documents* (Paris: Calmann-Lévy, 1898), 336. "La vie intérieure encore si mal connue de la famille royale."

INTRODUCTION

xi   *The throne is debased by indecency*: Maria Theresa, Comte Florimond-Claude de Mercy-Argenteau, and Marie-Antoinette, "Comte Florimond-Claude de Mercy-Argenteau," in *Correspondance secrète entre Marie-Thérèse et le Comte de Mercy-Argenteau avec les lettres de Marie-Thérèse et de Marie-Antoinette*, vol. 1 (Paris: Firmin Didot Frères, 1874), 154. "Le trône y est avili par l'indécence et l'extension du crédit de la favorite et par la méchanceté de ses partisans. La nation s'exhale en propos séditieux, en écrits indécents où la personne du monarque n'est point épargnée; Versailles est devenu le séjour des perfidies, des haines et des vengeances tout s'y opère par des intrigues et des vues personnelles, et il semble qu'on y ait renoncé à tout sentiment d'honnêteté."

xi   **By focusing on the enigmatic Versailles**: Stuart Lieberman, "A transgenerational theory," *Journal of Family Therapy* 1 (1979): 347–60. Such transgenerational transmission is the result of repetition of themes, perceptions, and behavioral patterns from one generation to the next. Although inheritance includes physical characteristics such as height, sex, and eye color, some mental traits are inherited as ranges of possibility depending on the environment, such as emotional reactivity or emotional responses to different situations.

Taking this a step further, Lebovici's "pathology of destiny" refers to trans-generational transmission in which a child is born with a predetermined role or mission in life. This aligns well with the Bourbons predetermining the roles and obligations of young princes and princesses, whereby parents interacted with and educated them in ways that represented their own upbringing and that of their royal ancestors. One of the most important roles of Bourbon princes and their princesses has been to produce an heir (and a spare) to the throne to guarantee the survival of the monarchy. But as we will see, Marie Antoinette's role was twofold; not only did she need an heir for the Bourbon line, she also needed an heir to secure her place without repudiation at court as the future queen of France and, subsequently, to exert the influence of her mother, Empress Maria Theresa of Austria, on French foreign policy.

xi   **this is called emotional genealogy**: Judith Lynn Fein, *The Spoon from Minkowitz: A Bittersweet Roots Journey to Ancestral Lands* (Santa Fe, NM: Global Adventure, 2013). Fein discusses emotional genealogy: "It is not only the stories that are told and have been handed down, but it is also the family behavior patterns that are transmitted. There are positive behaviors—like optimism, the thirst for social justice, kindness, an artistic or musical bent—but also the dark ones like rage, violence, lying, addiction, stonewalling silence."

xii   **The characters, however, are all far from simple**: Baron de Zur-Lauben, *Histoire militaire des Suisses au service de la France, avec les pièces justificatives*, vol. 3 (Paris: Desaint & Saillant, 1751), 389.

xii   **Ages of majority were set at the age of thirteen**: Sharon L. Jansen, *Anne of France: Lessons for My Daughter* (Cambridge, MA: Tamesis Books, 2012), 91–92. "By the terms of a statute of 1374, the age and legal majority of a king of France was defined as the heir's attainment of his 'fourteenth year.' There was some ambiguity in this law."

xii   **As we shall see, Louis XIV's governess would take her rank to the next level**: Roland Mousnier, *The Institutions of France under the Absolute Monarchy, 1598–1789: The Organs of State and Society*, vol. 2 (Chicago: University of Chicago Press, 1979), 5.

CHAPTER 1

3   *I am going to Versailles tomorrow*: Jean d'Elbée, *Le Mystère de Louis XIII* (Lyon: France: H. Lardanchet, 1943), 23. "Je m'en vais demain à Versailles pour deux ou trois jours. J'ai trouvé le sexe féminin avec aussi peu de sens et aussi impertinent en leurs questions qu'ils ont accoutumé. Il m'ennuie bien que la Reine ne soit accouchée pour m'en retourner en Picardie si vous le jugez à propos ou ailleurs pourvu que je sois hors d'avec toutes ces femmes, il m'importe où."

3   **a small river of sewer water**: Louis Dussieux, *Le château de Versailles: Histoire et description* (Versailles, France: L. Bernard, 1881), 2.

3 **Henri IV regularly hunted in this area**: Société des sciences morales, *Mémoires de la Société des sciences morales, des lettres et des arts de Seine-et-Oise* (Versailles, France: Author, 1880), 406.

3 **the melancholic Louis found joy**: Katherine Alexandra Patmore, *The Court of Louis XIII* (London: Methuen, 1909), 10–12.

3 **Louis decided to build his own pavilion**: Jean-Claude Guillou, "Le Domaine de Louis XIII à Versailles," *Versalia* 3 (2000): 87.

3 **the mason Nicolas Huaut began work**: Comte Alexandre de Laborde, *Versailles: Ancien et Moderne* (Paris: Imprimerie Schneider et Langrand, 1844), 158.

3 **a graceful, but small, castle**: Dussieux, *Le château de Versailles*, 2. "Versailles" appears for the first time in a charter of the eleventh century.

3 **But Louis was content**: André Pératé, *Versailles: The Palace, the Gardens, the Trianons, the Museum, the City* (Paris: H. Laurens, 1922), 5–8.

4 **better than sleeping on a mattress of straw**: Jean Héroard, *Journal sur l'enfance et la jeunesse de Louis XIII* (Paris: Firmin Didot, 1868), xxv.

4 **When the king stayed at the pavilion**: Jacques Levron, *Daily Life at Versailles in the Seventeenth and Eighteenth Centuries* (New York: Macmillan, 1968), 19.

5 **although legal oppression against homosexuality was severe**: Louis Crompton, *Homosexuality and Civilization* (Cambridge, MA: Harvard University Press, 2009), 321.

5 **had enfeebled her stuttering Louis**: Héroard, *Journal sur l'enfance*, xix.

5 **"that only death could extinguish"** (*seule la mort abolit*): Pierre Chevallier, "Les Étranges Amours du Roi Louis XIII," *Historama* 336 (1979): 1.

5 **the wedding night appeared to have been a disaster**: J. M. Guardia, *La médecine à travers les siècles: Histoire et philosophie* (Paris: J.-B. Baillière et fils, 1865), 318. "Revenons à Louis XIII, qui lisait peu ces auteurs, et à qui ce vers ne saurait s'appliquer tout entier; car il n'aima jamais une femme, non pas même la sienne, bien que, marié jeune et mis en demeure de faire acte de virilité avant l'âge d'homme, il eût été comme conduit par la main à cueillir les fruits précoces de l'amour."

6 **it only produced "pain and fatigue"**: Guardia, *La médecine*, 320. "La consommation était purement illusoire, et le roi avoua plus tard qu'il n'avait conservé que de douloureux souvenirs de cette nuit de noces dont la politique de la régente avait fait dresser le procès-verbal."

7 **The king's passion for the duke**: Kate van Orden, *Music, Discipline, and Arms in Early Modern France* (Chicago: University of Chicago Press, 2005), 111.

7 **who "lasted the longest but was loved the least"**: Chevallier, "Les Étranges Amours," 1.

7 **was susceptible to "bouts of jealousy"**: Guardia, *La médecine*, 316. "Remarquons toutefois que Tallemant des Réaux a dit expressément que les amours de Louis XIII étaient d'étranges amours, à l'endroit où il en parle comme d'un amoureux transi et susceptible tout au plus de jalousie."

7 **a handsome young subject selected as "an amusement"**: Robert Aldrich and Garry Wotherspoon, *Who's Who in Gay and Lesbian History: From Antiquity to World War II* (London: Routledge, 2002), 511.

8 **The king would summon Cinq-Mars**: A. Lloyd Moote, *Louis XIII, the Just* (Berkeley: University of California Press, 1991), 286.

8 **"his affections now belonged to Cinq-Mars"**: Moote, *Louis XIII*, 285.

8 **the king loved him "esperdument"**: Moote, *Louis XIII*, 285. "Louis *'l'aimait esperdument'*—that he loved the youth to distraction."

8 **When the court poet Boisrobert**: Wayne R. Dynes, *Encyclopedia of Homosexuality* (New York: Routledge, 2016), 156. Boisrobert also earned the sobriquet of "the mayor of Sodom."

8 **the king objected to the words "with desire"**: Tallemant des Réaux, *Les historiettes de Tallemant des Réaux* (Paris: J. Techener, 1854), 240.

8 **The poet then recounted unsurprisingly with a new verse**: Réaux, *Les historiettes*, 241.

8 **and a "large dormitory for men only"**: Lucy Norton, *The Sun King and His Loves* (London: H. Hamilton, 1983), 13.

9 **she openly vied for Gaston's admiration**: John Stevens Cabot Abbott, *Louis XIV* (New York: Harper & Brothers, 1898), 14.

9 **The king was forced to seek shelter**: d'Elbée, *Le Mystère*, 35.

9 **The royal marriage deteriorated**: Moote, *Louis XIII*, 147.

9 **Richelieu seemed to have foreseen this**: M. Wolowski, *Revue des cours littéraires de la France et de l'étranger littérature, philosophie, théologie, éloquence* (Paris: Germer Baillière, 1867), 657.

9 **the child was the son of Cardinal Mazarin**: Richard Wilkinson, *Louis XIV* (New York: Routledge, 2017), 14. One of Louis XIV's biographers, Anthony Levi, is convinced that Cardinal Mazarin, Anne's lover, future chief minister and possible husband, was the father of Louis XIV.

10 **The birth of the future Louis XIV**: Wilkinson, *Louis XIV*, 38.

CHAPTER 2

11 *Another motive further forced Louis XIV*: Charles Duclos, *Mémoires secrets sur le règne de Louis XIV, la Régence et le règne de Louis XV* (Paris: Firmin-Didot Frères, 1846), 112. "Un autre motif éloignait encore Louis XIV de sa capitale; il craignait d'abord d'exposer le scandale de ses amours aux yeux de la bourgeoisie, la seule classe de la société où la décence des mœurs subsiste ou subsistait encore. Mais bientôt il se lassa de tant de circonspection. Madame de la Vallière fut la première maîtresse déclarée, et il la fit duchesse de Vaujour. Cette femme, d'un caractère doux, incapable de nuire, même de se venger, en cédant à sa faiblesse pour le roi, regrettait sa vertu. Ses remords, encore plus que les dégoûts causés par une rivale, la conduisirent aux Carmélites, où elle vécut trente-six ans dans la plus dure pénitence. Elle n'était pas encore retirée de la cour, que la marquise de Montespan lui avait déjà enlevé le cœur du roi."

11 **A third nurse fled the scene**: Augustin Cabanès, *Le Cabinet secret de l'histoire* (Paris: Albin Michel, 1900), 151. "Il y a des enfants voraces, écrit un médecin contemporain du Grand Roi 2, qui, ne trouvant pas suffisamment de lait pour les

rassasier, sucent le mamelon avec tant de violence, qu'il y vient des fentes et des crevasses à la base, où il semble se vouloir séparer de la mamelle. Ce malheur est arrivé à plusieurs nourrices du Roi."

11 **Although she was warned**: Jean Balteau, *Dictionnaire de Biographie Française* (Paris: Letouzey et Ané, 1939), 82. "ANCELIN (Perrette DUFOUR, dame), nourrice de Louis XIV, était la femme d'Etienne Ancelin, voiturier de Poissy, lorsqu'elle fut choisie pour remplacer Elisabeth Ansel auprès du jeune dauphin, qui avait alors six mois. Elle le nourrit pendant 18 mois car on ne le sevra qu'en septembre 1640. La charge était assez dure; elle ne fut guérie des morsures de son nourrisson que par l'apposition du doigt de Sainte-Anne."

13 **thus magnifying Louis XIII's modest inheritance**: Pératé, *Versailles, France*, 10.

14 **"I do, sir, post this from my hand"**: Alfred Baudrillart, *Philippe V et la Cour de France: D'après les documents inédits tirés des archives espagnoles de Simancas et d'Alcala de Hénarès et des archives du Ministère des Affaires étrangères* (Paris: Firmin Didot, 1748), 47. "J'ai eu avis que cette Infante a toutes les dents pourries et qu'elle est rousse, deux choses, et surtout la seconde, qui seraient capables d'inspirer un grand dégoût à M. le Dauphin et d'avoir des suites très facheuses."

14 **"Girls swooned, their mothers shuddered"**: Amédée Renée, *Les nièces de Mazarin* (Paris: Firmin Didot, 1856), 178.

14 **Not unlike his father, Louis XIV**: Arthur Tilley, *The Decline of the Age of Louis XIV* (Cambridge: Cambridge University Press, 1929), 16.

14 **At an early age, Louis had shown**: Claude Dulong, *L'Amour au XVII Siècle* (Paris: Hachette, 1969), 114.

14 **The queen mother had Isabelle banished**: Alain Baraton, *L'Amour à Versailles* (Paris: Grasset & Fasquelle, 2009), 38–39.

15 **"what he would later practice so well with women"**: Edme Thédore Bourg, *Amours et galanteries des rois de France: Mémoires historiques sur les concubines, maitresses et favorites de ces princes* (Brussels, Belgium: Louis Tencé, 1830), 7. "Catherine-Henriette Belier, femme de Pierre de Beauvais, seigneur de Gentilly, première femme de chambre de la reine-mère (Anne d'Autriche), et sa favorite, est la première personne qui ait touché le cœur de Louis XIV. Le roi avait alors quatorze ou quinze ans, et la dame de Beauvais environ quarante-cinq; sa fille, Jeanne-Baptiste de Beauvais, qui épousa, le 6 novembre 1656, le marquis de Richelieu, était née en 1635, trois ans avant le roi."

15 **she had more than one such liaison**: Bourg, *Amours et galanteries*, 151.

15 **In the beginning of May, in the year 1655**: Henri Fournier, *Journal des maladies cutanées et syphilitiques* (Paris: Administration et Rédaction, 1898), 122. "Au commencement du mois de mai de l'année 1655, poursuit Vallot, un peu auparavant que d'aller à la guerre, l'on me donna avis que les chemises du roi étaient gâtées d'une matière qui donna soupçon de quelque mal, à quoi il était besoin de prendre garde. Les personnes qui me donnèrent les premiers avis n'étaient pas bien informées de la nature et de la qualité du mal, croyant d'abord que c'était ou quelque pollution, ou quelque maladie vénérienne; mais après avoir bien examiné toutes choses, je tombai dans d'autres sentiments et me persuadai que cet accident était de plus grande importance je n'avais pour lors de doute de la pureté de sa vie, non plus que de sa chasteté."

15 **As for the cause of the problem**: Fournier, *Journal des maladies*, 125. Moreover, the therapy, quite bizarre as it is, put into use by Vallot, is in favor of the hypothesis of a venereal disease. In the beginning, the first doctor administers antiphlogistics (bleeding) and purgatives. More quickly, he submits his patient for three weeks to a tonic treatment. "His Majesty drank, for the usual drink, a decoction of rind of stag horn and ivory, in which I sometimes dissolve two or three grains of salt of March. Then it varies with other tablets, made with "diaphoretic gold, prepared pearls and *specificum stomachicum*." It less explained "the enemas on the parts and the chest with the essence of ants, the spirit of crayfish prepared according to my recipe, and the balm of Peru."

16 **Vallot added that the infection**: Fournier, *Journal des maladies*, 124.

16 **"Under which show for us"**: Fournier, *Journal des maladies*, 125. "Sous quel spectacle pour nous, / Et d'où peut procéder en nous / Le changement qu'on y remarque? / Sur quelle herbe avez-vous marché, / Quoy, faut-il qu'un si grand monarque / Devienne un si grand desbauché? / C'est l'ordre que vos jeunes ans / S'attachent aux sujets plaisants, / Et qu'ils ne demandent qu'à rire; / Mais ne soyez point emporté, / Esvitez la desbauche, sire, / Passe pour la fragilité. / Il n'est ny censeur, ny Régent / Qui ne soit assez indulgent / Aux vœux d'une jeunesse extresme, / Et pour embellir vostre cour, / Qui ne trouve excusable mesme / Que vous ayez un peu d'amour. / Mais d'en user comme cela / Et de courir par ci par là / Sans vous arrester à quelqu'une, / Que tout vous soit bon, tout égal, / La blonde autant que la brune / Ha! Sire c'est un fort grand mal."

16 **Among these mistresses**: I.W.F., *The Story of Louise de la Vallière* (Norwich, UK: Fletcher and Son, 1870), 11.

16 **Ashamed of her affair**: Eleanor Herman, *Sex with Kings* (New York: HarperCollins, 2004), 222.

17 **He was in his father's good graces until**: Guillaume Dubois, *Memoirs of Cardinal Dubois* (London: Leonard Smithers, 1899), 103.

17 **"These young people had pushed their debauchery"**: Marquis de Sourches, *Mémoires du Marquis de Sourches sur le Règne de Louis XIV* (Paris: Librairie Hachette, 1882), 110. "Tous ces jeunes gens avoient poussé leurs débauches dans des excès horribles, et la cour étoit devenue une petite Sodome."

17 **"The Looseness of all the ladies"**: Edmond Locard, *Les crimes de sang et les crimes d'amour au XVIIe siècle* (Lyon, France: A. Storck et Cie., 1903), 211.

18 **The brotherhood grew momentum**: Locard, *Les crimes de sang*, 212–14.

19 **The young Comte de Vermandois**: Dynes, *Encyclopedia of Homosexuality*, 423.

20 **Consequently, the count died**: M. Zimmerman, *The Edinburgh magazine, or Literary miscellany* (Edinburgh: J. Sibbald, 1789), 345. Count de Vermandois was taken ill on the twelfth of November in the evening, a malignant fever appeared the next day, and he died on the eighteenth.

20 **"I ought to weep"**: Crompton, *Homosexuality and Civilization*, 340.

20 **Louis XIV thus had a homosexual father**: Louis-Georges Tin, *The Dictionary of Homophobia: A Global History of Gay and Lesbian Experience* (Vancouver: Arsenal Pulp Press, 2008), 68.

20 **The scandal was so public**: Mademoiselle de Montpensier, *Memoires* (Amsterdam: Jean-Frederic Bernard, 1729), 168.

21 **The eccentric prince Philippe**: James Eugene Farmer, *Versailles and the Court Under Louis XIV* (Versailles, France: Century, 1905), 302.

21 **especially his court composer**: Edouard Foucaud, *Histoire du théâtre en France* (Paris: Publications Modernes, 1845), 361. "Lully composait presque tous ses opéras lorsque la débauche avait exalté son cerveau."

21 **Louis XIV's own adulterous affairs**: These included Catherine Charlotte de Gramont, Bonne de Pons d'Heudicourt, Isabelle de Ludres, Marie Mancini, Claude de Vin des Œillets, Anne de Rohan-Chabot, Olympia Mancini, and Countess of Soissons, to name a few.

21 **"Is this the Madame that scandalizes all France?"**: Chad Denton, *Decadence, Radicalism, and the Early Modern French Nobility: The Enlightened and Depraved* (Lanham, MD: Lexington Books, 2017), 97.

21 **After a short separation**: Eliakim Littell, "Madame de Maintenon," *Living Age* 21 (1849): 151.

21 **Curiously, the upbringing of the children**: M. de la Beaumelle, *Memoirs for the History of Madame de Maintenon and of the Last Age* (London: A. Millar and J. Nourse, 1757), 287–88.

22 **Many found the ambitions**: Richard Bentley, *Bentley's Miscellany* (London: Richard Bentley, 1860), 314–15.

22 **Madame de Montespan said**: Bentley, *Bentley's Miscellany*, 315.

23 **"Ah!" said the former mistress**: Jean G. D. Armengaud, *Les Reines du monde par Nos Premiers Ecrivains* (Paris: Lahure, 1862), 7.

23 **Mademoiselle de Fontanges did not add**: Bentley, *Bentley's Miscellany*, 316.

23 **"teeming hotbed of subservience"**: Winston Churchill, *Marlborough: His Life and Times* (London: C. Scribner's Sons, 1933), 258.

23 **and the stench was becoming unbearable**: Anonymous, "A Victim of Paris and Versailles," *Macmillan's Magazine* 24 (1871): 494.

23 **There were no bathrooms**: Marie-Luise Gothein and Walter P. Wright, *History of Garden Art* (London: J. M. Dent & Sons, 1913), 746.

23 **along with a propensity for scandal**: George Potts, *The Preacher and the King* (London: T. Nelson & Sons, 1853), 6.

23 **These included luxuries**: Tilley, *Decline of the Age*, 42.

24 **The result of his carnal appetite**: Gerald James Stine, *The Biology of Sexually Transmitted Diseases* (Dubuque, IA: W. C. Brown, 1992), 259. Louis was thoroughly riddled with syphilis and gout, among other ailments.

CHAPTER 3

25 *All the passions at Versailles*: Jeanne Antoinette Poisson de Pompadour, *Mémoires de Madame la marquise de Pompadour* (Liège, Belgium: À Liège, 1766), 8.

25 **"Never forget your obligations"**: Ernest Moret, *Quinze ans du règne de Louis XIV* (Paris: Didier et Cie, 1859), 443.

25 **While Louis was on his deathbed**: Ragnhild Marie Hatton, *Louis XIV and Absolution* (London: Springer, 1976), 130. "Louis XIV designates his son the duke of Maine, bastard legitimized, to exercise the real power (regency), while the Duke of Orleans, nephew and son-in-law of the king (he had to marry in 1692 a legitimate girl, sister of the duke of Maine, whom the late king had also had from Madame de Montespan), returns to the charge, purely honorific, of 'president of the council of regency.' On September 2, 1715, Philippe d'Orléans, who won the support of the members of the Parliament of Paris, was proclaimed Regent of the kingdom and effective owner of power, during the minority of the young Louis XV."

26 **Madame de Sévigné, sitting nearby**: Marie de Rabutin-Chantal, *Letters of Madame de Rabutin Chantal, Marchioness de Sévigné* (London: J. Hinton, 1745), 24.

26 **The household of the dauphin**: Mousnier, *Institutions of France*, 6.

26 **provided instructors in various disciplines**: Mousnier, *Institutions of France*, 5–6.

27 **The court returned to Versailles**: Jules Mazé, *La Cour de Louis XIV* (Paris: Hachette, 1944), 17.

27 **His buxom, fat-cheeked daughter**: Bentley, *Bentley's Miscellany*, 423. "The Duchess of Berry was called Joufflotte, from her fat cheeks, and *Beau Paon* [beautiful peacock] from her ostentatious manners."

28 **She could have complained**: Louis Bertrand, *La Vie amoureuse de Louis XIV* (Paris: Frédérique Patat, 1924), 1644.

28 **She certainly could have complained**: Mazé, *La Cour de Louis XIV*, 44.

28 **He neglected his queen**: Sylvanus Urban, *The Gentleman's Magazine* (London: John Bowyer Nichols & Son, 1850), 526. "Educated in such a state of society, what could be expected of Louis XV? Amiable, effeminate, indolent, sensual, he allowed the country to govern itself, and gave himself up to the companionship of a succession of mistresses."

29 **"There is talk of a Madame d'Etioles"**: Eugène Pelletan, *Décadence de la monarchie* (Paris: Pagnerre, 1861), 298.

30 **She therefore moved**: Pelletan, *Décadence de la monarchie*, 305.

30 **He then drove them at night**: Pelletan, *Décadence de la monarchie*, 306.

30 **These ladies were required to be virgins**: Pelletan, *Décadence de la monarchie*, 304. "La marquise voulut régulariser ce commerce; elle en prit la surintendance. Le Trébuchet faisait scandale au château; on le relégua au Parc-aux-Cerfs, rue Saint Méderic. Ce fut là, dans une petite maison borgne, tenue par la femme d'un commis de marine, nommée Bertrand, que la marquise établit le harem, au jour le jour, de Sa Majesté. Le recrutement puisait dans tous les états et dans toutes les conditions; des voitures fermées apportaient ou remportaient indéfiniment, toute l'année, aux heures muettes de la nuit, les voluptés anonymes du roi chrétien."

32 **The Parc-aux-Cerfs normally accommodated**: Mazé, *La Cour de Louis XIV*, 170.

32 **But the health of the king's mistress**: James Anthony Froude, *Fraser's Magazine* (London: John W. Parker, 1850), 163.

33 **"other than this creature"**: Mazé, *La Cour de Louis XIV*, 173.

34 **"The king honors me with his company"**: Leitch Ritchie, *Versailles* (London: Longman, 1839), 201.

34 **The Austrian chancellor, Prince Kaunitz**: Lady Younghusband, *Marie-Antoinette: Her Early Youth, 1770–1774* (London: Macmillan, 1912), iii. "Quant à notre petite, tout ira bien, pourvu qu'on ne la gâte pas."

À SAVOIR: MARIE ANTOINETTE'S HANDWRITING (VIENNA, AUSTRIA)

35 *Graphology is a scientific method*: Pierre Menard, *L'Ecriture et le Subconscient* (Avignon, France: Edouard Aubanel, 1951), 9.

35 **It is not an exact science**: Steven G. Rogelberg, *The SAGE Encyclopedia of Industrial and Organizational Psychology* (London: SAGE, 2016), 560.

35 **According to Menard**: Menard, *L'Ecriture et le Subconscient*, 22.

36 "Ma docilité vous récompensera de tous les soins que vous coûtent mon éducation, continuez-les-moi, ma chère amie, et soyez assurée de la tendresse de votre fidèlle élève. Antoine." [I hope that in the future] my docility will reward you for all the care that you cost my education, continue me, my dear friend, and be assured of the tenderness of your faithful pupil. Antoine.

36 "Soyez persuadée chère Durieu que je penserai toujours à vous et que je ne n'oublierai jamais les peines que vous avez eu avec moi ce dont vous assure / votre très fidèle / Antoine Archiduchesse." Be persuaded dear Durieu that I will always think of you and that I will never forget the sorrows you had with me is assured by you / your very faithful / Antoine Archiduchesse.

CHAPTER 4

41 *The education of Marie Antoinette*: Madame Jeanne-Louise-Henriette Campan, *Memoirs of the Private Life of Marie Antoinette, Queen of France and Navarre* (Philadelphia: A. Small, 1823), 45.

41 **Life at court was simple**: Hillaire Belloc, *Marie Antoinette* (New York: Doubleday, Page, 1909), 28.

41 **"I wager this diamond"**: Henry Francis, "Marie Antoinette," *Era Magazine: An Illustrated Monthly* 9 (1902): 503.

42 **"I have lost"**: Francis, "Marie Antoinette," 504. Metastasio: "Ho perduto: l'augusta figlia / A pagar m'ha, condamnato / Ma s'e vero ch'a voi simiglia / Tutto l'mundo ha guadagnato."

42 **The following day, the Archbishop of Vienna**: Thomas Edward Watson, *From the End of the Reign of Louis the Fifteenth to the Consulate of Napoleon* (London: Macmillan, 1900), 89–91.

42 **The king and queen of Portugal**: Christophe Félix Louis Ventre de la Touloubre, *Histoire de Marie Antoinette . . . Reine de France* (Paris: H. L. Perronneau, 1797), 13.

42 **"He seemed greatly pained"**: Lady Younghusband, *Marie Antoinette, Her Early Youth, 1770–1774* (London: Macmillan & Co., 1912), 4.

43 **Supper parties unknown to her**: Catherine Mary Charlton Bearne, *A Sister of Marie Antoinette: The Life-Story of Maria Carolina, Queen of Naples* (London: T. Fisher Unwin, 1907), 25–26.

43 **"By the court I mean the empress"**: Carl Eduard Vehse, *The Austrian Court* (Philadelphia: George Barrie & Sons, 1896), 223.

43 **Although Francis secretly arranged suppers**: Carl Eduard Vehse, *Memoirs of the Court and Aristocracy of Austria* (London: H. S. Nichols, 1896), 226. "Even as early as 1747, Podewils mentions in his despatch: 'He is fond of women, and formerly showed a particular attachment for the Countess Colloredo, the wife of the vice-chancellor; for Countess Palffy, maid of honour to the Empress, who afterwards married the Sardinian envoy, Count Canales; and for several others. He even secretly arranged suppers and other small gay parties with them; but the jealousy of the Empress compelled him to restrain himself. As soon as she remarks that he is particularly attentive to any lady, she pouts with him, and lets him feel her displeasure in a thousand ways. Being aware of his propensity for gallantry, she has him watched everywhere. People, however, will have it that, notwithstanding all these jealous precautions, he, under the pretext of going out shooting, still finds means to arrange parties fines.'"

44 **When the empress gave advice**: C. Beem and M. Taylor, *The Man behind the Queen: Male Consorts in History* (London: Palgrave Macmillan, 2014), 118.

44 **Francis eventually grew weary**: Vehse, *Memoirs of the Court*, 228.

44 **However, she "could not resist"**: Beem and Taylor, *Man behind the Queen*, 119.

45 **Francis lost upward of ten thousand ducats**: Vehse, *Memoirs of the Court*, 229.

45 **"My daughter must never behold"**: Horace Walpole, *Letters of Horace Walpole to Horace Mann* (London: Richard Bentley, 1843), 249.

46 **Having been so engaged**: Derek Beales, *Joseph II*, vol. 1, *In the Shadow of Maria Theresa, 1741–1780* (London: Cambridge University Press, 2008), 39.

46 **Marie Antoinette shared**: Maureen Fleming, *Elisabeth: Empress of Austria* (New York: C. Kendall & W. Sharp, 1935), 84.

48 **Unfortunately, the court of Versailles disapproved**: Francis, "Marie Antoinette," 507.

48 **The abbé did his best to correct the results**: Arthur Kleinschmidt, *Charakterbilder aus der französischen Revolution* (Vienna: A. Hartleben, 1889), 23. "Das Porträt der Erzherzogin von Ducreux bezauberte Ludwig XV., der neue Botschafter Graf Mercy d'Argenteau unterhandelte fortgesetzt mit Choiseul und sandte 1768 den Abbé Vermond nach Wien, um die Erzherzogin in der französischen Literatur zu unterrichten; aus Vermond's Berichten erfahren wir, wie leicht die Erzherzogin zerstreut und wie weit sie noch in allem zurück war, aber auch wie ihr Charakter, Herz und Verstand, vereint mit dem Liebreize ihres Aeusseren, alle Welt entzückten."

48 **she did learn to speak it gracefully**: Francis, "Marie Antoinette," 509–10.

48 **She had succumbed**: Edward Crankshaw, *The Habsburgs: Portrait of a Dynasty* (New York: Viking, 1971), 38.

48 **The empress was aware of her daughter's stubbornness**: Hannes Etzlstorfer, "Marie Antoinette," *Quarterly Review* 149–50 (1880): 76.

48 **troubling "high forehead"**: Will Bashor, *Marie Antoinette's Head: The Royal Hairdresser, the Queen, and the Revolution* (Guilford, CT: Lyons Press, 2013), 34.

48 **her pale strawberry blond hair**: Bashor, *Marie Antoinette's Head*, 33.

49 **She would have preferred**: Younghusband, *Marie Antoinette*, 100.

49 **"She has a rather high forehead"**: Younghusband, *Marie Antoinette*, 101.

49 **One eyewitness wrote**: Maxime de la Rocheterie, *Histoire de Marie-Antoinette* (Paris: Perrin, 1890), 12.

50 **As the procession of fifty-seven carriages**: Bashor, *Marie Antoinette's Head*, 21.

CHAPTER 5

51 *It is certain that this princess*: Antoine de Rivarol, *Mémoires de Rivarol, avec des notes et éclaircissements historiques* (Paris: Baudoin Frères, 1824), 514. "L'affaiblissement de l'étiquette est une autre source d'objections contre la reine. Par-là, dit-on, elle a diminué la considération et le respect des peuples. Il est certain que cette princesse, toujours plus près de son sexe que de son rang, s'est trop livrée aux charmes de la vie privée. Les rois sont des acteurs condamnés à ne pas quitter le théâtre."

51 **The two courts spared no expense**: John Stevens Cabot Abbott, *History of Maria Antoinette* (New York: Harper & Brothers, 1868), 21.

51 **The princess surely noticed**: Campan, *Memoirs of the Private Life*, 50.

52 **Louis XV, however, was enchanted**: Abbott, *History of Maria Antoinette*, 50–51.

52 **the old man seemed more inclined**: Stefan Zweig, *Marie Antoinette: The Portrait of an Average Woman* (New York: Grove Press, 2002), 16.

52 **Marie Antoinette arrived at the Château de La Muette**: Joseph Weber, *Mémoires concernant Marie-Antoinette, archiduchesse d'Autriche, reine de France* (London: G. Schulze, 1809), viii.

52 **Among those invited to dine**: Hugh Noel Williams, *Memoirs of Madame du Barry of the Court of Louis XV* (New York: Collier & Son, 1910), 130.

52 **When Marie Antoinette was asked**: Robert Bruce Douglas, *The Life and Times of Madame du Barry* (London: Léonard Smithers, 1896), 146.

54 **The table, adorned with twenty-two place settings**: Pierre Ennès, "Le surtout de mariage en porcelaine de Sèvres du Dauphin, 1769–1770," *Revue de l'Art* 76 (1987): 63–73. "La table compte vingt-deux couverts réservés à la famille du Roi et au sang royal; elle est entourée d'une balustrade de marbre, qui sépare les officiers servants de la foule des spectateurs incessamment renouvelée, suivant l'usage du grand couvert. Le premier service s'y fait en vaisselle d'or, les autres en vaisselle de vermeil. La Cour occupe les loges et les galeries. Sur l'avant-scène, au-dessous de l'écusson de France soutenu par des Renommées, deux salons latéraux fermés par des portières bleu et argent permettent le service par le fond de la scène. Au milieu, s'ouvre un grand salon de musique dans le style de la salle; sous l'arcade décorée des chiffres du Dauphin et de la Dauphine, on aperçoit M. Rebel, surintendant de la musique du Roi, le bâton d'orchestre à la main, et sur les gradins quatre-vingts symphonistes, qui jouent sans interruption pendant les deux heures et demie du souper."

54   **The radical press**: Pierre de Nolhac, *Versailles et la Cour de France: Marie Antoinette Dauphine* (Paris: L. Conard, 1929), 96. "Dix-neuf ans plus tard, un autre souper célèbre, et le dernier, aura lieu au même endroit, ce banquet des gardes-du-corps du 1er octobre 1789, où la Reine malheureuse sera acclamée et qui provoquera les journées révolutionnaires. La vie de Marie-Antoinette à Versailles va d'une soirée à l'autre, et son souvenir demeure inséparable de cette salle achevée pour son mariage et inaugurée par ses premiers triomphes."

54   **Louis XV jokingly told the dauphin**: Clifton Fadiman and Andre Bernard, *Bartlett's Book of Anecdotes* (Boston: Little, Brown, 2000), 336.

55   *Rien,* **meaning**: Abbé Guillaume Honoré Rocques de Montgaillard, *Histoire de France, depuis la fin du règne de Louis XVI jusqu'à l'année 1825* (Paris: Moutardier, 1827), 171.

55   **Under such a governor**: Charles Duke Yonge, *The Life of Marie Antoinette, Queen of France* (London: Harper & Brothers, 1876), 14.

55   **When a courtier once complimented**: Armand Fouquier, *Causes célèbres de tous les peuples* (Paris: Lebrun, 1858), 89. "Comme un courtisan le complimentait un jour sur la précocité de son intelligence: 'Vous vous trompez, répondit-il; ce n'est pas moi qui ai de l'esprit, c'est mon frère de Provence.'"

55   **"Nature seems to have denied"**: Justin C. Vovk, *In Destiny's Hands: Five Tragic Rulers, Children of Maria Theresa* (New York: iUniverse, 2010), 94.

55   **Finally, the curtain was closed**: André Castelot, *Les grandes heures de la Révolution française* (Paris: Perrin, 1962), 216.

56   **Newly arrived princesses**: Bashor, *Marie Antoinette's Head*, xix.

56   **Marie Antoinette detested**: Joan Haslip, *Madame du Barry: The Wages of Beauty* (London: Tauris Parke, 2005), 58.

56   **Her lively spirit and grace**: Alexandre Dumas, *Louis Quinze* (Paris: Cadot, 1849), 94.

56   **"The King has a thousand kindnesses"**: Alfred Ritter von Arneth, *Marie-Antoinette: Correspondance secrète entre Marie-Thérèse et le Comte de Mercy-Argenteau* (Paris: Firmin Didot Frères, 1875), 17. "Le Roi a mille bontés pour moi, et je l'aime tendrement, mais c'est à faire pitié la faiblesse qu'il a pour Mme du Barry, qui est la plus sotte et impertinente créature qui soit imaginable. Elle a joué tous les soirs avec nous à Marly; elle s'est trouvée deux fois à côté de moi, mais elle ne m'a point parlé et je n'ai point tâché justement de lier conversation avec elle; mais quand il le fallait, je lui ai pourtant parlé."

56   **This would give her husband's two younger brothers**: Zweig, *Marie Antoinette*, 30.

56   **"It's necessary to let him be"**: Maria Theresa, Mercy-Argenteau, and Marie-Antoinette, "Comte Florimond-Claude de Mercy-Argenteau," 13. "M. la dauphine renouvela ses promesses de suivre sans interruption les heures destinées à quelque occupation sérieuse, et j'en pris occasion d'entrer dans le plus grand détail sur la nécessité et l'utilité de cette méthode, et sur les inconvénients inévitables qu'il y aurait à s'en écarter. S. A. R. me dit qu'elle était contente du dauphin, qu'elle attribuait sa timidité et sa froideur au genre d'éducation qu'il avait reçu, mais que d'ailleurs il paraissait avoir un bon caractère, qu'elle était intimement persuadée que le dauphin

tenait au duc de la Vauguyon par l'habitude, par la crainte, mais nullement par affection ni confiance, qu'au reste ce prince était si réservé sur le chapitre des gens qui
l'entourent, que malgré plusieurs petites tentatives, elle n'avait jamais pu tirer de lui
un mot de nature à éclaircir ses doutes."

57 **And Madame du Barry reported**: Haslip, *Madame du Barry*, 68.

57 **Overall, the king was healthy**: Cabanès, *Le Cabinet Secret*, 114.

57 **The prince had to be castrated**: M.R.D.W., *Vie de Louis-Philippe-Joseph, Duc
d'Orléans* (London: Palais Saint-James, 1790), 27.

57 **The Princesse de Lamballe, however**: Arneth, *Marie-Antoinette*, ii–iii.

58 **which only created a stronger bond**: Eliakim Littell, "Memoirs of Marie Antoinette," *Living Age* 60 (1849): 26.

58 **Such scenes occurred, however**: Michel de Decker, *La Princesse de Lamballe* (Paris:
Librairie Académique Perrin, 1979), 84–85.

58 **The Comte de Mercy reported**: Blanche Christable Hardy, *The Princess de Lamballe: A Biography* (London: Archibald Constable, 1908), 52.

58 **As the dauphine's favorite**: Mathurin François Adolphe de Lescure, *La princesse de
Lamballe, Marie-Thérèse-Louise de Savoie-Carignan* (Paris: H. Plon, 1864), 64–68.

58 **When apart, Marie Antoinette would**: Arneth, *Marie-Antoinette*, ii. "Lorsqu'elle
était encore Dauphine, sa dame d'honneur, la comtesse de Noailles, lui donnait tous
les hivers, pendant le carnaval, un bal par semaine. L'appartement de la comtesse à
Versailles était petit et resserré, et ne pouvait réunir que les personnes » qui tenaient
à la cour par leurs charges, et un petit » nombre de celles qu'on choisissait parmi les
plus distinguées de Paris. Le Dauphin, Monsieur, M. le comte d'Artois, les princes
et princesses du sang, venaient à ces bals. Parmi ces princesses, madame de Lamballe
fut, dès les premiers bals, distinguée par la Reine, qui ne tarda pas à la traiter avec
amitié et avec confiance; c'était avec elle que la Reine s'entretenait le plus souvent
à part, et leur liaison devint bientôt très intime."

59 **It was with the Princesse de Lamballe**: Lescure, *La princesse de Lamballe*, 69.

60 **It was rumored**: Yonge, *Life of Marie Antoinette*, 42.

60 **Marie Antoinette, on the other hand**: Yonge, *Life of Marie Antoinette*, 56.

61 **This scandal was confirmed**: Mathurin François Adolphe de Lescure, *Correspondance secrète inédite sur Louis XVI, Marie-Antoinette, la cour et la ville de 1777 à 1792*
(Paris: H. Plon, 1866), 334.

61 **She told her mother**: Arneth, *Marie-Antoinette*, x. "Quant au comte d'Artois, il se
rendait agréable par cet esprit de dissipation et ce goût de plaisir qui devinrent fort
dangereux à sa belle-sœur, en l'entraînant au Bois, aux courses, aux bals de l'Opéra,
à tant de fêtes où son mari ne venait pas, et qui furent l'occasion de beaucoup de
calomnies. Marie-Antoinette ne conserva d'illusions, si jamais elle en eut aucune, ni
sur l'un ni sur l'autre de ces deux princes."

61 **The Comte d'Artois was also rumored**: Dena Goodman and Thomas E. Kaiser,
Marie Antoinette: Writings on the Body of a Queen (New York: Routledge, 2013), 18.

62 **However, the three aunts at court**: Rocheterie, *Histoire de Marie-Antoinette*, 31.

62 **Clumsy and plump**: Rocheterie, *Histoire de Marie-Antoinette*, 97.

62 **Madame Campan, the dauphine's reader**: Vovk, *In Destiny's Hands*, 94–95.

62   **The words "Moi, Carmelite, et le roi tout à Dieu"**: Anna Emma Challice, *Heroes, Philosophers, and Courtiers of the Time of Louis XVI* (London: Hurst and Blackett, 1863), 358.

62   **With the ascension of the favorite**: Rocheterie, *Histoire de Marie-Antoinette*, 51.

62   **Pretending to be caring advisers**: Arneth, *Marie-Antoinette*, 190.

63   **It was also rumored that Adélaïde**: Comtesse de Boigne, *Memoirs of the Comtesse de Boigne* (London: Charles Scribner's Sons, 1907), 49–50. "Current scandal asserted that Comte Louis de Narbonne was a son of Madame Adelaide, a rumour utterly false and absurd, though it is true that the Princess made enormous sacrifices to his caprices. Mme. de Narbonne, imperious as she was, was entirely dominated by the whims of Comte Louis. When he had committed any foolishness and was in want of money, her ill-temper was unbearable, and she vented it chiefly upon Madame Adelaide, making her house intolerable. After a few days the poor Princess would buy back her peace of mind in hard cash. In this way the Comte de Narbonne became possessed of enormous sums, which he procured without the least trouble and accepted as easily."

63   **"This will be precious"**: François Buloz, *Revue des deux mondes* (Paris: Au Bureau de la revue des deux mondes, 1874), 781.

63   **Finding his sister "more spirited"**: J. Michelet, *Histoire de France: Louis XV et Louis XVI* (Librairie Internationale, 1874), 28.

CHAPTER 6

65   *It is not necessary for a queen*: Rivarol, *Mémoires de Rivarol*, 514. "Il ne faut pas qu'une reine, qui doit vivre et mourir sur un trône réel, veuille goûter de cet empire fictif et passager que les grâces et la beauté donnent aux femmes ordinaires, et qui en fait des reines d'un moment."

65   **On the day of the wedding**: Philippe Delorme, *Marie-Antoinette: Épouse de Louis XVI, mère de Louis XVII* (Paris: Pygmalion Editions, 1999), 50.

65   **The wedding basket also included**: Susan Hiner, *Accessories to Modernity: Fashion and the Feminine in Nineteenth-Century France* (Philadelphia: University of Pennsylvania Press, 2011), 72.

65   **The culture of Versailles**: Pierre-Henri Biger, "Introduction à l'éventail européen aux XVII et XVIII siècles," *Seventeenth-Century French Studies* 36 (2014): 84–92.

65   **there were a number of ways to flutter**: J.P.A., *L'Esprit d'Addisson* (Yverdon, Switzerland: Société Littérature, 1777), 10. "Il y a une variété infinie de mouvements dont on peut faire usage dans l'agitation de l'éventail; il y a le mouvement fâché, le mouvement modeste, le mouvement craintif, le mouvement confus, le mouvement enjoué, & le mouvement amoureux; en un mot, il n'y a presque pas une passion de l'âme qui ne produise, dans un éventail, un mouvement analogue; en sorte, qu'à la seule inspection de l'éventail d'une femme disciplinée, je vous dirai fort bien si elle est de bonne humeur, si elle fait la mine, ou si elle rougit. J'ai vu quelquefois dans un éventail tant de courroux, qu'il eût été dangereux, pour

l'amant qui l'avait irrité, de s'approcher de son tourbillon; & dans d'autres moments, je l'ai vu exprimer une langueur si tendre, que j'étais charmé pour la dame, que son amant fût à une distance raisonnable."

67 **The ladies all opened their fans**: Gaston Maugras, *Le Duc de Lauzun et la Cour de Marie-Antoinette* (Paris: Plon-Nourrit, 1895), 337. "La Reine a paru affligé en apprenant cette mort. Le dimanche au soir, elle faisait assez tristement son jeu, lorsqu'un accident bien léger, mais rare, a égayé la scène. Le marquis du Lau, qui jouait au lansquenet, a laissé échapper un vent bruyant qui a étonné tout le cercle. Les dames ont joué de l'éventail pour cacher le rire que cet événement excitait, mais la Reine n'a pu s'empêcher d'éclater, et tout le monde en a fait autant."

67 **Studying the fan's intrinsic symbolism**: V. Pokrovski, *L'Élégante dans la littérature satirique du XVIIIe siècle* (Moscow: Musée Ostankino, 1903), 43. "Bâiller derrière son éventail: va-t-en, tu m'ennuies. Lever l'éventail vers l'épaule droite: je te hais. Abaisser l'éventail fermé vers le sol: je te méprise. Effleurer son œil droit de son éventail fermé: quand te verrai-je? Faire signe vers soi de l'éventail fermé: j'ai tout le temps envie d'être avec toi. Menacer de l'éventail fermé: ne sois pas trop audacieux. Soulever l'éventail de sa main droite: m'es-tu fidèle? Cacher ses yeux derrière son éventail: je t'aime. Proposer un éventail: tu me plais beaucoup. Dissimuler son oreille gauche sous son éventail fermé: ne dévoile pas notre secret. Porter l'éventail à son cœur: je t'appartiens pour la vie. Refermer très lentement son éventail: j'accepte tout."

67 **However, when the Duc de Lauzun presents**: Georges Bernier and Rosamond Bernier, *L'œil* (Paris: Imprimeries réunies, 1959), 58.

68 **When the dauphine visited the gardens**: Emmanuel de Valicourt, *Les favoris de la reine: Dans l'intimité de Marie-Antoinette* (Paris: Tallandier, 2019), 34.

68 **When Choiseul was exiled**: Julian Swann, *Exile, Imprisonment, or Death: The Politics of Disgrace in Bourbon France* (Oxford: Oxford University Press, 2017), 216.

69 **To everyone's astonishment**: Hugh Noel Williams, *Memoirs of Madame du Barry of the Court of Louis XV* (New York: Collier & Son, 1910), 238.

69 **So awkward that even Louis XV himself**: Yonge, *Life of Marie Antoinette*, 82.

69 **In January 1774, the Comte de Creutz**: Hans Axel von Fersen, *Le comte de Fersen et la cour de France* (Paris: Firmin-Didot et Cie, 1878), xv. "Il fallait aller à Versailles faire sa cour au Roi et voir la cérémonie de l'ordre du Saint-Esprit. J'avais commandé ma voiture à 8 heures; mais je fus obligé d'attendre et pestant comme un malheureux, jusqu'à 8 heures ¾ que le tailleur m'apportât un habit de fourrure que je lui avais commandé le matin de la veille. A 10 heures j'étais à Versailles. La cérémonie n'est qu'une messe où le Roi et tous les chevaliers assistent en habit de cérémonie, après avoir dîné j'allais avec le comte Creutz faire une visite à Madame du Barry. Elle me parla alors pour la première fois. Au sortir de là nous revînmes à Paris et j'allais chez moi me coucher assez fatigué."

70 **"I spoke to the dauphine for some time"**: Émile Baumann, *Marie-Antoinette et Axel Fersen* (Paris: Grasset, 1931), 13.

71 **Madame du Barry certainly feared**: Donald R. Hopkins, *The Greatest Killer: Smallpox in History* (Chicago: University of Chicago Press, 2002), 70–71.

À SAVOIR: MARIE ANTOINETTE'S HANDWRITING (1770–1774)

74 **It was a private affair**: Zweig, *Marie Antoinette*, 17.

74 **According to the graphologist's analysis**: Bella Choji, email to author, July 30, 2019.

74 **A year later, the royal family attended**: Mathieu da Vinha, *Au service du roi: Les métiers à la cour de Versailles* (Paris: Tallandier, 2016), 274.

75 **However, she detested**: Zweig, *Marie Antoinette*, 35.

75 **"This person is a matter of fact person"**: Choji, email.

76 **He wrote that Louis**: Félix comte de France d'Hézecques and Charlotte Mary Yonge, *Recollections of a Page at the Court of Louis XVI* (London: Hurst & Blackett, 1873), 20.

76 **Three years later**: Campan, *Memoirs of the Private Life of Marie Antoinette*, xviii.

76 **Professional analysis of Marie Antoinette's letter**: Choji, email.

76 **She was also persistent**: Eliakim Littell, "Marie-Antoinette," *Living Age* 146 (1880): 581.

CHAPTER 7

79 *Every day she supplies the wicked*: Florimond-Claude Mercy-Argenteau, Joseph II, and Wenzel Anton von Kaunitz, *Correspondance secrète du comte de Mercy Argenteau avec l'empereur Joseph II et le prince de Kaunitz* (Paris: Imprimerie Nationale, 1891), 465.

79 **Unfortunately, Madame du Barry was not aware**: G. Touchard-Lafosse, *Chroniques pittoresques et critiques de l'oeil de boeuf des petits appartements de la cour et des salons de Paris, sous Louis 14, la Régence, Louis 15, et Louis 16* (Paris: Gustave Barba, 1845), 301–2. "Madame du Barry redoublait d'efforts pour dissiper ce nuage moral, lorsqu'on lui rapporta qu'en traversant un village des environs de Versailles, le roi avait paru voir avec quelque plaisir la fille d'un menuisier, jeune personne de treize ou quatorze ans, remplie de grâces et de gentillesse. La comtesse ordonne d'enlever cette enfant; on l'amène à Trianon, on la décrasse, on la parfume, et Louis XV la trouve dans son lit. La conquête eût été difficile pour un conquérant entré dans sa soixante-cinquième année, si des confortatifs violents ne l'eussent aidé dans cette victoire, plus laborieuse que satisfaisante. Or la fille du menuisier couvait en ce moment le germe de la petite vérole; sa majesté le puisa, pour la seconde fois, aux sources d'un plaisir imparfait. 1er mai. La petite vérole du roi est tout à fait déclarée; et quand elle le serait moins, on ne pourrait douter de son invasion, car la fille du menuisier est atteinte de cette maladie, avec des symptômes graves de malignité. Les médecins ne dissimulent point leur inquiétude sur la situation de sa majesté: le virus variolique est ici compliqué des ressentiments d'un mal d'origine galante, trop superficiellement, trop royalement traité à d'autres époques."

80 **"The gift of the King's illness to young"**: Touchard-Lafosse, *Chroniques pittoresques*, 301. "Les savants distingués qui veillaient à la conservation de la santé du roi n'ignoraient pas l'existence de ce reliquat; mais ils n'osaient l'attaquer à fond, se rangeant volontiers à l'avis du vieux Richelieu, de Bertin et de Lebel, qui était que:

Le don de la maladie du roi à de jeunes personnes robustes, vives et bien portantes, paraissait le seul spécifique convenable pour attirer au dehors les humeurs morbifiques de sa majesté, et pour rajeunir sa personne. On frémit à cette horrible dépravation de la pensée des courtisans. Cependant la plus grande agitation règne à la cour: le parti d'Aiguillon et du Barry est surtout alarmé. Ses inquiétudes sont partagées par la multitude d'intrigants, de fripons, d'espions titrés ou non, qui, satellites serviles, gravitent autour de ces deux puissances, dont la chute est assurée si le roi meurt."

80 **They were kept in quarantine**: Casimir Stryienski, *Mesdames de France, filles de Louis XV: Documents inédits* (Paris: Émile-Paul, 1911), 347.

80 **She wrote to her empress mother**: Maria Theresa, Mercy-Argenteau, and Marie-Antoinette, "Comte Florimond-Claude de Mercy-Argenteau," 207. "Pour mes tantes, on ne peut plus dire qu'elles me conduisent."

81 **"Tactful and complaisant"**: Zweig, *Marie Antoinette*, 107.

81 **"my brother is certainly mad"**: Geri Walton, *Marie Antoinette's Confidante: The Rise and Fall of the Princesse de Lamballe* (Havertown, UK: Pen and Sword, 2016), 99.

81 **He loved women**: Pierre Étienne Auguste Goupil, *Essais historiques sur la vie de Marie-Antoinette d'Autriche: Reine de France* (Paris: Chez Stampe, 1789), 18. "Ce prince n'aime à la fois que les femmes, le jeu & le vin."

82 **Some finally left the court for good**: Mousnier, *Institutions of France*, 5.

82 **In 1776, Madame de Marsan resigned**: Younghusband, *Marie-Antoinette*, 88.

82 **"women of ill repute"**: E. Welwert, "L'éminence grise de Marie Antoinette," *Revue de l'histoire de Versailles et de Seine-et-Otise* 23 and 24 (1919): 127.

82 **It was well known that the queen was especially keen**: Maugras, *Le Duc de Lauzun*, 97.

83 **The queen had never imagined**: Bashor, *Marie Antoinette's Head*, 82. "The art of flirtation depended on this back and forth dance with the gift—right beneath the eyes of the court. The slightest snub or gesture spoke volumes, only fanning court intrigues and petty jealousies. When the queen wore the plume of feathers later that evening, he overheard various courtiers remarking how indecent it was for the queen to wear such a sign of her affection for him in public."

83 **"His vanity magnified the value"**: Campan, *Memoirs of the Private Life*, 92.

83 **The queen replied**: Campan, *Memoirs of the Private Life*, 114.

83 **Moreover, Coigny told Madame**: Campan, *Memoirs of the Private Life*, 196.

83 **"We've managed to unmask the Duc de Lauzun"**: Maria Theresa, Mercy-Argenteau, and Marie-Antoinette, "Comte Florimond-Claude de Mercy-Argenteau," 8. "Nous sommes parvenus à lui démasquer le duc de Lauzun, qui était un des plus dangereux personnages, et la reine s'est décidée à lui refuser désormais tout accès de confiance. Il nous a réussi également de détruire le pernicieux crédit de la princesse de Guéméné, mais la reine, en la connaissant pour ce qu'elle vaut, la ménage encore pour pouvoir aller de temps en temps passer des heures de la soirée chez la dite princesse, qui rassemble chez elle la jeunesse de Versailles."

84 **"With her ladies at the palace"**: Jean-Louis Soulavie, *Mémoires historiques et politiques du règne de Louis XVI depuis son mariage jusqu'à sa mort* (Paris: Treuttel et Würtz, 1801), 47. "'La reine menait avec ses dames du palais,' une conduite peu propre à lui mériter le respect des français. 'Elle avait trouvé en charge, outre

madame de Noailles, dont j'ai parlé, plusieurs autres dames de la feue reine, qui tenaient de la cour de cette princesse le ton de la décence, et la dignité de leur rang.
Lorsque Louis XVI monta sur le trône, on comptait encore parmi les restes de
l'ancienne cour, les dames de Talleyrand, de, Grammont.de Tavannes, d'Adhemard,
de Chaulnes, de Duras, que. la reine trouvait vieilles et gênantes; elle leur riait au
nez, et se plaisait à les déconcerter, 'au point que plusieurs d'entre elles préférèrent
une retraite, à un service aussi désagréable.'"

84   **This imprudent act on the part of a queen**: Boigne, *Memoirs of the Comtesse de
Boigne*, 171–94. "Édouard Dillon était très beau, très fat, très à la mode. Il était de la
société de Madame de Polignac, et probablement adressait à la Reine quelques-uns
de ces hommages qu'elle réclamait comme jolie femme. Un jour, il répétait chez
elle les figures d'un quadrille qu'on devait danser au bal suivant. Tout à coup, il pâlit
et s'évanouit à plat. On le plaça sur un sofa, et la Reine eut l'imprudence de poser
sa main sur son cœur pour sentir s'il battait. Édouard revint à lui. Il s'excusa fort de
sa sotte indisposition et avoua que, depuis les longues souffrances d'une blessure à la
prise de Grenade, ces sortes de défaillances lui prenaient quelquefois, surtout quand
il était à jeun. La Reine lui fit donner un bouillon, et les courtisans, jaloux de ce
léger succès, établirent qu'il était au mieux avec elle."

85   **This act of kindness appeared**: Bashor, *Marie Antoinette's Head*, 85.

85   **He was just one of the rivals**: Louis Prudhomme, *Les crimes des reines de France:
Depuis le commencement de la monarchie* (Paris: Bureau des Révolutions de Paris,
1791), 444. "On peut encore joindre à la liste des rivaux de d'Artois, Coigny,
Fersen, & beaucoup d'autres, disoit-on, ou égaux en dignités, ou excessivement
inférieurs aux premiers: les parties de plaisir, les promenades nocturnes, les séjours
fréquents à Trianon, à St. Cloud, les voyages à Paris, les bals, les spectacles, les liaisons intimes, avec des hommes & des femmes perdus de réputation, la protection
accordée à des gens indignes."

85   **The defamatory work accused**: Ursula Haskins Gonthier, *Opinion, Voltaire, nature
et culture* (Paris: Voltaire Foundation, 2007), 199.

85   **After receiving one thousand gold coins**: Anonymous, "Libels on the Queen of
France," *Anglo American* 1 (1843): 234.

85   **suspiciously close friendships with women**: Alison Johnson, *Louis XVI and the
French Revolution* (Jefferson, NC: McFarland, 2013), 34.

85   **And the dauphine would dismiss everyone**: Jacques Castelnau, *La princesse de
Lamballe* (Paris: Librairie Hachette, 1956), 84.

86   **"My heart reminds me"**: Eugene Louis Guérin, *La Princess Lamballe et Madame
de Polignac* (Paris: Charles Lachapelle, 1858), 143.

86   **Moreover, the family was given apartments**: Hardy, *The Princesse de Lamballe*, 91.

87   **"I will receive them in my cabinet"**: Campan, *Memoirs of the Private Life of Marie
Antoinette*, 175.

87   **She was now destined to the shadows**: Campan, *Memoirs of the Private Life of
Marie Antoinette*, 92.

87   **The Comtesse Diane**: Campan, *Memoirs of the Private Life of Marie Antoinette*, 195.

87   **The Princesse de Lamballe was still superintendent**: Campan, *Memoirs of the
Private Life of Marie Antoinette*, 93.

88 **News of the queen's excessive favoritism**: Paul Girault de Coursac, *Louis XVI et Marie Antoinette: Vie conjugale, vie politique* (Paris: O.E.I.L., 1990), 714. "La comtesse de Polignac n'a ni l'esprit, ni le jugement, ni même le caractère à jouir de la confiance d'une grande princesse."

89 **"Undoubtedly, the most eager"**: Louis Petit de Bachaumont, *Marie-Antoinette, Louis XVI et la famille royale* (Paris: E. Thunot, 1866), 34.

89 **All of Paris, informed of the arrival**: Bachaumont, *Marie-Antoinette*, 163–64.

89 **"The Queen can no longer"**: Maria Theresa, Mercy-Argenteau, and Marie-Antoinette, "Comte Florimond-Claude de Mercy-Argenteau," 114.

90 **"Write to me everything you know"**: Vovk, *In Destiny's Hands*, 64.

90 **"Madame," he said, "within your circle"**: Arneth, *Marie-Antoinette*, 38. "Par exemple, madame, répliquai-je, vos sociétés, vos amis et amies: vous êtes devenue fort indulgente sur les mœurs et la réputation. Je pourrais prouver qu'à votre âge cette indulgence, surtout pour les femmes, fait un mauvais effet; mais enfin je passe que vous ne preniez garde ni aux mœurs ni à la réputation d'une femme, que vous en fassiez votre société, votre amie, uniquement parce qu'elle est aimable. Certainement ce n'est pas la morale d'un prêtre; mais que l'inconduite en tous genres, les mauvaises mœurs, les réputations tarées et perdues soient un titre pour être admis dans votre société, voilà ce qui vous fait un tort infini. Depuis quelque temps vous n'avez pas même la prudence de conserver liaison avec quelques femmes qui aient réputation de raison et de bonne conduite. — La reine a écouté tout ce sermon avec sourire et une sorte d'applaudissement et d'aveu. J'avais le ton de la douceur, mais d'une douceur de pitié et d'affliction."

90 **The Prince de Ligne described him**: Maugras, *Le Duc de Lauzun*, 83.

90 **"The queen said impudently"**: Pierre de Nolhac, *La Reine Marie-Antoinette* (Paris: Alphonse Lemerre, 1892), 27. "La reine dit impudemment a Besenval son confident: / "Mon mari est un pauvre sire!" / L'autre répond d'un ton léger: / "Chacun le pense sans le dire, / vous le dites sans y penser.""

91 **"You will not take care of yourself"**: Hardy, *The Princesse de Lamballe*, 82.

CHAPTER 8

93 *They introduced a taste for trifling games*: Campan, *Memoirs of the Private Life of Marie Antoinette*, 147.

93 **Although she was the only royal**: Haslip, *Marie Antoinette*, 128.

94 **Whether these games were played**: Campan, *Memoirs of the Private Life of Marie Antoinette*, 145.

94 **he was also known to attend**: N. W. Wraxall, *Waldie's Octavo Library* (Philadelphia: Adam Waldie, 1836), 417.

94 **On pronouncing the word "décampativos"**: Goupil, *Essais historiques*, 89.

94 **However, the Comte de Vaudreuil generally played**: Campan, *Memoirs of the Private Life of Marie Antoinette*, 333.

94 **Sir Nathaniel Wraxall, an English author**: Andrew Haggard, *Louis XVI and Marie Antoinette* (New York: D. Appleton, 1909), 110. "The hatred of the populace towards the Queen became naturally inflamed by this supposed mixture of a species

of incest with matrimonial infidelity; and it was to the base passions of the multitude that such atrocious fabrications were addressed by her enemies. If Marie Antoinette ever violated her nuptial vow, either Count Fersen or Monsieur de Vaudreuil were the favoured individuals."

94 **Messieurs Coigny, Guines, Esterhazy**: Anonymous, "Secret Correspondence on Marie Antoinette," *Living Age* 21 (1849): 554.

95 **"It is very true that the king"**: Arneth, *Marie-Antoinette*, lxii.

95 **"Thank Heaven," wrote Mercy**: F. de Albini, *Marie Antoinette and the Diamond Necklace from Another Point of View* (London: Swan Sonnenschein, 1900), 144.

95 **"Writers like Madame Campan"**: Thomas Wright, *The History of France* (London: London Printing Co., 1858), 404.

96 **The king laughed**: Anonymous, *La Revue hebdomadaire* (Paris: Plon, 1916), 448.

96 **The queen's brother Emperor Joseph II**: Zweig, *Marie Antoinette*, 78.

96 **Marie Antoinette's imperial brother was shocked**: Anonymous, "The Marriages of the Bourbons," *Spectator* 64 (1890): 273.

97 **"Certainly there was something to worry about"**: Arneth, *Marie-Antoinette*, 44.

97 **"I left Versailles with difficulty"**: Arneth, *Marie-Antoinette*, 45.

97 **"The situation of my sister"**: Arneth, *Marie-Antoinette*, 46.

97 **One wonders how this monarch**: Lady Sydney Morgan, *France in 1829–30* (New York: J. & J. Harper, 1830), 49.

97 **Among Louis XV's personal effects**: Yonge, *Life of Marie Antoinette*, 79.

98 **"It is truly deplorable"**: Littell, "Marie Antoinette," 584.

98 **"Do not delude yourself"**: Maria Theresa, Mercy-Argenteau, and Marie-Antoinette, "Comte Florimond-Claude de Mercy-Argenteau," 143.

98 **"I play only in public"**: Olivier Bernier, *Secrets of Marie Antoinette* (Garden City, NY: Doubleday Religious Publishing Group, 1985), 229.

98 **"I am almost tempted to doubt it"**: Maria Theresa, Mercy-Argenteau, and Marie-Antoinette, "Comte Florimond-Claude de Mercy-Argenteau," 251.

98 **He had also been sent by his father**: Sixto Sánchez Lorenzo, *El amante de la reina* (Barcelona: Roca editorial, 2012), 68.

99 **"The queen, who is the prettiest"**: Hans Axel von Fersen, *Diary and Correspondence of Count Axel Fersen: Grand Marshal of Sweden, Relating to the Court of France* (London: Heinemann, 1902), 12.

99 **"I am to go Thursday thus dressed"**: Fersen, *Diary and Correspondence of Count Axel Fersen*, 12.

99 **But when she broke etiquette**: Zweig, *Marie Antoinette*, 229.

99 **The court had also noticed**: Zweig, *Marie Antoinette*, 126.

99 **her eyes lit up and she gazed at Fersen**: Zweig, *Marie Antoinette*, 231. "Ah! que je fus bien inspirée, Quand je vous reçus dans ma cour!"

99 **Fortunately, the court's attention was soon directed**: Haggard, *Louis XVI*, 141.

99 **"For you, France, a dauphin must be born"**: Mathurin François Adolphe de Lescure, *Marie Antoinette et sa famille* (Paris: Ducrocq, 1865), 157. "Pour vous, la France, un dauphin doit naître / Une princesse arrive pour être témoin / sitôt qu'on voit une grâce paraître / Croyez que l'amour n'est pas loin."

100 **"Nothing can undo Coigny's work"**: Bashor, *Marie Antoinette's Head*, 283. "De Coigny cependant rien ne défit l'ouvrage, / Les caresses de Jule et sa lascive main, / En vain de la nature insultent à l'ouvrage, / Au compte de Louis arrive un gros Dauphin, / Juste au bout de neuf mois, à dater de l'époque / Où Coigny le jetta dans le moule royal."

100 **he insisted that the Duc de Coigny**: Vincent Woodrow Beach, *Charles X of France: His Life and Times* (London: Pruett, 1971), 9.

100 **This caused an uproar**: Weber, *Mémoires concernant Marie-Antoinette*, 65–69.

101 **They formed a circle called the *société***: Munro Price, *The Road from Versailles: Louis XVI, Marie Antoinette, and the Fall of the French Monarchy* (New York: St. Martin's Press, 2003), 15.

101 **"It was the queen who was sucked into"**: John Hardman, *Marie-Antoinette: The Making of a French Queen* (London: Yale University Press, 2019), 30.

CHAPTER 9

103 *You have become very indulgent of morals and reputation*: Maugras, *Le Duc de Lauzun*, 84.

103 **The queen even mentioned the hearsay**: Henri Guillemin, *Parcours* (Paris: Editions du Seuil, 1989), 360. "On me prête le goût des femmes et des amants."

103 **"Marie Antoinette at this juncture involuntarily turned"**: Zweig, *Marie Antoinette*, 120.

103 **"Such unofficial alliances and liaisons"**: Elizabeth Susan Wahl, *Invisible Relations: Representations of Female Intimacy in the Age of Enlightenment* (Stanford, CA: Stanford University Press, 1999), 76.

104 **"I think that you do not consider"**: Littell, "Secret Correspondence on Marie Antoinette," 554.

104 **After their wedding night**: Olivier Bernier, *The Eighteenth Century Woman* (New York: New Word City, 2018), 153.

104 **she could love Ferdinand "only out of duty"**: Bearne, *Sister of Marie Antoinette*, 71.

105 **Carolina was known to be**: Cinzia Recca, *The Diary of Queen Maria Carolina of Naples, 1781–1785* (London: Palgrave Macmillan, 2016), 102.

105 **Carolina became so obsessed with Emma**: Jean-Baptiste Honoré Raymond Capefigue, *L'Europe pendant la Révolution française* (Brussels, Belgium: Société belge de librairie, 1843), 58. "La reine Marie-Caroline se prit d'une si vive tendresse pour elle, qu'elle ne voulut pas d'autre compagne; la même chambre les reçut, souvent la même couche, et sans cesse réunies, elles donnaient simultanément leurs ordres, ainsi que deux sœurs, au ministre Acton, leur confident, esprit fin et national, comme Nelson, l'amant heureux et aimé."

106 **"I'm letting you know that you will be totally separated"**: Maria Theresa (Empress of Austria), *Briefe der Kaiserin Maria Theresia an ihre Kinder und Freunde* (Vienna: W. Braumüller, 1881), 30–34. "Voulant vous traiter en personne âgée, je vous avertis que vous serez totalement séparée de votre sœur 1). Je vous défends

tout secret, intelligence ou discours avec elle; si la petite recommençait, vous n'avez qu'à ne pas y faire attention ou à le dire à la Lerchenfeld ou à vos dames; tout ce tripot finira ainsi tout de suite. Ces secrets ne consistent d'ailleurs que dans des remarques contre votre prochain ou votre famille, ou vos dames. Je vous avertis que vous serez exactement observée, et que je me tiendrai à vous, comme l'aînée, la plus raisonnable par conséquent, pour faire revenir votre sœur. Évitez tout secret ou discours en passant à l'église, à la table, à l'appartement."

106 **"Write to me all the little circumstances"**: Vovk, *In Destiny's Hands*, 43.

106 **Carolina wrote Lerchenfeld again**: Henry Vallotton, *Marie-Thérèse: Impératrice* (Paris: Fayard, 1963), 244. "Dites à ma sœur *que je l'aime extraordinairement.*"

107 **"I am told that the day begins"**: Michael Farquhar, *A Treasury of Royal Scandals: The Shocking True Stories of History's Wickedest, Weirdest, Most Wanton Kings, Queens, Tsars, Popes, and Emperors* (New York: Penguin, 2001), 91.

107 **Christina and Isabella continued their relationship**: Farquhar, *Treasury of Royal Scandals*, 92.

107 **To show her contempt**: John Kiste, *Emperor Francis Joseph: Life, Death and the Fall of the Habsburg Empire* (Stroud, UK: History Press, 2005), 64.

107 **She made it a point to break with**: Kiste, *Emperor Francis Joseph*, 65.

107 **Unlike Marie Antoinette's husband**: Vovk, *In Destiny's Hands*, 121.

107 **Comte Mercy wrote the empress**: Lillian C. Smythe, *The Guardian of Marie Antoinette: Letters from the Comte de Mercy-Argenteau, Austrian Ambassador to the Court of Versailles, to Marie Thérèse, Empress of Austria, 1770–1780* (London: Hutchinson, 1902), 33.

107 **but Marie Antoinette persisted for two reasons**: Smythe, *Guardian of Marie Antoinette*, 34.

108 **The court was shocked**: Jules Flammermont, *Les correspondances des agents diplomatiques étrangers en France avant la révolution* (Paris: Ernest Leroux, 1896), 333. "La retraite de M. Thierry donne lieu aux propos les plus scandaleux dans Paris, a ce qu'une personne arrivée hier de cette ville m'a confié. L'on prétend que le duc de Coigny, premier écuyer du Roi a des entrées à de certaines heures dans l'appartement de cette princesse, qui fournissent matière à bien des remarques, que je serais cependant porté d'envisager comme des calomnies, que la légèreté de la conduite de la Reine suffit pour autoriser."

108 **it was said that the Duc de Coigny**: Smythe, *Guardian of Marie Antoinette*, 41.

108 **Because Madame du Barry was enchanted**: Smythe, *Guardian of Marie Antoinette*, 41–42.

108 **This would be the date**: Hector Fleischmann, *Le cénacle libertin de Mlle Raucourt de la comédie française* (Paris: Bibliothèque des Curieux, 1912), 274. "10 janvier 1773—Le roi a fait à Mlle de Raucoux la faveur de rester à la Comédie pendant tout le temps de la représentation de Didon, où elle jouait. Cette circonstance a été d'autant mieux remarquée, que S. M. n'aime point le spectacle en général et surtout la tragédie. Elle a eu la bonté de la présenter ensuite à madame la dauphine, sous le nom de la reine Didon. Elle l'a agréée, comme on a dit, pour entrer dans la troupe des Comédiens François et a ordonné qu'on lui donnât 50 louis pour marque de sa satisfaction. Mlle de Raucoux a emporté aussi les suffrages de Mme Dubarri. Cette belle comtesse lui a demandé ce qu'elle aimeroit mieux, ou de

trois robes pour son usage ou d'un habit de théâtre? L'actrice de répondre que, puisque la comtesse lui en laissoit le choix, elle préferoit l'habit de théâtre, dont le public profiteroit aussi. Cette note est intéressante, car elle fixe la date exacte de la première rencontre de Marie-Antoinette, alors dauphine, et de la tragédienne. On rappellera ici en passant, que Theveneau de Morande, mince autorité, évidemment, a accusé la Du Barry d'avoir, à cette représentation, facilité une entrevue amoureuse entre le roi et la débutante."

109 **"Her taste for tribades"**: Bryant T. Ragan, *Homosexuality in Modern France* (Oxford: Oxford University Press, 1996), 41.

109 **Rumors gave rise to**: Ragan, *Homosexuality in Modern France*, 40–42.

109 **the queen was willing to pay Raucourt's debts**: Hugh Noel Williams, *Later Queens of the French Stage* (New York: Harper & Brothers, 1906), 171.

109 **She was expelled**: Ragan, *Homosexuality in Modern France*, 41. "Marie-Antoinette's ongoing interest in Raucourt later earned her a place in the catalogue of the queen's female lovers published during the Revolution."

109 **Raucourt, the "young priestess of Lesbos"**: Ragan, *Homosexuality in Modern France*, 42.

109 **the hissing became so loud**: Williams, *Later Queens*, 75.

110 **Lesbian relationships at the time**: Ragan, *Homosexuality in Modern France*, 62.

110 **Even the famous artist Élisabeth Louise Vigée Le Brun**: Julien Arbois, *Dans le lit de nos ancêtres* (Paris: City Edition, May 25, 2016), 117. "In the years before the Revolution, the queen's 'dazzling' patronage of public women such as Mlle Arnould of the Opéra and Mlle de Raucourt of the Comédie Française reciprocally confirmed their (bad) reputations. Even the renowned artist Vigée Lebrun came under sexual suspicion."

110 **The pose was the same**: Mary D. Sheriff, "Hermaphrodite? History Painter? On the Self-Imaging of Elisabeth Vigée Lebrun," *Eighteenth Century: Theory and Interpretation* 35 (Spring 1994): 3–27.

111 **"But the most remarkable thing about her face"**: W. H. Helm, *Vigee-Lebrun 1755–1842* (Boston: Small, Maynard, 1915), 30.

111 **When Le Brun, in advanced pregnancy**: Frantz Funck-Brentano, *The Diamond Necklace: Being the True Story of Marie-Antoinette and the Cardinal de Rohan* (Philadelphia: J. B. Lippincott, 1901), 39–44.

111 **"The saphists have their places"**: Richard Krafft-Ebing, *Psychopathia Sexualis: With Especial Reference to the Antipathic Sexual Instinct* (New York: Rebman, 1906), 609.

111 **The former was practiced only by women**: Krafft-Ebing, *Psychopathia Sexualis*, 407. "The author declares that this vice ('saphism') is met with more frequently among ladies of the aristocracy and prostitutes."

112 **Cunnilingus, on the other hand**: Krafft-Ebing, *Psychopathia Sexualis*, 406–7.

112 **His name was either the Chevalier d'Eon**: Simon Burrows, Jonathan Conlin, Russell Goulbourne, and Valerie Mainz, *The Chevalier d'Eon and His Worlds: Gender, Espionage and Politics in the Eighteenth Century* (London: Continuum UK, 2011), 106.

112 **When the royal family visited Fontainebleau**: Maxime de la Rocheterie, *The Life of Marie Antoinette* (London: Dodd, Mead, 1893), 51.

113   **Also, Maria Theresa had told her**: Rocheterie, *Life of Marie Antoinette*, 14. "I counsel you, my dear daughter, to re-read my paper on the 21st of every month. I beg you to be true to me on this point. My only fear for you is negligence in your prayers and studies; and lukewarmnedness succeeds negligence. Fight against it, for it is more dangerous than a more reprehensible, even wicked, state; one can conquer that more easily. Love your family; be affectionate to them, — to your aunts as well as to your brothers-in-law and sisters-in-law. Suffer no evil-speaking; you must either silence the persons or escape it by withdrawing from them. If you value your peace of mind, you must from the start avoid this pitfall, which I greatly fear for you, knowing your curiosity."

À SAVOIR: MARIE ANTOINETTE'S HANDWRITING (1774–1778)

116   **The following notes refer**: Arneth, *Marie-Antoinette*, 361. "Je suis bien fâchée que vous ayez de si bonnes raisons de ne pas continuer les voyages; c'est un grand malheur pour mon frère. J'espère que vous l'aurez bien prêché avant son départ; vous savez qu'il faut un style un peu vif pour l'animer. Dieu veuille que vous en soyez venu à bout. Je ne vous pardonne pas vos excuses sur la longueur de votre lettre; il faudrait que vous me crussiez bien fausse pour douter de mes sentiments pour vous et du plaisir que j'aurai à recevoir de vos lettres. J'y compte."

116   **"Marie Antoinette was cold at heart"**: Littell, "Marie Antoinette," 581.

116   **"Marie-Antoinette's letters exhibit"**: Littell, "Marie Antoinette," 581.

117   **"I am more and more convinced"**: Littell, "Marie Antoinette," 581.

CHAPTER 10

121   *Scilicet is superis labor est*: Virgil, *The Aeneid*, quoted in Maurice Tourneux, *Marie-Antoinette devant l'histoire: Essai bibliographique* (Paris: Techener, 1895), 42.

122   **After buying up the entire edition**: Funck-Brentano, *Diamond Necklace*, 60. "It is necessary here to observe that in 1774 Beaumarchais had been sent to London by Louis XVI and Sartine to buy up the entire edition of a frightful pamphlet against Marie-Antoinette. It was called 'Important Notice to the Spanish Branch on its Rights to the Crown of Prance in Default of Heirs, and which may be very useful to all the Bourbon Family, especially King Louis XVI.' Signed G.A. (Guillaume Angelucci), at Paris, 1774. This Angelucci was a Jew. Beaumarchais put himself into relations with him and bought up the edition. He had the copies destroyed and did the same with a second edition at Amsterdam. He was about to return in triumph, when he heard that Angelucci had escaped with a copy saved from the general destruction."

122   **King Louis XVI's impotence**: Simon Burrows, *A King's Ransom: The Life of Charles Théveneau de Morande, Blackmailer, Scandalmonger and Master-Spy* (London: Bloomsbury, 2010), 132.

122 **"A young and frisky queen"**: Anonymous, *Les Amours de Charlot et Toinette* (France: n.p., 1789), 3–4.

124 **"Since the revolution, the monarchical club"**: Charles-Joseph Mayer, *Vie de Marie-Antoinette d'Autriche, reine de France, femme de Louis XVI, roi des Français* (Paris: Chez l'auteur et ailleurs, 1793), 128. "Depuis la révolution, le club monarchien dont Antoinette est l'âme, n'a cessé de faire des tentatives. Chacun des membres qui le composent, a puisé, dans le vagin de l'Autrichienne, le poison qu'il s'efforce de distiller. Cet antre pestifère est le réceptacle de tous les vices, et là, chacun vient se pourvoir abondamment de la dose qui lui est propre."

125 **"Her Heart is beating"**: Anonymous, *Les Amours de Charlot et Toinette*, 5–6.

126 **"While love tenderly"**: Anonymous, *Les Amours de Charlot et Toinette*, 6–7.

126 **"It was impossible to see anything"**: Smythe, *Guardian of Marie Antoinette*, 488. "She was dressed in silver, scattered over with laurier-roses; few diamonds, and feathers much lower than the Monument. They say she does not dance in time, but then, it is wrong to dance in time."

128 **"Dear reader, our lovers"**: Anonymous, *Les Amours de Charlot et Toinette*, 7–8.

128 **"A loud ring of the bell"**: Anonymous, *Les Amours de Charlot et Toinette*, 8.

128 **Some historians have attributed**: Jacques Peuchet, *Mémoires tirés des archives de la police de Paris* (Paris: A. Levavasseur et Cie., 1838), 31. "Il est plus que probable que Beaumarchais avait composé et porté à Londres, pour le faire imprimer, le libelle intitulé les Amours de Charlot et Toinette, imprimé avec des graywrqs [gravures] obscènes."

128 **The first edition was purchased**: Peter-Eckhard Knabe, *Opinion* (Berlin: Verlag Arno Spitz, 2000), 228. In 1773 Boissière was involved in the negotiation for Morande's *Mémoires secrets d'une femme publique*, and in 1781 he was paid 18,600 livres to suppress an illustrated edition of the scurrilous poem *Les Amours de Charlot et Toinette*, attributed to Beaumarchais.

128 **In March 1783, all editions found**: Knabe, *Opinion*, 288.

CHAPTER 11

131 **"Here is the King"**: F. M. Mayeur, *L'Autrichienne en goguettes, ou, L'orgie royale: Opéra proverb* (France: n.p., 1789), 3–6.

131 **who was the "most beautiful of mortals"**: Jeffrey M. Duban, *The Lesbian Lyre: Reclaiming Sappho for the 21st Century* (Hoathly, UK: Sussex Clairview Books, 2016), 55.

131 **Even the queen's official portrait painter**: Louise-Elisabeth Vigée-Lebrun, *The Memoirs of Mme. Elisabeth Louise Vigée-Le Brun, 1755–1789* (New York: George H. Doran, 1927), 162.

131 **However, the term "Ganymede"**: Claude J. Summers, *Homosexuality in Renaissance and Enlightenment England: Literary Representations in Historical Context* (New York: Routledge, 2013), 645.

132 **Because he went to bed like clockwork**: Claude Arnaud, *Chamfort* (Chicago: University of Chicago Press, 1992), 96.

134 **Let him have his fill and we'll make the most of it**: Mayeur, *L'Autrichienne en goguettes*, 7–9.

134 **The journalist and politician Bertrand Barrère wrote**: Cabanès, *Le Cabinet Secret*, 115.

134 **Historian Louis Gottschalk reported**: Stephen Mennell, *All Manners of Food: Eating and Taste in England and France from the Middle Ages* (Chicago: University of Illinois Press, 1996), 31.

139 **"A rogue Prince and a prostitute Queen"**: Mayeur, *L'Autrichienne en goguettes*, 9–16.

140 **His cure included emasculation**: Jean Charles Gervaise de Latouche, *Histoire de Dom B . . . portier des Chartreux* (Rome: Philotanus, 1750), 167. "Je ne revins de ma faiblesse que pour me voir dans un misérable lit, au milieu d'un hôpital. Je demandai où j'étais. A Bicêtre, me dit-on. A Bicêtre! m'écriai-je; ciel! à Bicêtre! La douleur me pétrifia, la fièvre me saisit, je n'en revins que pour tomber dans une maladie plus cruelle, la vérole! Je reçus sans murmurer ce nouveau châtiment du ciel. Suzon, me dis-je, je ne me plaindrais pas de mon sort, si tu ne souffrais pas le même malheur. Mon mal devint insensiblement si violent que, pour le chasser, on eut recours aux plus violents remèdes: on m'annonça qu'il fallait me résoudre à subir une petite opération. Il faut vous épargner ce spectacle de douleur. Que puis-je vous dire? Je tombai dans une faiblesse que l'on prit pour le dernier moment de ma vie. Que ne l'était-il? J'aurais été trop heureux! La douleur qui avait causé mon évanouissement m'en retira. Je portai la main où je sentais la douleur la plus vive. Ah! je ne suis plus un homme! Je poussai un cri qui fut entendu jusqu'aux extrémités de la maison." Translation: I only came back from my weakness to see myself in a miserable bed in the middle of a hospital. I asked where I was. At Bicêtre, I am told. At Bicêtre! I exclaimed; heaven! in Bicêtre! The pain petrified me, the fever seized me, I returned only to fall into a more cruel disease, the pox! I received without murmuring this new punishment from heaven. Suzon, I said to myself, I would not complain of my fate if you did not suffer the same misfortune. My illness became imperceptibly so violent that, in order to expel him, the most violent remedies were resorted to. I was told that I had to submit to a small opera-tion. You must spare yourself this spectacle of pain. What can I tell you? I fell into a weakness that was taken for the last moment of my life. What was it? I would have been too happy! The pain that had caused my fainting pulled me away. I put my hand where I felt the most pain. Ah! I am no longer a man! I uttered a cry that was heard to the ends of the house.

CHAPTER 12

141 *Established in the Tuileries*: F. Dantalle, *Description de la ménagerie royale d'animaux vivants, établie aux Tuileries, près de la terrasse nationale; Avec leurs noms, qualités, couleurs et propriétés* (Paris: De l'imprimerie des patriotes, n.d.).

143 **"What a swarm of parasites"**: Henry Smith Williams, *France, 1715–1815* (London: The Times, 1907), 184.

CHAPTER 13

149   *The unpleasant odours in the park*: Alain Corbin, *The Foul and the Fragrant: Odor and the French Social Imagination* (Cambridge, MA: Harvard University Press, 1986), 27.

149   **The lodgings in the dark, narrow mezzanines**: Pérate, *Versailles*, 43.

150   **Although an army of valets was constantly collecting**: Pérate, *Versailles*, 44. "Il était en effet interdit de jeter les excréments par les fenêtres, une pratique très courante dans le royaume—on criait alors « gare à l'eau! » pour avertir les pauvres passants. Ces fosses, régulièrement récurées, étaient reliées à des égouts qui déversaient la fange dans différents endroits de la ville. Une grande partie s'écoulait ainsi dans deux étangs, celui du marais au sud, baptisé « l'étang puant », et au nord dans celui de Clagny, qui fut comblé plus tard."

150   *Special Police of Versailles*: Denis-Laurian Turmeau de La Morandière, *Police sur les Mendians, les Vagabonds, les Joueurs de Profession, les Intrigans, les Filles Prostituées, les Domestiques hors de maison depuis longtemps et les Gens sans aveu* (Paris: Dessain, 1764), 333.

150   **The existence of private latrines**: Mathieu da Vinha, *Vivre à la cour de Versailles en 100 questions* (Paris: Tallandier, 2018), 23. "Versailles n'est pas Fontainebleau et Louis XIV souhaitait pour sa cour le meilleur et le plus moderne dans son château flambant neuf—à l'aune du XVIIe siècle. il y a bien des toilettes construites à Versailles, aujourd'hui disparues, que l'on retrouve tracées dans les anciens plans. Ces latrines publiques étaient situées dans plusieurs ailes du château et permettaient aux nombreux visiteurs de se soulager en toute quiétude. Mais le palais est vaste et, pour éviter les accidents, on plaçait régulièrement des chaises percées derrière des paravents dans certains couloirs. Ce qui n'empêchait pas les sujets de Sa Majesté de s'oublier dans les recoins ou dans les jardins—on tentait de masquer les odeurs en plantant des parterres aux senteurs puissantes: jacinthes, narcisses, et jasmin."

151   **The perfumed plants may not have helped much**: La Morandière, *Police sur les Mendians*, 334. "The unpleasant odours in the park, gardens, even the château, make one's gorge rise. The communicating passages, courtyards, buildings in the wings, corridors, are full of urine and faeces; a pork butcher actually sticks and roasts pigs at the bottom of the ministers' wing every morning; the avenue Saint-Cloud is covered with stagnant water and dead cats; livestock defecated in the great gallery; the stench reached even the king's chamber."

151   **"Pet dogs were often"**: Godfrey Fox Bradby, *The Great Days of Versailles: Studies from Court Life in the Later Years of Louis XIV* (New York: Charles Scribner's Sons, 1906), 60.

151   **During the reign of Louis XIV**: Eleanor Herman, *The Royal Art of Poison: Filthy Palaces, Fatal Cosmetics, Deadly Medicine, and Murder Most Foul* (New York: St. Martin's, 2018), 64.

151   **"The people stationed in the galleries"**: Herman, *Royal Art of Poison*, 63.

151   **while sitting upon their chaises percées**: Tony Spawforth, *Versailles: A Biography of a Palace* (New York: St. Martin's, 2010), 112. "Even members of the royal family—women as well as men, the king included—thought nothing of giving audiences or chatting to intimates while installed on the closestool."

151 **Because the chimneys did not draw well**: Anonymous, "Secret of the Satisfaction We Derive from Certain Stenches," *Current Opinion* (New York: Current Literature Publishing, 1913), 182. "But probably among those to the manner born it caused no inconvenience, and the recollection of the stenches of the Louvre and Versailles in later days was even associated in loyal breasts with tender feelings of regret for the past. The famous architect Viollet-le-Duc says that even in the unsavory details that have been referred to the old tradition was revived at the Restoration. He remembered the stenches which pervaded the corridors of Saint Cloud in the days of Louis XVIII. One day when a mere boy he visited the palace at Versailles in the company of an elderly lady who had been an ornament of the court of Louis XV. In going about they found their way into a passage where their nostrils were assailed by the foulest odors. The old lady inhaled these with the deepest pleasure, exclaiming rapturously, 'Ah! that reminds me of the beautiful past.' It is well known that the olfactory nerve often retains impressions more vividly than any of the other senses; hence the smell of a flower will call up in an old man the memory of a scene of youthful love or awaken forgotten associations. It is natural enough, therefore, that a once familiar stench should bring back a vanished past. But an old court beauty finding food for a fine sentiment in a stink is what Carlyle would call a comic-pathetic figure."

151 **Believing that "evil humors" could**: Bradby, *Great Days of Versailles*, 60.

152 **She had her own English toilet**: Simone Bertière, *The Indomitable Marie-Antoinette* (Paris: Editions de Fallois, 2014), 170.

152 **When an elderly noble lady**: Bradby, *Great Days of Versailles*, 13.

152 **Louis XV's daughter, Madame Adélaïde**: Spawforth, *Versailles*, 114.

152 **They also complained that the area**: Spawforth, *Versailles*, 113.

152 **And to conceal his lodging here**: Evelyn Farr, *I Love You Madly: Marie-Antoinette and Count Fersen; The Secret Letters* (London: Peter Owen, 2017), 117. "Versailles, 30 September 1789. I've been here for five days, and I'm going to put into place the economies I spoke of in my last letter. The Comte d'Esterházy, who isn't coming back this winter, is lending me his apartment and I shall settle here for the winter. In consequence, I shall give up my house in Paris and instead rent a very small apartment there as a pied-à-terre."

153 **Marie Antoinette also had another special hideaway**: Suellen Diaconoff, *Through the Reading Glass: Women, Books, and Sex in the French Enlightenment* (Albany: State University of New York Press, 2012), 21–22.

153 **naming a chamber as one's boudoir**: Diaconoff, *Through the Reading Glass*, 21.

153 **"The books from the boudoir"**: Albert Cim, *Les Femmes et les livres* (Paris: Ancienne Librairie, 1919), 9.

153 **He reasoned that the most honest**: Charles Augustin Sainte-Beuve, *Nouveaux lundis* (Paris: Michel-Lévy frères, 1887), 345–49.

153 **"Try to furnish out your mind"**: Rocheterie, *Life of Marie Antoinette*, 43.

153 **Then calming herself**: Rocheterie, *Life of Marie Antoinette*, 44.

154 **Surprisingly, in the afternoon**: Rocheterie, *Life of Marie Antoinette*, 46.

154 **And she replied with her usual good faith**: Rocheterie, *Life of Marie Antoinette*, 46.

154   **"The days are suitably well filled"**: Rocheterie, *Life of Marie Antoinette*, 47.

154   **However, most women at that time**: Diaconoff, *Through the Reading Glass*, 22.

154   **"What is scandalous about a worldly"**: Rocheterie, *Life of Marie Antoinette*, 197.

154   **The ceilings were still in ruin**: Smythe, *Guardian of Marie Antoinette*, 258.

155   **Patience was not one of the dauphine's virtues**: Nolhac, *La Reine Marie-Antoinette*, 135–54.

155   **The architect, Ange-Jacques Gabriel**: Bertière, *Indomitable Marie-Antoinette*, 132.

155   **This new interest was not due to the princess's taste**: Louis Lacour de La Pijardière, *Livres du boudoir de la reine Marie-Antoinette* (Oxford: Oxford University Press, 1862), 71.

155   **"Monsieur, Madame la Dauphine told Mr. Lecuyer"**: Nolhac, *Versailles et la Cour de France*, 288. "Monsieur, Madame la Dauphine a dit à M. Lécuyer, dès avant le voyage de Compiègne, de lui former une bibliothèque dans un cabinet près de sa chambre. La crainte de faire un objet de dépense, dont les fonds auraient été difficiles à obtenir, et la nécessité de faire cette besogne pendant ce voyage ont fait simplifier l'ouvrage, de sorte qu'on s'est contenté de faire des montants et des tablettes. Madame la Dauphine, n'ayant pas trouvé cela de son goût, a fait tout démolir en sa présence. Il y a deux jours qu'elle me fit aller chez elle pour m'expliquer ses intentions; elle veut un corps d'armoires avec des glaces et de la sculpture. Je viens en conséquence d'en faire le projet et je vais me mettre à portée d'en connaître la dépense. Comme Madame la Dauphine m'a dit qu'elle voulait jouir de cette bibliothèque au retour de Fontainebleau, je l'ai suppliée de recommander à M. le contrôleur général, la première fois qu'elle le verrait, de faire les fonds que l'on lui demanderait à ce sujet. M. Lécuyer et moi nous nous portons en avant pour remplir les vues de Madame la Dauphine; mais nous arrêterons, si les fonds ne viennent pas. J'espère que vous ne blâmerez point cette précaution de notre part, qui anticipe des ordres que nous aurions dû attendre de vous. Je suis avec un très profond respect, Monsieur."

155   **the old king could not refuse**: Maria Theresa, Mercy-Argenteau, and Marie-Antoinette, "Comte Florimond-Claude de Mercy-Argenteau," lxiv.

156   **Another risqué book**: Madame Beccary, *Mémoires de Fanny Spingler* (Paris: Chez Knapen & Fils, 1781).

156   **The primary stage could be treated**: Allan H. Pasco, *Revolutionary Love in Eighteenth and Early Nineteenth-Century France* (Farnham, UK: Ashgate, 2009), 167.

157   **More licentious than *Mémoires de Fanny Springler***: Michèle Bokobza Kahan, *Libertinage et folie dans le roman du 18e siècle* (Paris: Peeters, 2000), 180.

157   **"I've seen more than fifty people die"**: Pasco, *Revolutionary Love*, 167.

157   **"She who I respect"**: Restif de La Bretonne, *Le paysan perverti, ou, Les dangers de la ville* (Paris: La veuve Duchene, 1776), 350.

158   **In 1784, Marie Antoinette acquired the work**: Anonymous, *Les confessions d'une courtisane devenue philosophe* (Se trouve aux foires des principales villes des Pays-Bas, de France, d'Allemagne et de la Hollande, 1784), 2–3.

158   **The preface of this book is reminiscent**: Anonymous, *Les confessions d'une courtisane*, 2. "C'est en parcourant le cercle des faux plaisirs qu'elle en a connu le vuide & la satiété; c'est après que son âme ait été accablée par le poids de la dépravation,

qu'elle a savouré avec plus de délice, la douceur inexprimable d'une vie tranquille, exempte de reproche, et qui, employée à la pratique de ces devoirs, peut, seule, conduire au véritable bonheur."

À SAVOIR: MARIE ANTOINETTE'S HANDWRITING (1778–1792)

160 **"Madame, my very dear mother"**: Maria Theresa, *Maria Theresa und Marie Antoinette* (Vienna: Köhler, 1866), 349. "Madame ma très-chère mère, La santé de ma fille m'a occupée et un peu inquiétée depuis trois semaines. Plusieurs dents qui ont voulu sortir toutes à la fois, lui ont causé de grandes douleurs, et donné une fièvre. . . . Je suis touchée de la douceur et de la patience de cette pauvre petite au milieu de ses souffrances, qui dans certains moments ont été fort vives."

161 **"Here play went on madly"**: Littell, "Marie Antoinette," 582.

161 **"I am angry, Mr. Marshal"**: Marie Antoinette, *Lettre de Marie-Antoinette au maréchal de Castries, 30 août 1786* (Paris: Vente Collections Aristophil, 2019), 4. "Je suis fachée, Mr le maréchal, que vous ne m'ayez pas fait demander à me voir hier; malgré le peu de temps que j'avois a moi, j'en aurois toujours trouvé pour vous voir."

163 **Individualism and egocentricity**: Bashor, *Marie Antoinette's Head*, 77.

163 **"I don't need to tell you"**: "Souvenirs Historiques," *La Gazette Drouot* 1 (2020): 147. "Je n'ai pas besoin de vous dire, mon coeur, quel plaisir a éprouvé le roy à terminer l'affaire de M. de Luxembourg."

164 **Marie Antoinette may not have drunk alcohol**: William Procter Jr., "On Hoffman's Anodyne Liquor," *American Journal of Pharmacy* 28 (1852): 213–18. "Quand elle devient reine en 1774, elle conserve le même personnel pharmaceutique qui l'avait servi comme dauphine, c'est à dire Pierre-Alexandre Martin comme apothicaire du corps et Jamar de Libois, comme apothicaire du commun. Les médicaments lui sont alors fournis par Robert dont nous avons étudié le rôle comme apothicaire du roi. C'est ainsi que sur la couverture intérieure on peut lire la Potion pour la Reine: R. Syrop de capilaire une once; Eau de fleurs d'oranger une once; Eau de fleurs de tilleul trois onces; Gouttes d'Hoffmann g. 50. Avec cette dose, ou rempli le petit flacon de ce qu'il en peut contenir."

164 **"I showed your letter to the king"**: Marie Antoinette, *Lettre au Duc Jules de Polignac* (Paris: Vente Collections Aristophil, 2019), 2. "J'ai montré votre lettre au roi, et vous ne devez pas douter monsieur, du plaisir que nous avons à consentir au mariage de votre fils."

CHAPTER 14

171 ***The best treatment is mercury***: James Eustace Radclyffe McDonagh, *Venereal Diseases: Their Clinical Aspect and Treatment* (St. Louis, MO: C.V. Mosby, 1920), 4.

171 **Also, physicians were reluctant**: Linda Evi Merians, *The Secret Malady: Venereal Disease in Eighteenth-Century Britain and France* (Lexington: University Press of Kentucky, 1996), 118. "*He was unwilling to associate syphilis with the infants of*

'people of rank and fortune' with deaths being attributed to other causes like consumption. A child's tubercular osteitis could have been caused by venereal disease."

172   **"surprisingly cavalier attitude toward the disease"**: Pasco, *Revolutionary Love*, 165.

172   **Voltaire wrote that two-thirds of the French army**: Allan H. Ropper and Brian Burrell, *How the Brain Lost Its Mind: Sex, Hysteria, and the Riddle of Mental Illness* (New York: Penguin, 2019), 68.

172   **Syphilis was largely unknown in Europe**: Alfred Bollet and Alfred Jay, *Plagues and Poxes: The Impact of Human History on Epidemic Disease* (New York: Demos Medical, 2004), 72.

172   **Francis, the ninth king of the House of Valois**: John Bacot, *A Treatise on Syphilis* (London: Longman, Rees, Orme, Brown, and Green, 1829), 24. "François Ier, porteur du tréponème de la syphilis (nom de la bactérie responsable du mal), infecte la reine, Claude, qui en meurt en 1524."

173   **Other monarchs were likely infected**: Gérard Tilles and Daniel Wallach, "Histoire de la nosologie en dermatologie," *Annales de dermatologie et de vénéréologie* 116 (1989): 9–26.

173   **Elisabeth died while giving birth**: Bartolomé Bennassar, *Le Lit, le Pouvoir et la Mort: Reines et Princesses d'Europe de la Renaissance aux Lumières* (Paris: Editions de Fallois, 2006), 64.

173   **Historians have speculated**: Henri de Romeges, *Sexo-Monarchie* (Paris: Michel Lafon, 2013), 211. "Il lui refilera aussi une maladie vénérienne que lui avait transmise le chevalier de Lorraine."

173   **It is documented that King Louis XIV**: Augustin Cabanès, *La chronique médicale: Revue de médecine scientifique, littéraire et anecdotique* (Paris: Rédaction & administration, 1899), 380.

174   **Being generous, Philippe also gave**: Dirk Van der Cruysse, *Madame Palatine* (Paris: Fayard, 2014), 43. "L'homme n'est ni un ange ni un chêne."

174   **"Thanks to mercury's speed in the circulation"**: Jean Astruc, *Traité des maladies vénériennes: Où, après avoir expliqué l'origine, la propagation, & la communication de ces maladies en général, on décrit la nature, les causes & la curation de chacune en particulier* (Paris: La Veuve Cavelier, & Fils, 1773), 223. "Le mercure dit Astruc, grâce à sa vitesse dans la circulation détruira le virus vénérien quel qu'il soit et en quelque endroit où il se trouve . . . il sera détruit, déraciné et chassé au dehors par tous les conduits excrétoires. Cette modalité mécanique de destruction mérite d'être retenue. Elle dispensait en effet d'une salivation excessive qui au XVIIIe siècle n'était donc plus considérée comme indispensable."

174   **It could be used as an ointment**: Henri Hallopeau, *Du Mercure* (Paris: J. B. Baillière, 1878), 13.

174   **The excretion caused**: J. Felix Larrieu, *Cure Prompte et Radicale de la Syphilis* (Paris: Societe d'Editions Scientifiques, 1899), 15.

174   **A stove in which tablets of mercury**: James Copland and Charles Alfred Lee, "P. Lalouette, the New Method of Treating Venereal Diseases by Fumigation, Paris, 1776," in *A Dictionary of Practical Medicine: Comprising General Pathology, the Nature* (New York: Lilly, Wait, Colman, and Holden, 1859), 1493.

174 **It is uncertain whether Louis XV had treatment**: Jean-Frédéric Phélypeaux, comte de Maurepas, *Mémoires du comte de Maurepas* (Paris: Chez Buisson, 1792), 265. "Vos manières nobles et franches, / Pompadour, enchainent les cœurs; / Tous vos pas sont semés de fleurs; / Mais ce ne sont que des fleurs blanches."

175 **Such an epigram may have appeared**: Maurepas, *Mémoires*, 266.

175 **Historians have reported that the king's favorite**: Leslie Carroll, *Royal Romances: Titillating Tales of Passion and Power in the Palaces of Europe* (London: Penguin, 2012), 140.

175 **The prince had been drawn**: Pasco, *Revolutionary Love*, 164.

175 **And at the end of each banquet**: Walton, *Marie Antoinette's Confidante*, 18.

176 **The Duc de Chartres's grandmother wrote**: Pasco, *Revolutionary Love*, 166.

176 **"A young, lively and amiable Princess"**: Louis Petit de Bachaumont, *Mémoires secrets pour servir à l'histoire de la république des lettres en France* (London: John Adamson, 1784), 301. "Une jeune Princesse vive, aimable, mariée l'hiver dernier à un époux fort jeune aussi, n'a pu supporter tranquillement les infidélités réitérées de son mari, quelques funestes qu'elles aient été à son amour, même pour ce moderne Thésée; elle n'a pu voir, sans une jalousie marquée, son éloignement, ses écarts: elle a conçu de l'envie centre les objets les plus méprisables que le Prince honorait de ses regards; elle a eu contracté une mélancolie profonde et des vapeurs convulsives. Les médecins à la mode n'ayant pu calmer ce mal plus moral que physique, elle s'est mise entre les mains d'un nommé Pillara, charlatan en vogue."

176 **"The symptoms announced"**: Augustin Cabanès, *La princesse de Lamballe, intime: D'après les confidences de son médecin; Sa liaison avec Marie-Antoinette, son rôle secret pendant la Révolution* (Paris: A. Michel, 1922), 154. "Les symptômes annoncés par Saiffert se manifestèrent comme il l'avait prévu: la malade eut de la fièvre, en même temps qu'une éruption rouge, assez analogue à une éruption miliaire, sur toute la peau du corps."

177 **This would suggest that the princess**: Sarah Grant, *Female Portraiture and Patronage in Marie Antoinette's Court* (New York: Routledge, 2018), 41.

177 **Considering her wealth and status**: Castelnau, *La princesse de Lamballe*, 46. "Elle ne pouvait voir, sans un accès de jalousie marqué, l'éloignement et les excès de son époux; elle en conçut de l'envie contre les objets les plus méprisables que le prince honorait de ses regards. Elle en contracta une maladie profonde et des vapeurs convulsives. Cette maladie, les témoins contemporains l'identifient à celle de son mari, ce qui es possible."

177 **This chocolate remedy was actually sold**: Jean-Sylvain Bailly, *Vie privée de Charles-Philippe, ci-devant comte d'Artois, et sa correspondance* (Turin, Italy, 1749), 49.

CHAPTER 15

179 *Chlamydia in females was seldom detected*: Lemuel B. Bangs and William A. Hardaway, *An American Textbook of Genito-Urinary Diseases, Syphilis and Diseases of the Skin* (Philadelphia: W. B. Saunders, 1898), 347.

179   **Those close to the queen**: In her early and midtwenties Marie Antoinette had four children. At the age of twenty-two, she had child 1: a daughter born without complications who lived to the age of seventy-two. However, this daughter was unable to bear children in her marriage and was also known to have bad eyesight, bad teeth, and red blotches on her face. At the age of twenty-five, she had child 2: a son who was always sickly and feverish until his death at the age of seven. He became "hideously" crippled with curvature of the spine (referred to as vertebral decay or gangrene by the doctors), and he was plagued with tumors in his last year. It was also thought that symptoms of tuberculosis were the cause of his death. At the age of twenty-nine, she had child 3: a son who stooped at an early age, was often ill and frail, and was thought to have tuberculosis before dying at the age of ten. At the age of thirty, she had child 4: a daughter born prematurely who died a month before her first birthday. It was said that she was underdeveloped and fragile, and she died of convulsions (either due to cutting baby teeth or tuberculosis, according to an autopsy). In her midthirties it was reported that Marie Antoinette was becoming weaker and weaker, was suffering from uterine hemorrhaging, had bad eyes, and was almost blind in one eye before dying at the age of thirty-seven.

180   **These miscarriages could have been the result**: Lisa Marr, *Sexually Transmitted Diseases: A Physician Tells You What You Need to Know* (Baltimore: Johns Hopkins University Press, 2007), 47. "An infant born to a mother who has chlamydia can become infected when passing through an infected birth canal. Such an infant may develop infection in several different areas. About 10 percent have infection in the lungs, often developing symptoms several months after birth. Chlamydia can also cause miscarriage, premature rupture of membranes, preterm delivery, and delivery of a low-birth-weight infant."

180   **When the prince was taken from his governess**: François Fabre, *La Gazette des hôpitaux* (Bibliothèque du médecin-praticien, 1848), 622.

181   **"The queen gave birth"**: Louis Nicolardot, *Journal de Louis XVI* (Paris: E. Dentu, 1873), 43. "Couches de la reine du duc de Normandie à sept heures et demie; tout s'est passé de même qu'à mon fils."

181   **"And the miscarriage?"**: Mathurin François Adolphe de Lescure, *Correspondance secrète inédite sur Louis XVI, Marie-Antoinette, la cour et la ville de 1777 à 1792* (Paris: H. Plon, 1866), 483: "A cette occasion on se rappelle cette anecdote scandaleuse. Un jour la Reine dit à la comtesse Diane: 'Est-il vrai que le bruit raurt que j'ai des amants? — « On tient bien d'autres propos sur Votre Majesté,' répondit la comtesse. — 'Quels sont-ils?' — 'On dit que le beau Fersen est père du Dauphin, M. de Coigny de Madame Royale, le comte d'Artois de M. de Normandie. . . .' — 'Et la fausse couche?' reprit vivement la Reine."

181   **Even the Comte de Provence**: Labreli de Fontaine, *Révélation sur l'existence de Louis XVII, duc de Normandie* (Paris: Carpentier-Méricourt, 1831), 43. "Mais, monsieur l'abbé, il serait pourtant nécessaire de savoir quel est le père de l'enfant que vous allez baptiser. » L'ecclésiastique lui répondit avec dignité : « Cette question n'est point à » faire, Monseigneur : celui auquel je vais adminis» trer le sacrement de baptême, est le fils de votre » souverain et du mien. » Cette anecdote, fort au-

thentique, témoignait à elle seule la haine que le Comte de Provence avait vouée à Louis XVII, même au berceau."

181   **His sister, Marie-Thérèse**: Marie-Thérèse Charlotte Angoulême, *The Ruin of a Princess* (New York: Lamb, 1912), 263. "For some time past my brother had complained of a stitch in his side [point de côté]. May 6th, at seven in the evening, a rather strong fever seized him, with headache and the pain in his side. At first he could not lie down, for it suffocated him. My mother was uneasy and asked the municipals for a doctor. They assured her the illness was nothing and that her motherly tenderness was needlessly frightened. Nevertheless, they spoke to the Council and asked in my mother's name for Dr. Brunier. The Council laughed at my brother's illness, because Hébert had seen him five hours earlier without fever. They positively refused Brunier, whom Tison had recently denounced. Nevertheless, the fever became very strong. My aunt had the goodness to take my place in my mother's room, that I might not sleep in a fever atmosphere, and also that she might assist in nursing my brother; she took my bed, and I went to hers. The fever lasted several days, the attacks being worse at night."

182   **A history of miscarriages**: Merians, *Secret Malady*, 175.

182   **Furthermore, the child had been treated**: Will Bashor, *Marie Antoinette's Darkest Days: Prisoner No. 280 in the Conciergerie* (Lanham, MD: Rowman & Littlefield, 2016), 333.

182   **"Could a mother, or a woman of a certain age"**: Anonymous, *La Chronique médicale* (Paris: Rédaction & administration, 1898), 184. "Il y a un autre point sur lequel vous avez appelé mon attention: Une mère, ou une femme d'un certain âge, couchant avec son enfant, et affectée de leucorrhée ne peut-elle, sans qu'il y ait de sa part la moindre tentative de corruption, contaminer son enfant? Assurément: il suffit qu'il y ait contact, même involontaire, pour que la contagion se produise; encore dans ce cas, l'écoulement ressemblera à un écoulement blennorragique et il n'y aura que l'examen microscopique. la constatation du gonocoque de Neisser qui permettra de trancher la difficulté, et encore. . . . Voyez combien il faut être prudent dans ces questions délicates."

182   **chlamydia could have been the cause**: Gordon Edlin and Eric Golanty, *Health and Wellness* (Burlington, MA: Jones & Bartlett Learning, 2015), 433. "Left untreated, the chlamydial bacteria can multiply and cause inflammation and damage to the reproductive organs in both sexes. In men, untreated chlamydia can result in inflammation of the epididymis (epididymitis), characterized by pain, swelling, and tenderness in the scrotum and sometimes by a mild fever. . . . In women, chlamydial infections affect the cervix, uterus, fallopian tubes, and peritoneum. Often chlamydial infections of the reproductive tract produce no symptoms until the infection is advanced. A woman may then experience chronic pelvic pain, vaginal discharge, intermittent vaginal bleeding, and pain during intercourse."

182   **Syphilis of the lung might not have been as uncommon**: L. S. T. Burrell, *Syphilis in Relation to the Etiology and Diagnosis of Tuberculosis* (London: BMJ, 1929), 290.

183   **She was treated with medicinal soups**: Bashor, *Marie Antoinette's Darkest Days*, 193.

183   **"I immediately cut up one"**: Deborah Cadbury, *The Lost King of France: How DNA Solved the Mystery of the Murdered Son of Louis XVI and Marie Antoinette* (New York: St. Martin's Griffin, 2003), 109.

183   **the queen removed her bloody linen**: Bashor, *Marie Antoinette's Darkest Days*, 231.

183   **another cause could have been pelvic inflammatory disease**: Sarah Watstein and John Jovanovic, *Statistical Handbook on Infectious Diseases* (London: Greenwood, 2003), 93. "Up to 40% of women with untreated chlamydia will develop PID [pelvic inflammatory disease]."

183   **Another condition caused by chlamydia**: Gordon Edlin, Eric Golanty, and Kelli McCormack Brown, *Essentials for Health and Wellness* (Burlington, MA: Jones & Bartlett Learning, 2000), 179. "Chlamydia can reside in the cervix for many years, damaging uterine tubes and resulting in PID."

183   **chlamydia in females was seldom detected**: Bangs and Hardaway, *American Textbook*, 347.

184   **"Sunday 19: Rain and wind"**: Eugène Soubeiran, *Nouveau traité de pharmacie théorique et pratique* (Paris: Société Belge de Librairie, 1837), 472.

185   **On the twenty-sixth day patients**: Maximilian Joseph Chelius, *A System of Surgery* (London: Henry Renshaw, 1847), 664–68.

CHAPTER 16

187   *It is said that the astrologer*: Henry C. Hodges, "The Case of Marie Antoinette," *The Gateway: A Magazine Devoted to Literature, Economics, and Social Service* (Detroit, MI: Gateway, 1905), 38.

187   **In some parts of the report**: Corrine Kenner, *Astrology for Writers: Spark Your Creativity Using the Zodiac* (Woodbury, MN: Llewellyn Worldwide, 2013), 302–18.

SUN	Spirit, life force and identity. Masculine principle
MOON	Soul, emotions and instincts. Domesticity. Feminine principle
MERCURY	Intellect and power of communication. The reasoning mind
VENUS	Love, beauty, art and attraction
MARS	Energy, action, aggression and conflict
JUPITER	Wisdom, expansion, optimism and success
SATURN	Restriction, limitation, restraint and sorrow
URANUS	Change, originality, revolution and eccentricity
NEPTUNE	Imagination, spirituality, inspiration, illusion and deception
PLUTO	Power, forces beyond personal control and transformation

188   *Ascendant in Cancer*: Astrology House New Zealand (Orewa), chart wheel generated using Janus 5 Astrology Software, email to author, June 10, 2019. (All following chart readings are from this email.)

189   **Questionable, however, was her attention**: Arneth, *Marie-Antoinette*, 200. "Je suis bien touchée de la joie que ma chère maman veut bien me dire qui règne dans Vienne sur ma grossesse; s'il était possible, cela me ferait encore mieux aimer ma patrie. J'ai vu hier matin Caironi; je l'ai chargé de bien dire à toutes les personnes

qui veulent bien s'intéresser à moi qu'il m'a vue lui-même et très bien portante. J'oubliais de dire à ma chère maman qu'à ma seconde révolution j'ai demandé au roi 500 louis, ce qui fait 12,000 francs, que j'ai cru à propos d'envoyer à Paris pour les pauvres qui sont retenus en prison pour dettes des mois qu'ils doivent aux nourrices, et 4,000 francs ici à Versailles, aussi pour les pauvres. C'était une manière de faire une charité en même temps que de constater mon état aux yeux de tout le peuple. Je connais trop le bon cœur de ma chère maman pour ne pas espérer qu'elle m'approuvera."

189   **She was also a fervent supporter of convents**: Françoise de Motteville, *Memoirs of Madame de Motteville on Anne of Austria and her Court* (Boston: Hardy, Pratt, 1902), 186.

189   **she unabashedly and without embarrassment**: Arneth, *Marie-Antoinette*, 35. "La reine en a marqué un peu d'humeur au roi qui, avec sa douceur et complaisance naturelles, n'a presque pas osé avouer les ordres prohibitifs qu'il avait été obligé de donner; aussi la reine ne s'en gênait—elle aucunement; on joue presque tous les jours chez elle au pharaon."

189   **The queen and her architect**: Rocheterie, *The Life of Marie Antoinette*, 175. "The queen and Hubert Robert thought of everything."

190   **Her lightheartedness was well known**: Zweig, *Marie Antoinette*, 54.

190   **However, the count was worried**: Nolhac, *La Reine Marie-Antoinette*, 244. "The correspondent of Maria Theresa was not without anxiety for the future. The favour that he had received was extended to some other persons. The Queen yielded to the desire of being seen and applauded, and to the entreaties which were made to her on every side. But, as the royal representations were still kept to a certain exclusiveness, those who solicited admittance in vain resented the affront, and raised a clamour."

191   **"I can tell you I love you"**: Boigne, *Memoirs of the Comtesse de Boigne*, 306–310. "Je peux vous dire que je vous aime et je n'ai même le temps que de cela. Je me porte bien, ne soyez pas inquiet de moi. Je voudrais bien vous savoir de même. Ecrivez-moi en chiffre par la poste à l'adresse de M. Brown, une double enveloppe à M. Gougeno. Faites mettre les adresses par votre valet de chambre. Mandez-moi à qui je pourrais adresser celles que je pourrais vous écrire, car je ne peux plus vivre sans cela. Adieu le plus aimé et le plus aimant des hommes. Je vous embrasse de tout mon cœur (1). » Est-ce un premier aveu encouragé par les circonstances du dévouement et de la distance? Est-ce la preuve d'une intime et ancienne liaison? L'histoire ne le saura jamais."

191   **The letter was unquestionably passionate**: Boigne, *Memoirs of the Comtesse de Boigne*, 273.

191   **The French aristocrat**: Boigne, *Memoirs of the Comtesse de Boigne*, 273.

191   **Marie Antoinette definitely had Mars**: Hodges, "Case of Marie Antoinette," 38.

192   **"She had no idea of putting up with"**: Littell, "Marie Antoinette," 581.

192   **"There is no true warmth"**: Littell, "Marie Antoinette," 581.

192   **Marie Antoinette was also strong-willed**: Littell, "Marie Antoinette," 581. "Marie-Antoinette had no idea of putting up with anything irksome, or of not freely indulging in fancies. Not that she was a person of really warm affection. Marie-Antoinette was cold at heart, though she had an easily excited surface sen-

sibility, which made her hasty and impulsive. Maria Theresa writes anxiously and tenderly: Marie-Antoinette's letters exhibit only the frigid phrases of glib conventionality. There is no true warmth in her expression. This constitutional coldness was probably a lucky accident under the circumstances which marked the early years of her wedded life. If Marie Antoinette did not feel deeply, she was, however, given to quick likes and dislikes, which she indulged with petulant vehemence. Marie-Antoinette's friendships were merely a child's delight in a toy, that engrosses for a season, but subsides as soon as the sport has lost its attraction."

193 **Mercy added that Louis**: Alphonse Jobez, *La France sous Louis XVI* (Paris: Didier et Cie, 1881), 48.

193 **"The king feared her"**: Simone Bertière, *The Indomitable Marie-Antoinette* (Paris: Editions de Fallois, 2014), 127.

193 **Because her husband suffered**: Cabanès, *Le Cabinet secret de l'histoire*, 49. Did this surgery actually take place? According to the *Mémoires de Madame Campan* (Philadelphia: A. Small, 1823), 236, the question is not resolved. "Vers les derniers mois de 1777, la reine, étant seule dans ses cabinets, nous fit appeler, mon beau-père et moi, et, nous présentant sa main à baiser, nous dit que nous regardant l'un et l'autre comme des gens bien occupés de son bonheur, elle voulait recevoir nos compliments; qu'enfin elle était reine de France et qu'elle espérait bientôt avoir des enfants; qu'elle avait, jusqu'à ce moment, su cacher ses peines, mais qu'en secret elle avait versé bien des pleurs. A partir de ce moment heureux si longtemps attendu, l'attachement du roi pour la reine prit tout le caractère de l'amour. Le bon Lassone, premier médecin du roi et de la reine, me parlait souvent de la peine que lui avait faite un éloignement dont il avait longtemps à vaincre la cause, et ne me paraissait plus avoir alors que des inquiétudes d'un genre tout différent."

194 **He wrote to the queen**: Campan, *Memoirs of the Private Life of Marie Antoinette*, 204.

194 **On seeing her ring again**: Campan, *Memoirs of the Private Life of Marie Antoinette*, 204. "A few days after the Queen's recovery from her confinement, the curé of the Magdelaine de la Cité, at Paris, wrote to M. Campan, and requested a private interview with him; it was to desire he would deliver into the hands of the Queen, a little box, containing her wedding-ring, with this note written by the curé: 'I have received under the seal of confession, the ring which I send to your majesty; with an avowal, that it was stolen from you in 1771, in order to be used in sorceries, to prevent your having any children.' On seeing her ring again, the Queen said that she had, in fact, lost it about seven years before, while washing her hands; and that she had made it a rule with herself, to use no endeavour to discover the superstitious woman who had done her the injury."

194 **The king acquiesced**: Yonge, *Life of Marie Antoinette*, 207–11. "St. Cloud was bought; and Marie Antoinette, still eager to prevent her own acquisition from being too costly, proposed to the king that it should be bought in her name, and called her property; since an establishment for her would naturally be framed on a more moderate scale than that of any palace belonging to the king, which was held always to require the appointment of a governor and deputy-governors, with a corresponding staff of underlings, while she should only require a porter at the outer gate. The advantage of such a plan was so obvious that it was at once adopted."

195 **The queen's favorite, Besenval**: Haggard, *Louis XVI*, 269.

195 **"You yourself have said"**: Klara Mundt, *Marie Antoinette and Her Son* (New York: McClure, 1867), 38.

197 **"You are afraid"**: Zweig, *Marie Antoinette*, 54.

197 **Everything depends on the wife**: Rocheterie, *The Life of Marie Antoinette*, 14.

198 **She added that Marie Antoinette's**: Campan, *Memoirs of the Private Life of Marie Antoinette*, 24.

199 **She enjoyed the social life at court**: Zweig, *Marie Antoinette*, 89.

201 **Until the family was sent to the Temple**: Bashor, *Marie Antoinette's Darkest Days*, 262.

201 **The entire royal family was at risk**: Maria Theresa, Mercy-Argenteau, and Marie-Antoinette, "Comte Florimond-Claude de Mercy-Argenteau," 188.

201 **The craft landed safely after flying**: Roy Bainton, *The Mammoth Book of Unexplained Phenomena* (London: Little, Brown, 2013), 37.

202 **If one of the princesses was with child**: Vehse, *Memoirs of the Court*, 215–19.

202 **"When the mob arrived"**: Barry Edward O'Meary, *Napoleon in Exile; or, A Voice from St. Helena* (London: W. Simpkin and R. Marshall, 1822), 110.

203 **"These amours were not"**: Edouard et Jules Goncourt, "Queen Marie Antoinette," in *The Edinburgh Review* (New York: Leonard Scott, 1859), 75.

203 **"Paris, October 9, 1789"**: Fersen, *Le comte de Fersen*, 51: "Paris, le 9 octobre 1789. Tous les papiers publics vous instruiront, mon cher père, de ce qui s'est passé à Versailles le lundi 5 et le mardi 6, et de l'arrivée du roi à Paris avec toute la famille royale. J'ai été témoin de tout, et je suis revenu à Paris dans une des voitures de la suite du roi; nous avons été six heures et demie en chemin. Dieu me préserve de jamais voir un spectacle aussi affligeant que celui de ces deux journées. Le peuple paraît enchanté de voir le roi et sa famille."

203 **Charles-Maurice de Talleyrand, a historian**: Goncourt, "Queen Marie Antoinette," 77.

203 **Although it is still unclear**: Violette M. Montagu, *The Celebrated Madame Campan: Lady-in-Waiting to Marie Antoinette and Confidante to Napoleon* (Philadelphia: Lippincott, 1914), 96–99.

204 **When she left the balcony**: Imbert de Saint-Amand, *Marie Antoinette and the End of the Old Régime* (New York: Charles Scribner's Sons, 1890), 264–68.

204 **"The Queen is enchanted with her"**: Mary Monica Maxwell-Scott, *Madame Elizabeth de France, 1764–1794* (London: Edward Arnold, 1908), 25.

204 **"If sovereigns descended"**: Maxwell-Scott, *Madame Elizabeth de France*, 50.

205 **The former queen was taken to the Conciergerie**: Maxwell-Scott, *Madame Elizabeth de France*, 25–26.

206 **Simon told Hébert**: Zweig, *Marie Antoinette*, 57.

206 **When Simon asked**: Zweig, *Marie Antoinette*, 58.

207 **When Herman, the president of the tribunal**: Bashor, *Marie Antoinette's Darkest Days*, 166.

207 **Then, before Herman proceeded**: Mundt, *Marie Antoinette and Her Son*, 401.

207 **Then, she turned to face the people**: Émile Marc H. Saint-Hilaire, *Histoire des conspirations et des exécutions politiques en France* (Paris: Gustave Havard, 1849), 186.

208 **"Having a natural desire to go to her death clean"**: Zweig, *Marie Antoinette*, 449. "But even for this last occasion, a last humiliation had been kept in store. For many days, now, she had been losing blood, and the shift she was wearing was soiled with it."

208 **"Since the revolution, the monarchical club"**: Hector Fleischmann, *Marie-Antoinette Libertine* (Paris: Bibliothèque des Curieux, 1911), 267. "Depuis la Révolution, le club monarchien dont Antoinette est l'âme n'a cessé de faire des tentatives. Chacun des membres qui le composent a puisé dans le vagin de L'Autrichienne le poison qu'il s'efforce de distiller. Cet antre pestiféré est le réceptacle de tous les vices, et là chacun vient se pourvoir abondamment de la dose qui lui est propre."

À SAVOIR: MARIE ANTOINETTE'S HANDWRITING (1792–1793)

209 **The following letter**: Fersen, *Le comte de Fersen*, 111. "La personne qui vous porte celle-ci vous dira et fera connaître notre position telle qu'elle est. J'y ai entière confiance et il la mérite par son attachement et sa raison. Il porte un mémoire absurde, mais que je suis obligée d'envoyer. Il est essentiel que l'Emp. soit bien persuadé qu'il n'y a pas là un mot qui soit de nous, ni de notre manière de voir les choses; mais qu'il me fasse pourtant une réponse, comme s'il croyait que c'est là ma manière de voir, et que je puisse montrer; car ils sont si méfiants ici qu'ils exigeront la réponse."

211 **According to Barnave's biographer**: Anonymous, *Revue encyclopédique, ou Analyse raisonnée des productions les plus remarquables* (Paris: Bureau Central de la Revue Encyclopédique, 1831), 552. "Barnave sera la plus belle figure de la révolution. Pour ceux qui connaissent les détails de la vie convulsive du jeune tribun, pour ceux surtout qui savent l'histoire de sa mort, qui ont lu cette admirable lettre écrite de Dijon à sa mère et à ses sœurs, dans une halte de sa marche vers l'échafaud, il ne peut y avoir un doute sur la réalité de ce simple et ferme héroïsme qui constituait son génie et son caractère. Voilà l'homme dont M. Janin a fait un amant ridicule de la reine. A l'entendre, Barnave était amoureux de Marie-Antoinette, selon toute probabilité, long-tems avant qu'il ne l'eût vue."

211 **General François Jarjayes, along with the guard Toulan**: Clara Tschudi, *Marie Antoinette* (London: Swan Sonnenschein, 1902), 261–62.

211 **"You will be angry with me"**: Tschudi, *Marie Antoinette*, 262.

211 **"We have dreamed a lovely dream"**: Rocheterie, *The Life of Marie Antoinette*, 501.

CHAPTER 17

215 **He complied and then left her alone**: Bashor, *Marie Antoinette's Darkest Days*, 333. "C'est à vous, ma Sœur, que j'écris pour la dernière fois. Je viens d'être

condamnée non pas à une mort honteuse, elle ne l'est que pour les criminels, mais à aller rejoindre votre frère; comme lui innocente, j'espère montrer la même fermeté que lui dans ces derniers moments. Je suis calme comme on l'est quand la conscience [*sic*] ne reproche rien, j'ai un profond regret d'abandonner mes pauvres enfants; vous savez que je n'existois que pour eux, et vous, ma bonne et tendre Sœur: vous qui avez par votre amitié tout sacrifié pour être avec nous; dans quelle position je vous laisse! J'ai appris par le plaidoyer même du procès que ma fille étoit séparée de vous. Hélas! la pauvre enfant, je n'ose pas lui écrire, elle ne recevroit pas ma lettre je ne sais même pas si celle-ci vous parviendra, recevez pour eux deux ici, ma bénédiction. J'espère qu'un jour, lorsqu'ils seront plus grands, ils pourront se réunir avec vous, et jouir en entier de vos tendres soins. Qu'ils pensent tous deux à ce que je n'ai cessé de leur inspirer, que les principes, et l'exécution exacte de ses devoirs sont la première base de la vie; que leur amitié et leur confiance mutuelle, en feront le bonheur; que ma fille sente qu'à l'âge qu'elle a, elle doit toujours aider son frère pour les conseils que [*rature*] l'expérience qu'elle aura de plus que lui et son amitié pourront lui inspirer; que mon fils à son tour, rende à sa sœur, tous les soins, les services que l'amitié peut inspirer; qu'ils sentent enfin tous deux que, dans quelque position où ils pourront se trouver, ils ne seront vraiment heureux que par leur union. Qu'ils prennent exemple de nous, combien dans nos malheurs, notre amitié nous a donné de consolations, et dans le bonheur on jouit doublement quand on peut le partager avec un ami; et où en trouver de plus tendre, de plus cher que dans sa propre famille? Que mon fils n'oublie jamais les derniers mots de son père, que je lui répète expressément: qu'il ne cherche jamais à venger notre mort. J'ai à vous parler d'une chose bien pénible à mon cœur. Je sais combien cet enfant, doit vous avoir fait de la peine; pardonnez-lui, ma chère Sœur; pensez à l'âge qu'il a, et combien il est facile de faire dire a [*sic*] un enfant ce qu'on veut, et même ce qu'il ne comprend pas, un jour viendra, j'espère, où il ne sentira que mieux tout le prix de vos bontés et de votre tendresse pour tous deux il me reste à vous confier encore mes dernières pensées. J'aurois voulu les écrire dès le commencement du procès; mais, outre qu'on ne me laissoit pas écrire, la marche en a été si rapide, que je n'en aurois réellement pas eu le tem. Je meurs dans la religion catholique, apostolique et romaine, dans celle de mes pères, dans celle où j'ai été élevée, et que j'ai toujours professée, n'ayant aucune consolation spirituelle à attendre, ne sachant pas s'il existe encore ici des prêtres de cette religion, et même le lieu où je suis les exposeroit trop, s'il [*sic*] y entroient une fois. Je demande sincèrement pardon à Dieu de toutes les fautes que j'ai pu commettre depuis que j'existe. J'espère que dans sa bonté il voudra bien recevoir mes derniers vœux, ainsi que ceux que je fais depuis longtems pour qu'il veuille bien recevoir mon âme dans sa miséricorde et sa bonté. Je demande pardon à tout ceux que je connois, et à vous, ma Sœur, en particulier, de toutes les peines que, sans le vouloir, j'aurois pu vous causer. Je pardonne à tous mes ennemis le mal qu'ils m'ont fait. Je dis ici adieu à mes tantes [*rature*] et à tous mes frères et sœurs. J'avois des amis, l'idée d'en être séparée pour jamais et leurs peines sont un des plus grands regrets que j'emporte en mourant, qu'ils sachent, du moins, que jusqu'à mon dernier moment, j'ai pensé à eux. Adieu, ma bonne et tendre Sœur; puisse cette lettre vous arriver! pensez toujours à moi; je vous embrasse de tout mon cœur, ainsi que ces pauvres et chers enfants; mon Dieu! qu'il est déchirant de les quitter pour toujours. Adieu, adieu! je ne vais plus m'occuper que de mes devoirs spirituels. Comme je ne suis pas libre dans mes actions, on m'amènera peut-être, un prêtre, mais je proteste ici que je ne lui dirai pas un mot, et que je le traiterai comme un être absolument étranger."

215   **"This handwriting has a good standard"**: Bella Choji, email to author, July 30, 2019.

217   **However, the last three letters**: Adolphe Desbarrolles, *Les mystères de l'écriture: Art de juger les hommes sur leurs autographes* (Paris: Garnier Frères, 1872), 292. "L'écriture de Marie-Antoinette ne dit pas une sensibilité exquise, encore moins la sensibilité de l'abandon. Quand elle écrit pauvres en parlant de ses enfants, la mère se penche un peu plus: il en est de même au mot pour toujours. Mais la femme, la reine, la chrétienne se redresse dans les tortures mêmes de son cœur. Marie-Antoinette n'emploie de majuscules que pour les deux initiales de sa signature. L'écrit que nous étudions commence par une minuscule, signe classique, nous le savons, ou d'instruction incomplète, ou de simplicité, ou d'inattention. Remarquez ces barres fermes, rigides et épaisses qui coupent lest minuscules dans la ligne:'Avez par votre amitié tout sacrifié'; voyez le même signe de puissance de volonté et d'énergie intraitable dans le mot prêtre. Et dans la deénière ligne, cette nature inébranlable et héroïque se sert du même trait dur, implacable, inexorable, pour barrer deux T, qui appartiennent a deux mots distincts."

217   **"I write to you"**: Bashor, *Marie Antoinette's Darkest Days*, 227–29.

217   **The *Glaive vengeur***: H. G. Dulac, *Le glaive vengeur de la République française une et indivisible ou galerie* (Paris: Galletti, 1793), 116.

217   **And the *Moniteur* reported**: Eliakim Littell, "Lord Holland's Foreign Reminiscences," *Living Age* 29 (1851): 392.

217   **The following verse**: Louis Hastier, *Vieilles histoires, étranges énigmes* (Paris: A. Fayard, 1955), 183.

218   **"I wish that my death"**: Eliakim Littell, "Louis XVII," *Living Age* 39 (1853): 215.

218   **"Not a murmur, not a motion"**: Anonymous, *The Universal Magazine of Knowledge and Pleasure* (London: W. Bent, 1793), 77.

220   **However, evidence suggests that the queen**: Bashor, *Marie Antoinette's Darkest Days*, 280.

221   **"I say here adieu"**: Bashor, *Marie Antoinette's Darkest Days*, 229.

222   **The queen's daughter, Marie-Thérèse**: Belloc, *Marie Antoinette*, 419.

222   **The remark, "avait couché avec la reine"**: Charles Kunstler, *Fersen et son secret* (Paris: Hachette, 1947), 321.

CHAPTER 18

223   **The Comte de la Marck confirmed this**: Comte de Mirabeau, *Correspondance entre le comte de Mirabeau et le comte de La Marck* (Brussels, Belgium: Méline, Cans et

compagnie, 1851), 300. "Il a eu, il y a peu de jours, une longue conférence avec la reine: il a employé les moyens les plus odieux pour jeter le trouble dans son âme, et il a été jusqu'à lui dire que, pour obtenir le divorce, on la rechercherait en adultère."

224   **When Louis asked her**: Rocheterie, *Histoire de Marie-Antoinette*, 53.

224   **Historian Thomas Wright wrote**: Wright, *History of France*, 403. "Marie Antoinette passed her life in the bosom of a little private society, to which the high nobility who surrounded the throne were seldom admitted; while her party which found support only in her favour, consisted of persons generally of little character, and often of mere servile representatives of the interests of Austria, and stood as low in the consideration of the public as in that of the aristocracy. Her personal attachments were violent and unduly demonstrative, and, as is generally the result, of short duration."

224   **Witnessing such illicit acts**: David M. Turner, *Fashioning Adultery: Gender, Sex and Civility* (Cambridge: Cambridge University Press, 2002), 154.

225   **A confession on the part of the guilty party**: Turner, *Fashioning Adultery*, 153. "All evidence of adultery was therefore to some degree 'presumptive,' evaluated on the 'proximity and nearness of the Acts.' Strong proofs of adultery included witnessing 'the Man's lying on the Woman's Body with her Coats up,' viewing the man and woman 'both together naked and undressed in some secret place . . . or else from seeing them in Bed together and the like.'"

225   **"Letters in which the accused parties"**: "Criminal Laws," *Collins Dictionary of Law*, ed. William J. Stewart (Glasgow: HarperCollins, 1996).

225   **To the princess she wrote**: Lucien Faucou, *L'Intermédiaire des chercheurs et curieux* (Paris: L'Intermédiaire des chercheurs et curieux, 1894), 3. "Adieu, ma chère Lamballe, je vous embrasse du meilleur de mon cœur comme je vous aimerai toute ma vie."

225   **And to Madame de Polignac**: Marie Antoinette, *Lettres de Marie-Antoinette* (Paris: A. Picard et fils, 1895), xlii. "Je ne peux résister au plaisir de vous embrasser encore."

225   **sexual contact with other women**: Turner, *Fashioning Adultery*, 154.

225   **Finally, Marie Antoinette wrote Fersen**: Florian Kergourlay, *Les passages caches des lettres de Marie-Antoinette au comte de Fersen* (Paris: Communiqué de presse, 2015), 1. "Je vais finer, non pas sans vous dire mon bien cher et tendre ami que je vous aime à la *folie* et que *jamais* jamais je ne peux être un moment sans vous adorer."

225   **Fersen confirms staying overnight**: Saint-Amand, *Marie Antoinette*, 17.

226   **Fersen had entered the palace**: Zweig, *Marie Antoinette*, 338.

226   **The relationships may have been sporadic**: William Mack and William Benjamin Hale, *Corpus Juris: Being a Complete and Systematic Statement of the Whole Body of the Law as Embodied in and Developed by All Reported Decisions* (London: Butterworth, 1920), 128.

226   **From the viewpoint of the queen's subjects**: Sara F. Matthews-Grieco, *Cuckoldry, Impotence and Adultery in Europe* (New York: Routledge, 2017), 276.

226   **"All the youth of both sexes"**: Charlotte-Elisabeth Orléans, *Correspondance Complète de Madame Duchesse d'Orléans* (Paris: Charpentier, 1891), 366. "On a plus que jamais besoin des grâces de Dieu, car c'est une terrible époque que la nôtre;

on n'entend parler que de querelles, de discussions, de vols, de meurtres, de vices de tous genres; le vieux serpent, le diable, a été délivré de ses chaînes et règne dans l'air; il faut donc que tous les bons chrétiens se livrent à la prière."

226 **Interestingly enough, Louis XIII did**: Herbert Lockyer, *Last Words of Saints and Sinners: 700 Final Quotes from the Famous* (Grand Rapids, MI: Kregel, 1969), 81.

227 **When he became deathly ill**: Williams, *Memoirs of Madame du Barry*, 248.

227 **"We cannot recommence the scandal"**: Pierre de Nolhac, *Louis XV at Versailles* (Paris: Flammarion, 1934), 119.

227 **"I sincerely ask pardon of God"**: Bashor, *Marie Antoinette's Darkest Days*, 229.

227 **Although repentant, was Marie Antoinette still guilty**: Anonymous, *The Christian Library* (Philadelphia: E. C. & J. Biddle, 1851), 45.

SELECTED BIBLIOGRAPHY

I am referencing the sources that have been used in writing *Marie Antoinette's World: Intrigue, Infidelity, and Adultery in Versailles*, but due to the immense amount that has been written about Marie Antoinette, this bibliography does not include all the books and sources that I researched.

A., J. P. *L'Esprit d'Addisson.* Yverdon, Switzerland: Société Littérature, 1777.

Abbott, John Stevens Cabot. *History of Maria Antoinette.* New York: Harper & Brothers, 1868.

———. *Louis XIV.* New York: Harper & Brothers, 1898.

Albini, F. de. *Marie Antoinette and the Diamond Necklace from Another Point of View.* London: Swan Sonnenschein, 1900.

Aldrich, Robert, and Garry Wotherspoon. *Who's Who in Gay and Lesbian History: From Antiquity to World War II.* London: Routledge, 2002.

Anonymous. "A Victim of Paris and Versailles." *Macmillan's Magazine* 24 (1871): 494.

———. *The Christian Library.* Philadelphia: E. C. & J. Biddle, 1851.

———. *La Chronique médicale.* Paris: Rédaction & administration, 1898.

———. *Les confessions d'une courtisane devenue philosophe.* Se trouve aux foires des principales villes des Pays-Bas, de France, d'Allemagne et de la Hollande, 1784.

———. "Libels on the Queen of France." *Anglo American* 1 (1843): 234.

———. "Marie Antoinette." *London Quarterly Review.* New York: Leonard Scott Publishing, 1877.

———. "The Marriages of the Bourbons." *Spectator* 64 (1890): 273.

———. *Revue encyclopédique, ou Analyse raisonnée des productions les plus remarquables.* Paris: Bureau Central de la Revue Encyclopédique, 1831.

———. *La Revue hebdomadaire.* Paris: Plon, 1916.

———. "Secret Correspondence on Marie Antoinette." *Edinburgh Review* 144–45 (1876): 175.

———. "Secret of the Satisfaction We Derive from Certain Stenches." *Current Opinion.* New York: Current Literature Publishing, 1913.

———. "Souvenirs Historiques." *La Gazette Drouot* 1 (2020): 147.

———. *The Universal Magazine of Knowledge and Pleasure*. London: W. Bent, 1793.

Arbois, Julien. *Dans le lit de nos ancêtres*. Paris: City Edition, May 25, 2016.

Arnaud, Claude. *Chamfort*. Chicago: University of Chicago Press, 1992.

Arneth, Alfred Ritter von. *Marie-Antoinette: Correspondance secrète entre Marie-Thérèse et le Comte de Mercy-Argenteau*. Paris: Firmin Didot Frères, 1875.

Astruc, Jean. *Traité des maladies vénériennes: Où, après avoir expliqué l'origine, la propagation, & la communication de ces maladies en général, on décrit la nature, les causes & la curation de chacune en particulier*. Paris: La Veuve Cavelier & Fils, 1773.

Bachaumont, Louis Petit de. *Marie-Antoinette, Louis XVI et la famille royale*. Paris: E. Thunot, 1866.

———. *Mémoires secrets pour servir à l'histoire de la république des lettres en France*. London: John Adamson, 1784.

Bacot, John. *A Treatise on Syphilis*. London: Longman, Rees, Orme, Brown, and Green, 1829.

Bailly, Jean-Sylvain. *Vie privée de Charles-Philippe, ci-devant comte d'Artois, et sa correspondance*. Turin, Italy, 1749.

Bainton, Roy. *The Mammoth Book of Unexplained Phenomena*. London: Little, Brown, 2013.

Balteau, Jean. *Dictionnaire de Biographie Française*. Paris: Letouzey et Ané, 1939.

Baraton, Alain. *L'Amour à Versailles*. Paris: Grasset & Fasquelle, 2009.

Bashor, Will. *Jean-Baptiste Cléry: Eyewitness to Louis XVI and Marie-Antoinette's Nightmare*. Philadelphia: Diderot Press, 2011.

———. *Marie Antoinette's Darkest Days: Prisoner No. 280 in the Conciergerie*. Lanham, MD: Rowman & Littlefield, 2016.

———. *Marie Antoinette's Head: The Royal Hairdresser, the Queen, and the Revolution*. Guilford, CT: Lyons Press, 2013.

Baudrillart, Alfred. *Philippe V et la Cour de France: D'après les documents inédits tirés des archives espagnoles de Simancas et d'Alcala de Hénarès et des archives du Ministère des Affaires étrangères*. Paris: Firmin Didot, 1748.

Baumann, Émile. *Marie-Antoinette et Axel Fersen*. Paris: Grasset, 1931.

Beach, Vincent Woodrow. *Charles X of France: His Life and Times*. London: Pruett, 1971.

Bearne, Catherine Mary Charlton. *A Sister of Marie Antoinette: The Life-Story of Maria Carolina, Queen of Naples*. London: T. Fisher Unwin, 1907.

Beaumelle, M. de la. *Memoirs for the History of Madame de Maintenon and of the Last Age*. London: A. Millar and J. Nourse, 1757.

Beccary, Madame. *Mémoires de Fanny Spingler*. Paris: Chez Knapen & Fils, 1781.

Beem, C., and M. Taylor. *The Man behind the Queen: Male Consorts in History*. London: Palgrave Macmillan, 2014.

Belloc, Hillaire. *Marie Antoinette*. New York: Doubleday, Page, 1909.

Bennassar, Bartolomé. *Le Lit, le Pouvoir et la Mort: Reines et Princesses d'Europe de la Renaissance aux Lumières*. Paris: Editions de Fallois, 2006.

Bentley, Richard. *Bentley's Miscellany*. London: Richard Bentley, 1860.

Bernier, Georges, and Rosamond Bernier. *L'œil*. Paris: Imprimeries réunies, 1959.

Bertière, Simone. *The Indomitable Marie-Antoinette*. Paris: Editions de Fallois, 2014.

Bertrand, Louis. *La Vie amoureuse de Louis XIV*. Paris: Frédérique Patat, 1924.

Bible. New Oxford Annotated Version. 3rd ed. Oxford: Oxford University Press, 2001.

Biger, Pierre-Henri. "Introduction à l'éventail européen aux XVII et XVIII siècles." *Seventeenth-Century French Studies* 36 (2014): 84–92.

Boigne, Comtesse de. *Memoirs of the Comtesse de Boigne.* London: Charles Scribner's Sons, 1907.

Bollet, Alfred, and Alfred Jay. *Plagues and Poxes: The Impact of Human History on Epidemic Disease.* New York: Demos Medical, 2004.

Bourg, Edme Théodore. *Amours et galanteries des rois de France: Mémoires historiques sur les concubines, maitresses et favorites de ces princes.* Brussels, Belgium: Louis Tencé, 1830.

Bradby, Godfrey Fox. *The Great Days of Versailles: Studies from Court Life in the Later Years of Louis XIV.* New York: Charles Scribner's Sons, 1906.

Burrell, L. S. T. *Syphilis in Relation to the Etiology and Diagnosis of Tuberculosis.* London: BMJ, 1929.

Burrows, Simon. *A King's Ransom: The Life of Charles Théveneau de Morande, Blackmailer, Scandalmonger and Master-Spy.* London: Bloomsbury, 2010.

Burrows, Simon, Jonathan Conlin, Russell Goulbourne, and Valerie Mainz. *The Chevalier d'Eon and His Worlds: Gender, Espionage and Politics in the Eighteenth Century.* London: Continuum UK, 2011.

Cabanès, Augustin. *Le Cabinet secret de l'histoire.* Paris: Albin Michel, 1900.

———. *La chronique médicale: Revue de médecine scientifique, littéraire et anécdotique.* Paris: Rédaction & administration, 1899.

Campan, Madame Jeanne-Louise-Henriette. *Memoirs of the Private Life of Marie Antoinette, Queen of France and Navarre.* Philadelphia: A. Small, 1823.

Capefigue, Jean Baptiste Honoré Raymond. *L'Europe pendant la Révolution française.* Brussels, Belgium: Société belge de librairie, 1843.

Carroll, Leslie. *Royal Romances: Titillating Tales of Passion and Power in the Palaces of Europe.* London: Penguin, 2012.

Castelnau, Jacques. *La princesse de Lamballe.* Paris: Librairie Hachette, 1956.

Castelot, André. *Les grandes heures de la Révolution française.* Paris: Perrin, 1962.

Challice, Anna Emma. *Heroes, Philosophers, and Courtiers of the Time of Louis XVI.* London: Hurst and Blackett, 1863.

Chelius, Maximilian Joseph. *A System of Surgery.* London: Henry Renshaw, 1847.

Chevallier, Pierre. "Les Étranges Amours du Roi Louis XIII." *Historama* 336 (1979): 1.

Churchill, Winston. *Marlborough: His Life and Times.* London: C. Scribner's Sons, 1933.

Cim, Albert. *Les Femmes et les livres.* Paris: Ancienne Librairie, 1919.

Copland, James, and Charles Alfred Lee. "P. Lalouette, the New Method of Treating Venereal Diseases by Fumigation, Paris, 1776." In *A Dictionary of Practical Medicine: Comprising General Pathology, the Nature.* New York: Lilly, Wait, Colman, and Holden, 1859.

Corbin, Alain. *The Foul and the Fragrant: Odor and the French Social Imagination.* Cambridge, MA: Harvard University Press, 1986.

Coursac, Paul Girault de. *Louis XVI et Marie Antoinette: Vie conjugale, vie politique.* Paris: O.E.I.L., 1990.

Crompton, Louis. *Homosexuality and Civilization.* Cambridge, MA: Harvard University Press, 2009.

Dantalle, F. *Description de la ménagerie royale d'animaux vivants, établie aux Tuileries, près de la terrasse nationale; Avec leurs noms, qualités, couleurs et propriétés.* Paris: De l'imprimerie des patriotes, n.d.

Decker, Michel de. *La Princesse de Lamballe.* Paris: Librairie Académique Perrin, 1979.

d'Elbée, Jean. *Le Mystère de Louis XIII.* Lyon, France: H. Lardanchet, 1943.

Delorme, Philippe. *Marie-Antoinette: Épouse de Louis XVI, mère de Louis XVII.* Paris: Pygmalion Editions, 1999.

Denton, Chad. *Decadence, Radicalism, and the Early Modern French Nobility: The Enlightened and Depraved.* Lanham, MD: Lexington Books, 2017.

Diaconoff, Suellen. *Through the Reading Glass: Women, Books, and Sex in the French Enlightenment.* Albany: State University of New York Press, 2012.

Doran, Dr. John. *"Mann" and Manners at the Court of Florence, 1740–1786.* London: H. S. Nichols, 1896.

Douglas, Robert Bruce. *The Life and Times of Madame du Barry.* London: Leonard Smithers, 1896.

Duban, Jeffrey M. *The Lesbian Lyre: Reclaiming Sappho for the 21st Century.* West Hoathly, UK: Sussex Clairview Books, 2016.

Dubois, Guillaume. *Memoirs of Cardinal Dubois.* London: Leonard Smithers, 1899.

Duclos, Charles. *Mémoires secrets sur le règne de Louis XIV, la Régence et le règne de Louis XV.* Paris: Firmin-Didot Frères, 1846.

Dulac, H. G. *Le glaive vengeur de la République française une et indivisible ou galerie.* Paris: Galletti, 1793.

Dumas, Alexandre. *Louis Quinze.* Paris: Cadot, 1849.

Dussieux, Louis. *Le château de Versailles: Histoire et description.* Versailles, France: L. Bernard, 1881.

Dynes, Wayne R. *Encyclopedia of Homosexuality.* New York: Routledge, 2016.

Edlin, Gordon, and Eric Golanty. *Health and Wellness.* Burlington, MA: Jones & Bartlett Learning, 2015.

Edlin, Gordon, Eric Golanty, and Kelli McCormack Brown. *Essentials for Health and Wellness.* Burlington, MA: Jones & Bartlett Learning, 2000.

Ennès, Pierre. "Le surtout de mariage en porcelaine de Sèvres du Dauphin, 1769–1770." *Revue de l'Art* 76 (1987): 63–73.

Etzlstorfer, Hannes. "Marie Antoinette." *Quarterly Review* 149–50 (1880): 76.

F., I. W. *The Story of Louise de la Vallière.* Norwich, UK: Fletcher and Son, 1870.

Fabre, François. *La Gazette des hôpitaux.* Bibliothéque du médecin-praticien, 1848.

Fadiman, Clifton, and Andre Bernard. *Bartlett's Book of Anecdotes.* Boston: Little, Brown, 2000.

Farmer, James Eugene. *Versailles and the Court under Louis XIV.* Versailles, France: Century, 1905.

Farquhar, Michael. *A Treasury of Royal Scandals: The Shocking True Stories of History's Wickedest, Weirdest, Most Wanton Kings, Queens, Tsars, Popes, and Emperors.* New York: Penguin, 2001.

Farr, Evelyn. *I Love You Madly: Marie-Antoinette and Count Fersen; The Secret Letters.* London: Peter Owen, 2017.

Faucou, Lucien. *L'Intermédiaire des chercheurs and curieux*. Paris: L'Intermédiaire des chercheurs et curieux, 1894.

Fein, Judith Lynn. *The Spoon from Minkowitz: A Bittersweet Roots Journey to Ancestral Lands*. Santa Fe, NM: Global Adventure, 2013.

Fersen, Hans Axel von. *Diary and Correspondence of Count Axel Fersen: Grand Marshal of Sweden, Relating to the Court of France*. London: Heinemann, 1902.

———. *Le comte de Fersen et la cour de France*. Paris: Firmin-Didot et Cie, 1878.

Flammermont, Jules. *Les correspondances des agents diplomatiques étrangers en France avant la révolution*. Paris: Ernest Leroux, 1896.

Fleischmann, Hector. *Le cénacle libertin de Mlle Raucourt de la comédie française*. Paris: Bibliothèque des Curieux, 1912.

———. *Marie-Antoinette libertine*. Paris: Bibliothèque des Curieux, 1911.

Fleming, Maureen. *Elisabeth: Empress of Austria*. New York: C. Kendall & W. Sharp, 1935.

Fontaine, Labreli de. *Révélation sur l'existence de Louis XVII, duc de Normandie*. Paris: Carpentier-Méricourt, 1831.

Foucaud, Edouard. *Histoire du théâtre en France*. Paris: Publications Modernes, 1845.

Fouquier, Armand. *Causes célèbres de tous les peuples*. Paris: Lebrun, 1858.

Fournier, Henri. *Journal des maladies cutanées et syphilitiques*. Paris: Administration et Rédaction, 1898.

Francis, Henry. "Marie Antoinette." *Era Magazine: An Illustrated Monthly* 9 (1902): 503–10.

Funck-Brentano, Frantz. *The Diamond Necklace: Being the True Story of Marie-Antoinette and the Cardinal de Rohan*. Philadelphia: J. B. Lippincott, 1901.

Gonthier, Ursula Haskins. *Opinion, Voltaire, nature et culture*. Paris: Voltaire Foundation, 2007.

Goodman, Dena, and Thomas E. Kaiser. *Marie Antoinette: Writings on the Body of a Queen*. New York: Routledge, 2013.

Gothein, Marie-Luise, and Walter P. Wright. *History of Garden Art*. London: J. M. Dent & Sons, 1913.

Goupil, Pierre Étienne Auguste. *Essais historiques sur la vie de Marie-Antoinette d'Autriche: Reine de France*. Paris: Chez Stampe, 1789.

Grant, Sarah. *Female Portraiture and Patronage in Marie Antoinette's Court*. New York: Routledge, 2018.

Guardia, J. M. *La médecine à travers les siècles: Histoire et philosophie*. Paris: J.-B. Baillière et fils, 1865.

Guillemin, Henri. *Parcours*. Paris: Editions du Seuil, 1989.

Guillou, Jean-Claude. "Le Domaine de Louis XIII à Versailles." *Versalia* 3 (2000): 87.

Haggard, Andrew. *Louis XVI and Marie Antoinette*. New York: D. Appleton, 1909.

Hardman, John. *Marie-Antoinette: The Making of a French Queen*. London: Yale University Press, 2019.

Hardy, Blanche Christable. *The Princesse de Lamballe: A Biography*. London: Archibald Constable, 1908.

Haslip, Joan. *Madame du Barry: The Wages of Beauty*. London: Tauris Parke, 2005.

———. *Marie Antoinette*. London: Piper, 1987.

Hastier, Louis. *Vieilles histoires, étranges énigmes*. Paris: A. Fayard, 1955.

Hatton, Ragnhild Marie. *Louis XIV and Absolution*. London: Springer, 1976.

Helm, W. H. *Vigee-Lebrun 1755–1842*. Boston: Small, Maynard, 1915.

Herman, Eleanor. *The Royal Art of Poison: Filthy Palaces, Fatal Cosmetics, Deadly Medicine, and Murder Most Foul*. New York: St. Martin's, 2018.

———. *Sex with Kings*. New York: HarperCollins, 2004.

Hiner, Susan. *Accessories to Modernity: Fashion and the Feminine in Nineteenth-Century France*. Philadelphia: University of Pennsylvania Press, 2011.

Hodges, Henry C. "The Case of Marie Antoinette." *The Gateway: A Magazine Devoted to Literature, Economics, and Social Service*. Detroit, MI: Gateway, 1905.

Jansen, Sharon L. *Anne of France: Lessons for My Daughter*. Cambridge, MA: Tamesis Books, 2012.

Jobez, Alphonse. *La France sous Louis XVI*. Paris: Didier et Cie, 1881.

Kahan, Michèle Bokobza. *Libertinage et folie dans le roman du 18e siècle*. Paris: Peeters, 2000.

Kenner, Corrine. *Astrology for Writers: Spark Your Creativity Using the Zodiac*. Woodbury, MN: Llewellyn Worldwide, 2013.

Kiste, John. *Emperor Francis Joseph: Life, Death and the Fall of the Habsburg Empire*. Stroud, UK: History Press, 2005.

Knabe, Peter-Eckhard. *Opinion*. Berlin: Verlag Arno Spitz, 2000.

Krafft-Ebing, Richard. *Psychopathia Sexualis: With Especial Reference to the Antipathic Sexual Instinct*. New York: Rebman, 1906.

Kunstler, Charles. *Fersen et son secret*. Paris: Hachette, 1947.

Laborde, Comte Alexandre de. *Versailles: Ancien et Moderne*. Paris: Imprimerie Schneider et Langrand, 1844.

La Morandière, Denis-Laurian Turmeau de. *Police sur les Mendians, les Vagabonds, les Joueurs de Profession, les Intrigans, les Filles Prostituées, les Domestiques hors de maison depuis long-tems et les Gens sans aveu*. Paris: Dessain, 1764.

La Pijardière, Louis Lacour de. *Livres du boudoir de la reine Marie-Antoinette*. Oxford: Oxford University Press, 1862.

Lescure, Mathurin François Adolphe de. *Correspondance secrète inédite sur Louis XVI, Marie-Antoinette, la cour et la ville de 1777 à 1792*. Paris: H. Plon, 1866.

———. *La princesse de Lamballe, Marie-Thérèse-Louise de Savoie-Carignan*. Paris: H. Plon, 1864.

———. *Marie Antoinette et sa famille*. Paris: Ducrocq, 1865.

Levron, Jacques. *Daily Life at Versailles in the Seventeenth and Eighteenth Centuries*. New York: Macmillan, 1968.

Lieberman, Stuart. "A Transgenerational Theory." *Journal of Family Therapy* 1 (1979): 347–60.

Littell, Eliakim. "Lord Holland's Foreign Reminiscences." *Living Age* 29 (1851): 392.

———. "Madame de Maintenon." *Living Age* 21 (1849): 151.

———. "Marie Antoinette." *Living Age* 146 (1880): 581–84.

———. "Memoirs of Marie Antoinette." *Living Age* 60 (1849): 26.

———. "Secret Correspondence on Marie Antoinette." *Living Age* 21 (1849): 554.

Locard, Edmond. *Les crimes de sang et les crimes d'amour au XVIIe siècle*. Lyon, France: A. Storck et Cie., 1903.

Lockyer, Herbert. *Last Words of Saints and Sinners: 700 Final Quotes from the Famous*. Grand Rapids, MI: Kregel, 1969.

Lorenzo, Sixto Sánchez. *El amante de la reina*. Barcelona: Roca editorial, 2012.

Mack, William, and William Benjamin Hale. *Corpus Juris: Being a Complete and Systematic Statement of the Whole Body of the Law as Embodied in and Developed by All Reported Decisions.* London: Butterworth, 1920.

Maria Theresa (Empress of Austria). *Briefe der Kaiserin Maria Theresia an ihre Kinder und Freunde.* Vienna: W. Braumüller, 1881.

Maria Theresa, Comte Florimond-Claude de Mercy-Argenteau, and Marie-Antoinette. "Comte Florimond-Claude de Mercy-Argenteau." In *Correspondance secrète entre Marie-Thérèse et le Comte de Mercy-Argenteau avec les lettres de Marie-Thérèse et de Marie-Antoinette.* Vol. 1. Paris: Firmin Didot Frères, 1874.

Marie Antoinette. *Lettres de Marie-Antoinette.* Paris: A. Picard et fils, 1895.

Marie-Thérèse Charlotte Angoulême. *The Ruin of a Princess.* New York: Lamb, 1912.

Marr, Lisa. *Sexually Transmitted Diseases: A Physician Tells You What You Need to Know.* Baltimore: Johns Hopkins University Press, 2007.

Matthews-Grieco, Sara F. *Cuckoldry, Impotence and Adultery in Europe.* New York: Routledge, 2017.

Maugras, Gaston. *Le Duc de Lauzun et la Cour de Marie-Antoinette.* Paris: Plon-Nourrit, 1895.

Maurepas, Jean-Frédéric Phélypeaux comte de. *Mémoires du comte de Maurepas.* Paris: Chez Buisson, 1792.

Maxwell-Scott, Mary Monica. *Madame Elizabeth de France, 1764–1794.* London: Edward Arnold, 1908.

Mayer, Charles-Joseph. *Vie de Marie-Antoinette d'Autriche, reine de France, femme de Louis XVI, roi des Français, 1793.* Paris: Tuileries, 1793.

Mazé, Jules. *La Cour de Louis XIV.* Paris: Hachette, 1944.

McDonagh, James Eustace Radclyffe. *Venereal Diseases: Their Clinical Aspect and Treatment.* St. Louis, MO: C.V. Mosby, 1920.

Mennell, Stephen. *All Manners of Food: Eating and Taste in England and France from the Middle Ages.* Chicago: University of Illinois Press, 1996.

Merians, Linda Evi. *The Secret Malady: Venereal Disease in Eighteenth-Century Britain and France.* Lexington: University Press of Kentucky, 1996.

Michelet, J. *Histoire de France: Louis XV et Louis XVI.* Librairie Internationale, 1874.

Montgaillard, Abbé Guillaume Honoré Rocques de. *Histoire de France, depuis la fin du règne de Louis XVI jusqu'à l'année 1825.* Paris: Moutardier, 1827.

Montpensier, Mademoiselle de. *Mémoires.* Amsterdam: Jean-Frédéric Bernard, 1729.

Moote, Lloyd A. *Louis XIII, the Just.* Berkeley: University of California Press, 1991.

Moret, Ernest. *Quinze ans du règne de Louis XIV.* Paris: Didier et Cie, 1859.

Morgan, Lady Sydney. *France in 1829–30.* New York: J. & J. Harper, 1830.

Motteville, Françoise de. *Memoirs of Madame de Motteville on Anne of Austria and Her Court.* Boston: Hardy, Pratt, 1902.

Mundt, Klara. *Marie Antoinette and Her Son.* New York: McClure, 1867.

Mousnier, Roland. *The Institutions of France under the Absolute Monarchy, 1598–1789: The Organs of State and Society.* Vol. 2. Chicago: University of Chicago Press, 1979.

Nicolardot, Louis. *Journal de Louis XVI.* Paris: E. Dentu, 1873.

Nolhac, Pierre de. *Études sur la cour de France: Marie-Antoinette dauphine, d'après de nouveaux documents.* Paris: Calmann-Lévy, 1898.

———. *La Reine Marie-Antoinette*. Paris: Alphonse Lemerre, 1892.

———. *Louis XV at Versailles*. Paris: Flammarion, 1934.

———. *Versailles et la Cour de France: Marie Antoinette Dauphine*. Paris: L. Conard, 1929.

Norton, Lucy. *The Sun King and His Loves*. London: H. Hamilton, 1983.

Orden, Kate van. *Music, Discipline, and Arms in Early Modern France*. Chicago: University of Chicago Press, 2005.

Orléans, Charlotte-Elisabeth. *Correspondance Complète de Madame Duchesse d'Orléans*. Paris: Charpentier, 1891.

Pasco, Allan H. *Revolutionary Love in Eighteenth and Early Nineteenth-Century France*. Farnham, UK: Ashgate, 2009.

Patmore, Katherine Alexandra. *The Court of Louis XIII*. London: Methuen, 1909.

Pelletan, Eugène. *Décadence de la monarchie*. Paris: Pagnerre, 1861.

Pératé, André. *Versailles: The Palace, the Gardens, the Trianons, the Museum, the City*. Paris: H. Laurens, 1922.

Peuchet, Jacques. *Mémoires tirés des archives de la police de Paris*. Paris: A. Levavasseur et Cie., 1838.

Plato. *The Republic*. Translated by John Llewelyn Davies and David James Vaughan. 2nd ed. London: University Press for Macmillan, 1866.

Pokrovski, V. *L'Élégante dans la littérature satirique du XVIIIe siècle*. Moscow: Musée Ostankino, 1903.

Pompadour, Jeanne Antoinette Poisson de. *Mémoires de Madame la marquise de Pompadour*. Liège, Belgium: À Liège, 1766.

Potts, George. *The Preacher and the King*. London: T. Nelson & Sons, 1853.

Price, Munro. *The Road from Versailles: Louis XVI, Marie Antoinette, and the Fall of the French Monarchy*. New York: St. Martin's Press, 2003.

Procter, William, Jr. "On Hoffman's Anodyne Liquor." *American Journal of Pharmacy* 28 (1852): 213–18.

Prudhomme, Louis. *Les crimes des reines de France: Depuis le commencement de la monarchie*. Paris: Bureau des Révolutions de Paris, 1791.

Ragan, Bryant T. *Homosexuality in Modern France*. Oxford: Oxford University Press, 1996.

Réaux, Tallemant des. *Les historiettes de Tallemant des Réaux*. Paris: J. Techener, 1854.

Recca, Cinzia. *The Diary of Queen Maria Carolina of Naples, 1781–1785*. London: Palgrave Macmillan, 2016.

Renée, Amédée. *Les nièces de Mazarin*. Paris: Firmin Didot, 1856.

Ritchie, Leitch. *Versailles*. London: Longman, 1839.

Rivarol, Antoine de. *Mémoires de Rivarol, avec des notes et éclaircissements historiques*. Paris: Baudoin Frères, 1824.

Rocheterie, Maxime de la. *Histoire de Marie-Antoinette*. Paris: Perrin, 1890.

———. *The Life of Marie Antoinette*. London: Dodd, Mead, 1893.

Rogelberg, Steven G. *The SAGE Encyclopedia of Industrial and Organizational Psychology*. London: SAGE, 2016.

Romeges, Henri de. *Sexo-Monarchie*. Paris: Michel Lafon, 2013.

Ropper, Allan H., and Brian Burrell. *How the Brain Lost Its Mind: Sex, Hysteria, and the Riddle of Mental Illness*. New York: Penguin, 2019.

Saint-Amand, Imbert de. *Marie Antoinette and the End of the Old Régime.* New York: Charles Scribner's Sons, 1890.

Sainte-Beuve, Charles Augustin. *Nouveaux lundis.* Paris: Calmann-Lévy, 1885.

Saint-Hilaire, Émile Marc H. *Histoire des conspirations et des exécutions politiques en France.* Paris: Gustave Havard, 1849.

Sheriff, Mary D. "Hermaphrodite? History Painter? On the Self-Imaging of Elisabeth Vigée Lebrun." *Eighteenth Century: Theory and Interpretation* 35 (Spring 1994): 3–27.

Smythe, Lillian C. *The Guardian of Marie Antoinette: Letters from the Comte de Mercy-Argenteau, Austrian Ambassador to the Court of Versailles, to Marie Thérèse, Empress of Austria, 1770–1780.* London: Hutchinson, 1902.

Société des sciences morales. *Mémoires de la Société des sciences morales, des lettres et des arts de Seine-et-Oise.* Versailles, France: Author, 1880.

Soubeiran, Eugène. *Nouveau traité de pharmacie théorique et pratique.* Paris: Société Belge de Librairie, 1837.

Sourches, Marquis de. *Mémoires du Marquis de Sourches sur le Règne de Louis XIV.* Paris: Librairie Hachette, 1882.

Spawforth, Tony. *Versailles: A Biography of a Palace.* New York: St. Martin's, 2010.

Stine, Gerald James. *The Biology of Sexually Transmitted Diseases.* Dubuque, IA: W. C. Brown, 1992.

Stryienski, Casimir. *Mesdames de France, filles de Louis XV: Documents inédits.* Paris: Émile-Paul, 1911.

Summers, Claude J. *Homosexuality in Renaissance and Enlightenment England: Literary Representations in Historical Context.* New York: Routledge, 2013.

Swann, Julian. *Exile, Imprisonment, or Death: The Politics of Disgrace in Bourbon France.* Oxford: Oxford University Press, 2017.

Tilles, Gérard, and Daniel Wallach. "Histoire de la nosologie en dermatologie." *Annales de dermatologie et de vénéréologie* 116 (1989): 9–26.

Tilley, Arthur. *The Decline of the Age of Louis XIV.* Cambridge: Cambridge University Press, 1929.

Tin, Louis-Georges. *The Dictionary of Homophobia: A Global History of Gay and Lesbian Experience.* Vancouver: Arsenal Pulp Press, 2008.

Touchard-Lafosse, G. *Chroniques pittoresques et critiques de l'oeil de boeuf des petits appartements de la cour et des salons de Paris, sous Louis 14., la Régence, Louis 15. et Louis 16.* Paris: Gustave Barba, 1845.

Touloubre, Christophe Félix Louis Ventre de la. *Histoire de Marie Antoinette . . . Reine de France.* Paris: H. L. Perronneau, 1797.

Tourneux, Maurice. *Marie-Antoinette devant l'histoire: Essai bibliographique.* Paris: Techener, 1895.

Tschudi, Clara. *Marie Antoinette.* London: Swan Sonnenschein, 1902.

Turner, David M. *Fashioning Adultery: Gender, Sex and Civility.* Cambridge: Cambridge University Press, 2002.

Urban, Sylvanus. *The Gentleman's Magazine.* London: John Bowyer Nichols & Son, 1850.

Valicourt, Emmanuel De. *Les favoris de la reine: Dans l'intimité de Marie-Antoinette.* Paris: Tallandier, 2019.

Vallotton, Henry. *Marie-Thérèse: Impératrice*. Paris: Fayard, 1963.

Van der Cruysse, Dirk. *Madame Palatine*. Paris: Fayard, 2014.

Vehse, Carl Eduard. *Memoirs of the Court and Aristocracy of Austria*. London: H. S. Nichols, 1896.

Vigée-Lebrun, Louise-Elisabeth. *The Memoirs of Mme. Elisabeth Louise Vigée-Le Brun, 1755–1789*. New York: George H. Doran, 1927.

Vinha, Mathieu da. *Au service du roi: Les métiers à la cour de Versailles*. Paris: Tallandier, 2016.

———. *Vivre à la cour de Versailles en 100 questions*. Paris: Tallandier, 2018.

Vovk, Justin C. *In Destiny's Hands: Five Tragic Rulers, Children of Maria Theresa*. New York: iUniverse, 2010.

W., M. R. D. *Vie de Louis-Philippe-Joseph, Duc d'Orléans*. London: Palais Saint-James, 1790.

Walton, Geri. *Marie Antoinette's Confidante: The Rise and Fall of the Princesse de Lamballe*. Havertown, UK: Pen and Sword, 2016.

Watson, Thomas Edward. *From the End of the Reign of Louis the Fifteenth to the Consulate of Napoleon*. London: Macmillan, 1900.

Watstein, Sarah, and John Jovanovic. *Statistical Handbook on Infectious Diseases*. London: Greenwood, 2003.

Weber, Joseph. *Mémoires concernant Marie-Antoinette, archiduchesse d'Autriche, reine de France*. London: G. Schulze, 1809.

Wilkinson, Richard. *Louis XIV*. New York: Routledge, 2017.

Williams, Henry Smith. *France, 1715–1815*. London: The Times, 1907.

Williams, Hugh Noel. *Later Queens of the French Stage*. New York: Harper & Brothers, 1906.

———. *Memoirs of Madame du Barry of the Court of Louis XV*. New York: Collier & Son, 1910.

Wolowski, M. *Revue des cours littéraires de la France et de l'étranger littérature, philosophie, théologie, éloquence*. Paris: Germer Baillière, 1867.

Wraxall, N. W. *Waldie's Octavo Library*. Philadelphia: Adam Waldie, 1836.

Wright, Thomas. *The History of France*. London: London Printing Co., 1858.

Yonge, Charles Duke. *The Life of Marie Antoinette, Queen of France*. London: Harper & Brothers, 1876.

Younghusband, Lady. *Marie-Antoinette: Her Early Youth, 1770–1774*. London: Macmillan, 1912.

Zimmerman, M. *The Edinburgh Magazine, or Literary Miscellany*. Edinburgh: J. Sibbald, 1789.

Zur-Lauben, Baron de. *Histoire militaire des Suisses au service de la France, avec les pièces justificatives*. Vol. 3. Paris: Desaint & Saillant, 1751.

Zweig, Stefan. *Marie Antoinette: The Portrait of an Average Woman*. New York: Grove Press, 2002.

ILLUSTRATIONS AND CREDITS

PART I

A "resident" of Parc-aux-Cerfs, Marie-Louise O'Murphy. *Marie-Louise O'Murphy*, François Boucher (1758).

CHAPTER 1

Louis XIII's Versailles, as constructed circa 1630–1640. *Vue du premier château de Versailles*, Comtesse-Héloïse de Gomboust (1652).

Louis XIII and the Marquis de Cinq-Mars. *Louis XIII, King of France, with the Sash and Badge of the Order of Saint Esprit*, Frans Pourbus the Younger (seventeenth century); *Henri Coiffier de Ruzé, Marquis de Cinq-Mars*, Antoine le Nain (1630).

CHAPTER 2

Louis XIV's first nurse, Madame Longuet de la Giraudière. *Louis XIV et la Dame Longuet de La Giraudière*, Charles et Henri Beaubrun (seventeenth century).

Duchesse Louise de La Vallière and Louis XIV. *Louise, Duchess of la Valliere*, E. T. Parris, engraved by H. Robinson (1838); *Louis XIV of France*, Hyacinthe Rigaud (1701).

Duke Philippe I of Orléans, Philippe of Lorraine (depicted as Ganymede), and the Count of Vermandois. *Portrait of the Duke of Orléans, only sibling of Louis XIV*, Nicolas de Larmessin (seventeenth century); *Chevalier de Lorraine, depicted as Ganymede*, Baldassare Franceschini (second half of seventeenth century); *Louis, Count of Vermandois (illegitimate son of Louis XIV and Mademoiselle de La Vallière*, Pierre Mignard (1680).

CHAPTER 3

Young Louis XV of France. *Young Louis XV*, John Henry Wright, *A History of All Nations from the Earliest Times* (Philadelphia: Lea Brothers, 1905), 117.

Louise-Julie, Pauline, Diane, and Marie-Anne de Mailly. *Dame du Palais de la reine Marie Leszczynska*, Jean-Marc Nattier (n.d.); *Pauline Félicité de Mailly-Nesle, Comtesse de Vintimille (1712–1741), une favorite de Louis XV*, Jean-Marc Nattier (n.d.); *Diane Adélaïde de Mailly-Nesle, duchesse de Lauraguais*, Jean-Marc Nattier (n.d.); *Marquise de La Tournelle, Duchesse de Châteauroux*, Jean-Marc Nattier (1740).

Liaison dangereuse. Valmont entrant dans la chambre de Cécile endormie. Pierre Choderlos de Laclos, *Les Liaisons dangereuses* (Paris: P. E. G. Durand, 1782).

Jeanne Antoinette Poisson, Marquise de Pompadour, and Madame Jeanne Bécu, Comtesse du Barry. Theodor Griesinger, *Die Maitressenwirthschaft in Frankreich unter Ludwig XIV; XV* (Stuttgart, Germany: Pracht-Ausgabe, 1874), 188; *Portrait of Marie-Jeanne Bécu, comtesse du Barry*, Pierre Adrien Le Beau, after Marilly (1770–1780).

Traced note to Marie Antoinette's teacher (circa 1768). Auguste Geffroy, *Gustave III et la cour de France suivi d'une ètude critique* (Paris: Didier, 1867), 329.

PART II

Dauphine Marie Antoinette. *Archduchess Maria Antonia of Austria, the later Queen Marie Antoinette of France, at the age of 16 years*, Joseph Kreutzinger (1771).

CHAPTER 4

Marie Antoinette dancing with her brothers. *Fête Organized to Celebrate the Marriage of the Emperor Joseph II to Princess Marie-Josèphe of Bavaria*, Georg Weikert (1765).

Empress Maria Theresa and Emperor Francis I of Austria. *Empress Maria Theresia of Austria*, Martin van Meytens (1759); *Emperor Francis I of Austria, engraving by Meyer after A. Dumont*, Edward Baines, *History of the Wars of the French Revolution* (London: Longman, Hurst, Rees, Orme, Brown & Harper, 1817).

CHAPTER 5

The siblings: Comte de Provence, Comte d'Artois, Marie Clotilde, and Elisabeth. *Louis Stanislas Xavier de France, futur Louis XVIII*, Louis-Jacques Cathelin (1771); *Portrait of Charles X of France as Count of Artois*, Louis-Jacques Cathelin (1773); *Marie Clotilde de France while Princess of Piedmont*, Louis-Jacques Cathelin (1780); *Princess Elisabeth of France*, Marie-Louise-Adélaïde Boizot (1780).

Marie Thérèse Louise de Savoie Carignan. *Princesse de Lamballe*, Stich von Bosselman aus: Adolphe Thiers, *Histoire de la Révolution française* par M. A. Thiers, de l'Académie française (Paris: Furne et Cie Libraires-Éditeurs rue Saint-André-des-Arts, 1865), 45.

Mesdames Tantes Victoire, Adélaïde, and Sophie. *Madame Victoire de France*, Jean-Marc Nattier (1748); *Madame Adélaïde, Duchesse de Louvois*, Jean-Marc Nattier (1750); *Madame Sophie de France*, Jean-Marc Nattier (1748).

CHAPTER 6

Marie Antoinette signaling with her hand fan? *Marie Antoinette se promenant dans un jardin*, Élisabeth Louise Vigée Le Brun (1780–1785).

Hans Axel von Fersen. F. F. Flach, *Grefve Hans Axel von Fersen: Minnesteckning jemte utdrag ur hans dagbok och* (Stockholm: Fritzes Kongl., 1896), 62.

Marie Antoinette and Louis-Auguste's marriage contract (May 16, 1770). *Acte de mariage de Marie-Antoinette et Louis XVI* (1770).

Dauphine's letter to Maria Theresa (July 12, 1770). *Lettres de Marie-Antoinette: Recueil des lettres authentiques* (Paris: Picard, 1895), 8.

Duke d'Aumont's marriage contract (August 19, 1771). Alfred Hamy, *Essai sur les ducs d'Aumont gouverneurs du Boulonnais, 1662–1789* (Paris: G. Hamain, 1907), 221.

PART III

Peace Bringing Back Abundance. *La paix ramenant l'abondance*, Élisabeth Louise Vigée Le Brun (1780).

CHAPTER 7

Yolande Martine Gabrielle de Polastron, Duchess of Polignac. *Martine-Gabrielle-Yolande de Polastron*, Élisabeth Louise Vigée Le Brun (1783).

CHAPTER 9

"Love-à-la-mode" (Lady Hamilton and Queen Maria Carolina). *"Love-à-la-mode" (Lady Hamilton and Queen Maria Carolina)*, James Gillray (early nineteenth century).

Marie Antoinette and Maria Carolina. *Caroline, Archduchess of Austria Double Portrait with Her Sister Marie Antoinette*, Antonio Pencini (1764).

Mademoiselle Raucourt. *Mlle Raucourt in der Tragödie Mithridate von Racine*, Jean Michel Moreau (n.d.). *Sophie Arnould*, Jean-Baptiste Greuze (1786).

Original painting *en chemise* (left) and re-creation of the painting *en chemise* (right). *Marie Antoinette in a Muslin Dress* (Salon de Paris), Élisabeth Louise Vigée Le Brun (1783); *Marie-Antoinette à la Rose*, Élisabeth Louise Vigée Le Brun (1783).

Fencing match between the Chevaliers de Saint-Georges and d'Eon and Marie Antoinette in redingote. *The Assault, or Fencing Match, which took place at Carlton House on the 9th of April 1787, between Mademoiselle la Chevalière D'Eon de Beaumont and Monsieur de Saint George*, Victor Marie Picot after a painting by Charles Jean Robineau (1789); *Marie Antoinette hunting*, Louis Auguste Brun (1783).

Signature (November 16, 1774). *Marie Antoinette, Nov. 16, 1774*, Wesley Manning, *A Note on the Handwriting of Marie Antoinette* (London: Press Holdings, 1934), 36.

Letter from Marie Antoinette to the Count von Rosenberg (April 17, 1775). *Letter from Marie Antoinette, Queen of France, to Count Xavier von Rosenberg, 17 April 1775,* Alfred Ritter von Arneth, *Marie-Antoinette: Correspondance secrète entre Marie-Thérèse et le Comte de Mercy-Argenteau* (Paris: Firmin Didot Frères, 1875), 361.

Letter from Marie Antoinette to M. de Clugny (1776). Autographed letter to M. de Clugny (1776). Thierry Bodin, *Lettres et manuscrits* (Paris: Syndicat Français des Experts, 2012), 132.

PART IV

Louis XVI. *Gravure et mezzo-tinto avec aquarelle.* "Louis XVI, having put on the Phrygian cap, cried 'long live the nation.' He drank to the health of the sans-culottes and affected a show of great calm. He spoke high-sounding words about how he never feared the law, that he had never feared to be in the midst of the people; finally he pretended to play a personal part in the insurrection of June 20. Prints & Photographs Division, Courtesy of the Library of Congress, LC-USZC2-3561. Public domain.

CHAPTER 11

"What, Monsieur le Comte, you are usurping my rights?" Marie Antoinette, Madame de Polignac, and the Comte d'Artois, Charles-Joseph Mayer, *Vie de Marie-Antoinette d'Autriche, reine de France, femme de Louis XVI, 1793* (Paris: Tuileries, 1793), 31.

CHAPTER 12

The Rare Animals. *Marie Antoinette as an Austrian pantheress.* "October 1790, the King and Queen adopted the project of delivering themselves from slavery. Indeed Marie Antoinette played more than a passive part." *Vie de Marie-Antoinette d'Autriche, reine de France, femme de Louis XVI, roi des Français; Depuis la perte de son pucelage jusqu'au premier mai 1791, ornée de vingt-six figures et agrémentée d'une troisième partie* (Paris: Chez l'auteur et ailleurs, 1792), 77; *Louis XVI as a horned pig.* "Rights of Man and the Constitution of France. It must be said in extenuation of such attacks that Marie Antoinette actually was engaged in a plot to remove Louis XVI from Paris." *Vie de Marie-Antoinette d'Autriche, reine de France, femme de Louis XVI, roi des Français; Depuis la perte de son pucelage jusqu'au premier mai 1791, ornée de vingt-six figures et agrémentée d'une troisième partie* (Paris: chez l'auteur et ailleurs, 1792), 76; The Rare Animals: Or the Transfer of the Royal Zoo from Temple (1793). Charles-Joseph Mayer, *Vie de Marie-Antoinette d'Autriche, reine de France, femme de Louis XVI, roi des Français, 1793* (Paris: Tuileries, 1793), 39; *La Poulle d'Autruche.* Caricature of Marie Antoinette. French School (1791).

CHAPTER 13

Letter to Mother (1780). *Ci-après illustrée, une lettre de Marie-Antoinette adressée à Marie-Thérèse* (October 11, 1780). In A. Ritter von Arneth, *Maria Theresia und Marie Antoinette* (Paris: Jung Treuttel, 1865), 324.

Letter to Castries (1786). *Disgrâce du prince de Soubise, ancien ministre d'État, a dû se retirer après l'affaire du collier de la Reine, dans laquelle son parent, le cardinal de Rohan, avait été gravement compromis* (August 30, 1786).

Letter to Hans Axel von Fersen (1791). Lettre de la Reine à Fersen (December 28, 1791).

PART V

Marie Antoinette on the Way to the Guillotine, Jacques-Louis David. *The Last Days of Marie Antoinette, Queen of France* (London: Sampson Low, 1850).

CHAPTER 14

"For One Pleasure a Thousand Pains" (circa 1659). *A syphilis sufferer gets fumigated in a special oven.* The caption on the oven translates as "For one pleasure a thousand pains."

CHAPTER 15

Dauphin Louis Charles and Count Axel von Fersen. *Ludvig (XVII) Dauphin,* Artist unknown. Credit: Nationalmuseum (Stockholm); Axel von Fersen the Younger. Elise Amberg.

Pages from Fersen's journal. *Hans Axel von Fersens Samling.* Stafsundsarkivet, Dagböcker, SE/RA/720807/02/6/II/5 (1791–1794).

CHAPTER 16

Natal chart for Marie Antoinette, November 2, 1755, 19:30:00 LMT—01:05:20, Vienna, Austria, 16e20'00, 48n13'00. Geocentric Tropical Zodiac—Placidus House System. *Chart Wheel generated using Janus 5 Astrology Software.* Credit: Astrology House New Zealand.

"J'en appelle au cœur de toutes les mères ici présentes." *Marie Antoinette at Trial,* Louis Jean Joseph Blanc, *Histoire de la Révolution française* (Paris: Docks de la librairie, 1878).

Letter to Barnave (1791). *Revue encyclopédique, ou Analyse raisonnée des productions les plus remarquables* (Paris: Bureau Central de la Revue Encyclopédique, 1831).

Letter to General Jarjayes written from the Temple Prison. *Écriture et signature de Marie-Antoinette. Fragment d'une lettre écrite du Temple au général de Jarjayes*, in *Isographie des hommes célèbres* (Paris: Duchesne aîné, 1827–1830).

The Verdict. *Frontispice de l'édition originale, gravé par Palas sur un dessin de Charles Monnet,* Choderlos de Laclos, *Les Liaisons dangereuses* (Paris: P. E. G. Durand, 1782).

CHAPTER 17

Excerpt from Marie Antoinette's last letter. Ascendancy and then descendancy of first five lines. *Lettre de Marie-Antoinette à Madame Élisabeth* (October 16, 1793). Archives nationales.

Excerpts from Marie Antoinette's last letter. *Adieu, ma bonne et tendre soeur* (Farewell, my good and tender sister). *Lettre de Marie-Antoinette à Madame Élisabeth* (October 16, 1793). Archives nationales.

INDEX